DISCARDED

John Wiley & Sons, Ltd

D1341467

Emotional Freedom Technique For Dummies®

Published by
John Wiley & Sons, Ltd
The Atrium
Southern Gate
Chichester
West Sussex
PO19 8SQ
England

E-mail (for orders and customer service enquires): cs-books@wiley.co.uk

Visit our Home Page on www.wiley.com

For general information on our other products and services, please contact our Customer Care Department within the U.S. at 800-762-2974, outside the U.S. at 317-572-3993, or fax 317-572-4002.

For technical support, please visit www.wiley.com/techsupport.

Wiley also publishes its books in a variety of electronic formats. Some content that appears in print may not be available in electronic books.

Library of Congress Control Number is available from the publisher.

British Library Cataloguing in Publication Data: A catalogue record for this book is available from the British Library

ISBN: 978-0-470-75876-2

Printed and bound in Great Britain by Bell & Bain, Ltd., Glasgow

10 9 8 7 6 5 4

WILEY

D

A

About the Author

Helena Fone is an Advanced EFT Practitioner, presenter, Level 3 trainer and supervisor. She is also an Advanced Holistic Hypnotherapist, has trained in Neuro-linguistic programming, studied Cognitive Behavioural Therapy, and runs a busy private practice, Therapy4me, in the UK and in Gozo. She is founder of the Cheshire EFT Association, also founder of the only UK EFT Register solely for Energy Therapists, www.EFTRegister.com, a support group for like-minded therapists. Over the years she has helped hundreds of people eliminate issues arising from emotional and physical traumas, anxiety attacks, addictions, inhibitions, low self esteem, fertility issues, and bereavement. You can find more information at www.therapy4me.co.uk or www.tappingtherapy.net.

Helena delivers training in EFT to a diverse range of people including psychologists, counsellors, therapists, housewives, teachers, nurses, and sales executives. She has given several presentations on EFT to large groups and has a regular interview slot on her local radio station. Helena divides her time between her practice and her voluntary work with local hospices and cancer support centres. She has also been a local voluntary magistrate for 13 years. Her specialty in EFT is working with cancer patients, and she is currently delivering EFT to schools in Cheshire where there is great scope for helping children improve both academically and emotionally. Helena has used EFT successfully to free herself from her own past issues and improve her own physical problems.

Publisher's Acknowledgments

We're proud of this book; please send us your comments through our Dummies online registration form located at www.dummies.com/register/.

Some of the people who helped bring this book to market include the following:

Acquisitions, Editorial, and Media Development

Project Editor: Simon Bell

Executive Editor: Samantha Spickernell

Copy Editor: Martin Key

Proofreader: Charlie Wilson

Publisher: Jason Dunne

Executive Project Editor: Daniel Mersey

Cover Photos: © Yasuhide Fumoto/ Getty Images

Cartoons: Rich Tennant (www.the5thwave.com)

Composition Services

Project Coordinator: Lynsey Stanford

Layout and Graphics: Reuben W. Davis, Laura Pence

Proofreader: Jessica Kramer

Indexer: Ty Koontz

Publishing and Editorial for Consumer Dummies

Diane Graves Steele, Vice President and Publisher, Consumer Dummies

Joyce Pepple, Acquisitions Director, Consumer Dummies

Kristin A. Cocks, Product Development Director, Consumer Dummies

Michael Spring, Vice President and Publisher, Travel

Kelly Regan, Editorial Director, Travel

Publishing for Technology Dummies

Andy Cummings, Vice President and Publisher, Dummies Technology/General User

Composition Services

Gerry Fahey, Vice President of Production Services

Debbie Stailey, Director of Composition Services

Contents at a Glance

Introduction

Welcome to *Emotional Freedom Technique For Dummies*, written to empower you (whoever you are) to create and facilitate positive changes to your emotional and physical health. EFT, as it's better known, is fast becoming one of the leading energy therapies used by highly respected clinicians, psychologists, and psychiatrists. Counsellors, teachers, health workers, parents, athletes, cancer support workers, children, and addiction groups also use the technique.

EFT can reduce physical and emotional pains remarkably fast a very high percentage of the time, without the use of drugs or needles. You can also use it to release limiting beliefs and habitual mental patterns. EFT usually works when nothing else will, you can use it anywhere at any time, and the results are often long lasting. The most exciting part of EFT is that it puts you in control.

Different psychotherapies deal with the mind, but energy therapies such as reiki, reflexology, acupuncture, and shiatsu deal with the body. EFT works as a mind–body connection to remove unwanted negative emotions from the mind and, at the same time, improve the body. Many therapists of both mind and body incorporate EFT in their work with great effect. What started out almost ten years ago as a handful of EFT practitioners now runs into thousands as EFT rapidly spreads around the world as a new self-healing tool.

About This Book

This book has absolutely everything you need if you're looking to improve your own or other's emotional and physical health with EFT. It covers not just the basics, but the more advanced stuff on EFT – and almost everything else in between.

Whether you've never heard of EFT or you're an experienced practitioner, the book has something for you. Whatever your level of knowledge or experience, I've written this book as a useful source of reference and as a road map for your journey to self-healing.

I keep any scientific references and jargon to a minimum, and explain what I do use. Where I use the terms 'practitioner' or 'therapist', they refer to the leading person, and the 'client' may be your friend, child, spouse, or anyone you want to help with EFT.

I can't cover everything in this book, so I focus on:

- ✔ Introducing you to the background to EFT.
- ✔ Helping you understand what emotional health is and why it's as important as your physical health.
- ✔ Illustrating EFT's technique and how you can perform it on yourself and others for physical, psychological, and physiological issues.
- ✔ Providing you with some suggested phrases to get the most out of EFT.
- ✔ Making it easier to recognise what can interfere with EFT working.
- ✔ Offering some exercises so you can practise and experiment.

Conventions Used in This Book

To help you navigate through this book, I've set up a few conventions:

- ✔ *Italics* are used for emphasis and to highlight new words or terms that are defined.
- ✔ Monofont is used for web addresses.
- ✔ **Bold faced text** is used to indicate the action part of numbered steps.

What You Don't Need to Read

The sidebars (the grey shaded boxes dotted throughout the text) contain bonus bits of info not crucial to the topic at hand. They're fun, and they can round out your knowledge, but skip them if you like.

Foolish Assumptions

I have assumed, rightly or wrongly, that by reading this book you're intrigued by EFT and want to enhance your wellbeing. I've also assumed that you either have little or no knowledge of EFT or are familiar with EFT but want to expand on what you already know. Like many new discoveries, EFT spawns many a debate as to its scientific validity. The information in this book introduces you to the concept of EFT and you can judge for yourself. If you can answer 'yes' to any of the following, then this book is for you:

- ✔ Are you looking to improve your life?
- ✔ Would you like to know whether EFT may be useful in your work or practice?
- ✔ Do you already practise EFT but want to know more?
- ✔ Are you curious as to how EFT can help you and others?

How This Book Is Organised

I've divided this book into five parts, and broken each part into chapters. The table of contents gives you more detail on each chapter. I've added some exercises for you to experiment on yourself and others and keep you amused.

Part 1: The Path to Emotional Freedom

The best way to understand EFT is to try it for yourself and see how it works. So, if you don't read anything else in this book, I recommend that you read Part I. Basically, this part not only explains the background to EFT but it also defines what emotions are and how the mind and body are connected. More importantly, though, it gives you detailed instruction on how to carry out the basic EFT technique that you use throughout the rest of the book.

Part II: Venturing Further with EFT

In this part you can become more adventurous with your technique as you widen your experience and understanding of EFT. You develop the confidence to try EFT out on yourself and others who may just get in the way of your enthusiasm.

I realise that all problems aren't going to be as easy as ABC and sometimes people can't even talk about their problem. Don't panic: some techniques have exercises for you to practise that help you, such as 'Sneaking Up on the Problem' and the 'Movie Technique'. If you need to prompt those emotions, you'll find ways to do this as well.

Sometimes you find that you can't figure out why something isn't working, so I include some hints and tips for when EFT doesn't seem to work.

Part III: Finding Your Way to Inner Happiness

Everyone wants love in their life and to be free from fears, phobias, and stresses. I can't promise that by reading this part you'll achieve all that. What I can promise, though, is that you'll develop a deeper understanding of the importance of loving yourself. I can also promise that you'll have a therapeutic tool to control your fears and phobias.

This part also covers how to use EFT to release the deep-seated emotions attached to trauma, and how to deal with anger, grief, and relationship issues.

Part IV: Applying EFT to Physical Issues

I begin this part by zooming in on your bad habits, cravings, and addictions. I explain why you do the things you do and how you can get out of your bad habits if you want to.

I then move on to healing the body and touch on ailments from eyesight to infertility and even the more serious disease of cancer. EFT doesn't claim to cure cancer or other serious diseases, but what it can do is help manage the symptoms. The evidence shows that, by removing emotional problems, physical symptoms either improve or disappear altogether.

I end this part with helping you get a good night's sleep . . . aaaahh.

Part V: Exploring Other Avenues

This part takes you through what can get in the way of you getting what you want in life – apart from winning the lottery, unless you just happen to be lucky. Words can be very powerful, as you get to find out.

If you're considering contacting an EFT practitioner, I talk you through what to expect from an EFT session and what qualities to look for in a practitioner. You'll find this helpful if you're considering training as a practitioner yourself. If you want to work with children, you'll find some very useful information here.

Part VI: The Part of Tens

Contained here are those frequently asked questions that save you from searching through the book. If you want to contact a practitioner or train as one, there's some good reference material as well.

Icons Used in This Book

The icons in this book help you find particular kinds of information that may be of use to you:

Real-life experiences I've had when using EFT to help myself and others.

An opportunity to have a go for yourself with guided instruction.

Technical language for a fuller explanation of what's going on in EFT – skip it if you want.

This is the stuff you really need to hang on to. Be sure you understand it.

As it says. Steer clear of anything this icon tells you is a bad idea.

This icon flags up practical advice to help you along the way.

Where to Go from Here

You don't have to read this book from cover to cover. You can simply look up your topic of interest in the index or table of contents, flip to that page, and start reading.

If you're a beginner with EFT, you may start by familiarising yourself with the basic EFT technique in Chapters 3 and 4 before you jump ahead in the book and read the warning icons along the way. That way you're more likely to understand the exercises and get results. After you're familiar with the technique then you can go to whatever topic that takes your interest. If you decide you'd like to consult an EFT practitioner or if you're interested in training as a practitioner, you can find details in Chapter 17. Attending workshops is an ideal way to see EFT in action. A search on the Internet or a call to your local practitioner guides you in the right direction.

Most of all, I wish you a safe and peaceful journey on the road to emotional freedom.

Part I
The Path to Emotional Freedom

The 5th Wave   By Rich Tennant

"EFT is based on the belief that your strong, personal emotions can affect changes in the physical world, though apparently not on the golf course."

In this part . . .

This part introduces you to the key concepts in EFT, defining what emotions are and how the mind and body are connected. More importantly, though, it gives you detailed instruction on how to carry out the basic EFT routines that you use throughout the rest of the book.

Chapter 1

Explaining EFT

*E*motional Freedom Technique (or EFT as it is referred to in this book) is a simple healing technique that you can use by yourself or with a therapist/ practitioner. You can combine it effectively with some other therapies, or use it as a standalone technique. In this chapter, you discover how EFT evolved, how it works, and how you can benefit from using it on yourself and others. You also find out a small sample of the problems EFT can help with and, if using EFT on yourself, when you may want to find outside help from a therapist.

Meeting the EFT Family

Although you may not have heard of EFT, you may well be familiar with the therapies of acupuncture, acupressure, shiatsu, and kinesiology. All are part of the energy therapies family tree, shown in Figure 1-1. Broadly speaking, energy therapies are techniques that work on rebalancing the flow of energy that gets disrupted as it travels through channels in your body known as *meridians*. This bit is important to maintaining good emotional and physical health, and I talk more about this later in this chapter. There's also a bit of psychology thrown in here, which is why you also hear people referring to EFT as an energy therapy, energy psychology, or meridian therapy. I explain the most popular of the other energy therapies – and you can use them with EFT – in Chapter 18.

EFT is what you may call a modern-day version of these energy therapies, some of which go back more than 2,500 years. Other theorists say that EFT taps into a part of the brain that stores and processes information, used in neuro-physiology. No one exactly knows but, after all, do you need to know exactly how something works if it's doing you no harm, only good? Because many people use EFT to great effect, the best advice is to continue to use it until scientists come up with their own theory.

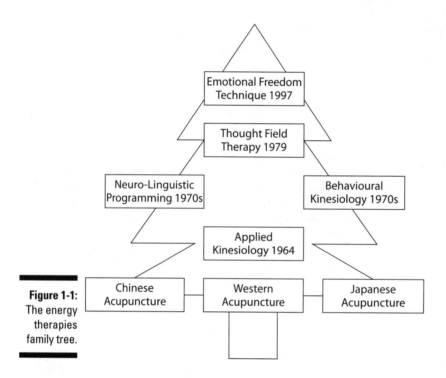

Figure 1-1:
The energy therapies family tree.

Discovering EFT in Action

Every day you encounter a multitude of experiences. You store specific experiences as memories into a filing cabinet in your brain, but because your brain can't store every single memory, it deletes what's irrelevant and stores the most important. With the memory, your brain stores any emotion that goes with it. Next time you need to remember a name or location, for instance, your brain searches around the filing cabinet and brings some or all the information back, together with any emotion. When you see someone you love your brain accesses that information and brings with it good feelings. What information your brain can't find readily it makes up as best it can, which is why you sometimes get names mixed up, for instance.

Alphabet soup: EFT and TFT

EFT's roots are in Thought Field Therapy (TFT), which was discovered by Dr Roger Callahan, a cognitive psychologist and hypnotherapist who specialised in phobias. In the 1980s, Dr Callahan had been studying the Chinese meridians and their effect on emotions when you tap on certain meridians. A patient, Mary, came to see him. Mary had an intense phobia of water and, up to that time, Dr Callahan hadn't had much luck in curing her with his conventional therapies. During this particular session, however, Mary complained of feeling sick in her stomach at the mere thought of being near water, and Dr Callahan asked her to think about her phobia while tapping several times under her eye, which is the stomach meridian. After several minutes of tapping, to Dr Callahan's amazement, Mary suddenly jumped up and announced that her phobia had gone. She went over to Dr Callahan's

pool (this was, of course, California), feeling no anxiety or sickness in her stomach, and even splashed water on her face.

Apart from the fact that her phobia disappeared so quickly, what was also interesting about this experiment was that, although Mary's phobia to water had disappeared, she said she had no intention of jumping into the pool because she couldn't swim.

Gary Craig, a Stanford engineer and ordained minister, trained with Dr Callahan in TFT and applied this method to his clients. Over the years, he simplified the method and found that it wasn't necessary to tap in sequence or on so many meridians. Others tried also to adapt the method but it was Gary's that was the simplest and most effective of all, and so Emotional Freedom Technique was born in the early 1990s.

Whether it's to protect you from future life-threatening events is unclear, but unfortunately bad or negative memories are easier to remember and recall than good or positive memories.

The cause of all negative emotions is a disruption in the body's energy system. In EFT this statement is known as the *discovery statement*. It was once thought that bad memories caused negative emotions, but we now know that the disruption in your body's energy system actually causes the negative emotions and responses. This disruption causes a blockage in your energy system, and can be triggered again either consciously or unconsciously. For example, say you were locked in a cleaning cupboard as a very small child and you were scared. Whether you remember the incident or not, as an adult you may not like being in dark places, a small room or even the smell of certain cleaning materials.

Each time something triggers a negative memory, your brain also brings with it the negative emotion such as fear, anger, or hurt. These bad memories send an alert message to your brain and at the same time create a negative emotion. Because these type of messages to your brain are like electrical impulses, they act like a bolt of lightning that short-circuits your body's energy system, causing a blockage or an imbalance. It's this disruption that causes emotional and physical problems. You can find out more on emotions and the brain in Chapter 2.

Unless you release these blockages, they can remain locked in your body's energy system for years or even a lifetime and are only evident when you start suffering from symptoms such as anger, fear, low self-esteem, addiction, and anxiety, for example. This endless re-triggering reinforces the belief that you can't remove the problem, which is why you often hear someone say 'I've always had this fear', or 'I can't change the way I feel (or behave); it's the way I am'.

What causes this energy disruption in some people and not in others depends upon:

- ✔ The way you were brought up or conditioned to respond to negative events.
- ✔ If you were affected by a psychological or emotional trauma.
- ✔ A birth defect.
- ✔ An emotional incident whether past or present.
- ✔ Possibly *geopathic stress* – a name given to natural or man-made energies emanating from the earth which are detrimental to our health.

Memories can also be triggered by any or all of your senses – sight, smell, touch, taste, sound – reactivating the energy disruption and resulting negative emotion.

Table 1-1 demonstrates how a person's energy system is disrupted on seeing a spider they believe will harm them. Notice how the negative disruption affects thoughts, feelings, and behaviour. The negative thought or memory triggers a disruption in the body's energy system, experienced as psychological, physical, or emotional pain.

Table 1-1	Disruption in the Body's Energy System
Thought	Spiders are deadly; they're dangerous; must send message to brain
Emotion	Fear
Physical feeling	Paralysis, heart racing, sweaty palms
Behaviour	Run, hit out, cower

Travelling the meridian highway

Physicists have changed people's understanding of energy by proposing that all 'solid' objects, including your body, are made up of energy. You know this because doctors can measure them when you have an electroencephalography (EEG) or a magnetic resonance imaging (MRI) scan. This energy that flows through your body can't be seen by the naked eye but if you were able to picture your body as a three-dimensional roadmap, you'd see a whole network of invisible pathways interconnecting with each other, acting like electrical circuits. These electrical circuits are known as meridians and they connect to the tissues,

organs, and every atom, cell, bone, and tendon in your body. The meridians interact with each other and transmit information faster than the speed of light, sending signals to alter body temperature or to regulate emotion, and also to signal you when you need to release water, for instance. Chinese medicine refers to this as a life-force called 'chi' (pronounced 'chee').

As long as you're in pretty good emotional health, these meridians maintain a constant balance and flow.

The figure shows you what the meridian highway looks like.

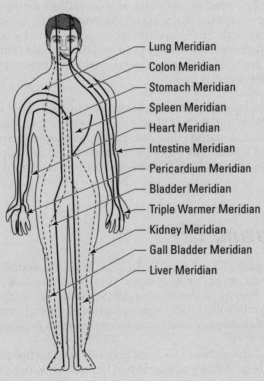

- Lung Meridian
- Colon Meridian
- Stomach Meridian
- Spleen Meridian
- Heart Meridian
- Intestine Meridian
- Pericardium Meridian
- Bladder Meridian
- Triple Warmer Meridian
- Kidney Meridian
- Gall Bladder Meridian
- Liver Meridian

Table 1-2 shows some further examples of how you can react to an memory or emotion that has been triggered.

Table 1-2	Reaction to a Trigger
Area Affected	*Results in . . .*
Emotion	Anger, shame, jealousy, fear
Behaviour	Hitting the bottle, hitting someone, running away
Physiology	Heart racing, sweating, feeling agitated
Belief	Can't achieve, mustn't do, not good enough

Soothing the negative

During an EFT session you're tapping on various meridian points around your body while concentrating on the problem. This sends vibrations along your energy path, and these vibrations get to work by unblocking, or in other words, *rebalancing* the energy system. This process removes the excess or irrational reaction but leaves the rational and normal reaction. If all this sounds like magic, it is.

Now before I get carried away, I must say that EFT isn't a universal remedy for everything and it can't claim to cure every ailment known to man or woman for that matter – nor can it give you longer eyelashes or whiter teeth. However, it's a therapy that has the potential to develop into a revolutionary new way of healing. With EFT, the philosophy is to try it on everything and see.

Practising EFT

You can apply EFT on anyone. Anyone? Well, yes actually. As long as you have a modicum of common sense, there's no reason why not. EFT enhances any other healing or self-help modality, whether it be counselling, hypnotherapy, reiki, reflexology, neurolinguistic programming, cognitive behaviour therapy, play therapy, and many more therapies besides.

Many ideas throughout this book enhance your techniques with EFT but here are three helpful tips you may like to remember before you begin:

✔ **Openness:** I can appreciate that you may still be a little sceptical even up to this point and, I have to admit, I was the same when I first heard about EFT. I had to see it work with my own eyes before I could truly believe. If you can leave your scepticism to one side while reading this book and carrying out the exercises, I'd greatly appreciate it. If you're willing to do this, I can promise you an amazing experience. Although you don't have to believe in EFT for it to work, it enhances your experience.

✔ **Humour:** Obviously, there's a time and place to use humour, especially when you're working on someone else. It helps not to take yourself too seriously. By injecting some humour when you're working with someone else you'll find that you achieve a greater rapport with them. In Chapter 5, I share with you some enlightening techniques and phrases I use with clients that can help break down the barriers.

✔ **Creativity:** Try thinking of EFT as more of an art than a science and you'll find that being creative with your approach is one way of getting good results. Time and time again people ask me what phrases they should use. I always say this comes with time and practice, but throughout the book I give suggestions to help you along the way. Meanwhile, let your creativity flow.

You use EFT on a problem like this:

1. **Tune into your problem or issue and measure its intensity on a scale between zero and 10, with 10 being the highest.**

   For example, say that you're afraid of flying. You travel a lot for work. So perhaps you'd rate this problem as an 8.

2. **Start tapping on certain parts of the body while saying a phrase acknowledging the problem and accepting yourself.**

   For example, perhaps you tap on the back of your hand while humming a song, counting from 1 to 5 out loud, and rolling your eyes, humming, and tapping again. You no doubt think that doing all this sounds wacky or like voodoo, but I assure you, it absolutely works.

One of EFT's many attractive qualities is that it's portable enough to be used on someone over the telephone and I work with a lot of my clients this way. If you want to know more, Chapter 17 takes you through the pros and cons and explains how this works in practice.

Remarkably, this healing tool works virtually without negative side effects so there's:

✔ No surgery.

✔ No needles.

✔ No medication.

✔ No months or years of therapy.

✔ No need to remove clothing.

✔ No need for you to revisit or remember all the traumatic event.

✔ Certainly no brainwashing.

I can't think of any other therapy that's as quick, safe, gentle, non-invasive, suitable for adults and babies, and even suitable for use on animals and pets. What's more, it's a therapy that you can self-apply.

Finding Help with EFT

It's difficult to measure, but it's estimated that practitioners have used EFT on millions of people for a variety of reasons. Here's a small example of what you can use EFT on:

Phobias	Relationship issues
Fears	Lack of motivation
Insomnia	Blushing
Panic attacks	Effects of chemotherapy
Addictions (smoking, alcohol, food, for example)	Performance
Cravings	Public speaking
Grief	Shyness
Stress	Enuresis (bedwetting)
Anxiety	Habits (nail-biting, hair-pulling, for instance)
Pain	Anger
Trauma and abuse	

Do tell your GP if you're experiencing an improvement in your symptoms as a consequence of EFT. The technique does deserve some credit, after all. The more reports the medical profession receive that EFT works, the more likely they are to either use it on patients or refer them to a qualified practitioner.

No matter how well it works for you, don't use EFT to replace any medication your GP prescribes.

Seeking a Therapist

As with any other therapies, you need to recognise when to seek professional help or advice. This section gives you some guidance in this respect.

Compared to other techniques, EFT is usually quite gentle and you can often achieve substantial relief with little or no pain. Some people's issues, however, are so intense that the mere mention of them causes emotional or physical pain. Although truly serious instances of a severe reaction to a memory such as a panic attack are most likely to occur in seriously emotionally damaged people (approximately less than 1 per cent of the population), beginners of EFT need to employ sensible precautions in this regard and not go where not qualified. I discuss how to handle such reactions in more detail in Chapter 4.

Although EFT produces remarkable clinical results, it's still in the experimental stage and practitioners and the public must take complete responsibility for their use of it. If you want to discuss the use of EFT for a specific emotional or physical problem with a professional in the mental health field, then you need to enquire where these practices are listed. Where appropriate, consult a qualified doctor.

Other occasions when you may need to seek the help or advice of an EFT practitioner are:

- ✔ Overwhelming emotions.
- ✔ Insufficiently trained.
- ✔ Lack of progress.
- ✔ Getting stuck.
- ✔ Childhood abuse cases.
- ✔ Intense trauma.
- ✔ Mental health issues.

If in doubt, seek guidance from a qualified practitioner.

Chapter 2

Understanding Emotions

• •

• •

*T*he medical profession has come to realise that negative emotions play havoc with your physical and mental health, individual development, and human relations. If you're emotionally healthy, you have the confidence and drive to achieve in life. You also have better physical health.

Still not sure that negative emotions link to your physical health? Ask yourself, when did your physical symptoms begin, and then try to think back to what was going on in your life around that time. More often that not, you find a link with the physical symptoms and the emotional event. Maybe the link is with an emotional event that happened some time ago but has been reawakened somehow. For instance, you may have found yourself crying at the funeral of someone you vaguely knew, and were surprised that you reacted so emotionally when you hadn't grieved as fully for the earlier loss of a parent.

In this chapter, I explain what it means to be emotionally healthy and how your brain reacts to emotional events. I encourage you to explore any buried emotions you may have and to discover how Emotional Freedom Technique (EFT) can help with these, without exposing yourself to any unpleasant memories. The more you know about your feelings and how you can deal with them, the better you feel about yourself.

As an emotional healing tool, EFT is very simple in its application and provides a range of approaches to clear emotional issues. At the same time EFT restores your emotional health and has a profound effect on improving your physical health.

Understanding the Basics of Emotions

Scientists and theorists still continue to debate on whether a connection exists between the way in which you behave and your emotions. The subject is complex so I won't even try to compete with scientists on this one. What experts do know is that emotional states aren't something that happen to you; rather, you create them based on how you view the world.

Your emotions are a series of electrical and chemical signals that your brain interprets to produce a particular feeling. This emotion then drives a series of decisions about what to do next.

Ask two people about memories of their last holiday and you may get two very different responses. Person A's holiday may have been fantastic because he had good weather, a fabulous hotel, and no flight delays. Person B's holiday may have been terrible because the hotel wasn't as the brochure described, the food was so bad she had food poisoning, and the travel company won't compensate her. If I ask Person A and Person B to visualise the experience of their holiday and to note what emotion they feel you can imagine they won't be the same. Person B may never go back to that destination again because she firmly believes that if she does she'll have a negative experience.

This simple demonstration shows how your emotions are split between psychological (what you think) and biological (what you feel). It also demonstrates how negative emotions can affect your behaviours and beliefs. Regardless of whether they're positive or negative, your brain responds to your thoughts and memories by releasing hormones and chemicals that send you into a state of arousal, causing you to feel an emotion. Arousal happens due to a 'trigger' and you may respond either positively and form an attachment, or negatively where you develop an aversion that you express as anger or hatred. Table 2-1 gives some examples of how your five senses can trigger an emotion, either positive or negative.

Table 2-1	Senses and Potential Triggers
Sense	*Trigger*
Sight	Visiting a particular place
Smell	The distinct smell of flowers, perfume, or smoke
Hearing	The sound of someone's voice or a certain noise
Touch	A particular touch or caress
Taste	Your first meal in a highly recommended restaurant

The negative emotions are the ones that cause the disruption to your body's energy system. Next time a scene in a film makes you cry or your partner makes you angry, take note where in your body you're feeling your emotion; perhaps you feel anxiety in your stomach or sadness in your heart.

Naming your emotions

An emotion is a type of feeling, and verbalising or naming your emotions can help to tame them. Brain scans show that putting negative emotions into words calms the brain's emotion centre. Although the words you use during an EFT session aren't that important, you can find it very helpful to express those feelings in a more accurate manner. As a practitioner, it's useful to recognise the many different meanings that people attach to emotions.

If you express yourself as feeling sad, this may actually mean you feel rejected, yet to someone else it may mean they feel heartbroken. Table 2-2 shows some common emotions and the different meanings they can contain.

Table 2-2	Emotions and Their Other Meanings
Emotion	*Other meanings*
Anger	Resentful, bitter, unjust, stubborn, unforgiving, hateful, fearful, offended, disgusted, shameful, disappointed, guilty, humiliated
Sadness	Unhappy, grief-stricken, lonely, abandoned, rejected, blamed, heartbroken, miserable, let down
Fear	Uneasy, terrified, anxious, petrified, worried, threatened, agitated, exposed, mistrusting, cautious, embarrassed

Build up a vocabulary of your negative emotions and their effect on you. Do you avoid certain people, for instance, because you feel inferior? Do you clench your teeth during meetings? Keep a note of all these occurrences of negative emotions in a diary and After you become skilled at recognising your emotions. After you get to grips with the EFT routine I describe in Chapters 3 and 4, you're better prepared to deal with those negative emotions. Remember, EFT works no matter how long you've had the problem.

Keeping a lid on emotions

You experience all kinds of emotional upsets during your lifetime and generally you deal with them in the proper manner. Regulating your emotions is important if you want to successfully interact with other people. For example, you may feel frustrated at not finding your shoe size in the shop, but you wouldn't scream and shout at the assistant!

When words can't describe

Alexithymia means literally 'no words for feelings'. It's a common condition, particularly among people who have experienced traumatic or deprived childhoods. Without words for feelings, it becomes impossible to deal with those feelings. When using EFT, you may find it easier to describe your emotions as a shape and/or colour instead. So, for example, you may describe 'anger' as a red ball, 'sadness' as a black bowling ball weighing 5 kilograms, ' abandonment' as an empty box, and so on.

How you respond to emotional experiences usually lies with your parents, teachers, upbringing, gender, or culture. In Iranian culture, for example, expressing negative emotions in a direct way isn't acceptable and Americans think that expressing anger rather than suppressing it is healthy. If your parents told you 'boys don't cry', 'put it to the back of your mind', or 'keep a stiff upper lip' then these beliefs become buried in your subconscious.

By the time you've reached adulthood you may be as good at burying your emotions as you are at letting them go. As the character in a Woody Allen movie cheerfully put it, 'I never get angry; I grow a tumour instead.'

It's well known that suppressed emotions can lead to depressed behaviour, though be reassured here that no matter how long you've modelled this behaviour, you can change.

Consciously suppressing emotions can happen because:

- ✔ You may not know how to react emotionally because you've not been in that situation before so you internalise the situation until you have accessed the facts.

- ✔ You may want to protect others: you witness someone being injured and go to help her, yet despite your own shock and upset, you can't let your feelings show while you're helping her.

- ✔ You may want to protect yourself: you may have been ridiculed for expressing your emotions at some time in your life or been hurt either physically or emotionally over a period of time. Either way, you make a decision never to allow yourself to show your feelings.

Examples like these show how you can easily suppress emotions.

Negative emotions stop you from thinking and behaving rationally, and seeing situations in their true perspective. When negative emotions take you over, you tend to see only what you want to see and remember only what you want to remember. This situation only prolongs the anger or grief and prevents you from enjoying life. The longer this situation goes on, the more entrenched the problem becomes.

Dealing with negative emotions inappropriately can also be harmful – for example, expressing anger with violence. Releasing your emotions acts like the valve on a pressure cooker, relieving your inner tensions. In a relationship, holding on to or disguising emotions can lead your partner to believe you lack feeling or even misinterpret your feelings. Chapter 8 explores relationships in more detail.

Holding back the tears?

Tears of joy and sadness relieve stress and stimulate healing. Dr William Frey made an interesting discovery. He revealed that emotional tears – such as when you're happy, upset, or stressed – contain different chemicals to the ones you produce when you, say, cut up onions. The emotional tears contain more protein-based hormones, which act as natural painkillers – which probably explains why you usually feel better after a good cry. So next time you feel like crying, go ahead, safe in the knowledge that you're doing your body a favour.

Few people cry for no reason but if you find yourself crying a lot in response to criticism take a look at Chapter 7. Many people find that they've forgotten all about these hidden emotions that they've stored away in their subconscious.

George arrives home from work and his wife casually asks if he's remembered to phone the electrician. George explodes and accuses his wife of not trusting him and shouts, 'Why do you treat me like a child?' George's wife is taken aback, as is George. What his wife didn't know, and what George hadn't realised, was that a subconscious reaction triggered his outburst. When George was younger, his father often blamed him when things went wrong and frequently told George that he couldn't be trusted to do anything.

You've probably surprised yourself at times by reacting out of character when you were least expecting it. Ask yourself if your behaviour may have stemmed from a past experience and make a note to treat it with EFT as I explain in Chapters 3 and 4.

How you deal with suppressed emotions depends on you. Maybe you go off to the gym and take it out on the squash court, or let off steam at anyone who gets in your way on the road. Perhaps you go down to the pub and tranquilise your negative emotions at the bar. Other ways that may help you to cope with your negative emotions include:

- Trying not to exaggerate things by going over and over them again in your mind.
- When negative thoughts enter your head, not trying to prevent them intruding. You're in control, so allow them to come in and allow them to go out.

> ✓ Working out how to relax with activities such as playing your favourite music, having a warm bath, or watching a funny movie.
>
> ✓ Accepting that the past is just that and letting it go.
>
> ✓ Exercising to release endorphins, which make you feel better.

Industries such as gambling, alcohol, drugs, fashion, and retail are just a few that profit very nicely out of providing people with temporary tranquilisers. Try stepping back and noticing what you resort to in times of emotional upset.

Pinpointing Emotional Health

Being emotionally healthy doesn't necessarily mean being happy all the time. Happiness comes and goes very quickly, and nobody's happy all the time: life throws things at you when you least expect it to.

If you're not emotionally healthy you may not have a sense of wellbeing and you probably find that coping with life's events is difficult. As a result, your emotions can manifest themselves as physical symptoms. (See the section 'Reaping the Rewards of Emotional Health,' later in this chapter.)

Emotional health means possessing:

> ✓ A sense of wellbeing and contentment in mind, body, and spirit.
>
> ✓ Self-realisation – taking part in life to the fullest, through meaningful activities and positive relationships.
>
> ✓ The ability to deal with stress in life and bounce back from misfortune.
>
> ✓ The ability to change, grow, and experience a range of feelings as life's circumstances change.
>
> ✓ The ability to enjoy life and have fun.
>
> ✓ A sense of balance in one's life – between solitude and sociability, work and play, sleep and wakefulness, rest and exercise, and so on.
>
> ✓ The ability to care for oneself and for others.
>
> ✓ Self-confidence and self-esteem.

Using EFT daily on each of your problems or just to start the day greatly improves your overall emotional health.

The World Health Organization Declaration

In 2005, 52 national health ministers of the World Health Organization signed a Mental Health Declaration for Europe, declaring, amongst other things, a commitment to promoting emotional wellbeing amongst children and young adults in education. This declaration demonstrates the growing awareness and importance of emotional health.

Reaping the Rewards of Emotional Health

Generally, people like to think they have good emotional heath without knowing exactly what it is. Poor emotional health generally arises from suppressing your emotions, which then affect your physical health. Recently, the medical profession has begun to recognise the importance of taking care of emotional health and the relationship between emotions and disease. Applying EFT on your suppressed emotions can restore both your emotional and, ultimately, your physical health.

While you're going through an emotionally stressful time you may recognise that you don't take care of your health as well as you should: you may not feel like exercising, eating nutritious foods, or taking medicine that your doctor prescribes. You may even increase your intake of alcohol, tobacco, or other drugs. All these are signs of poor emotional health. Physical symptoms can include:

✔ Back pain

✔ Bowel problems

✔ Chest pain

✔ Diabetes

✔ Insomnia

✔ High blood pressure

✔ Headaches

✔ Migraines

✔ Sexual problems

✔ Shortness of breath

✔ Skin disorders

Psychological symptoms may manifest themselves in:

✔ Addictions

✔ Avoidance behaviours

✔ Irritability

✔ Lack of confidence

✔ Low self-esteem

✔ Mood swings

✔ Relationship issues

✔ Unrealistic fears

✔ Weight problems

This advice may sound obvious, but try paying close attention to your body and question whether any of the symptoms in these lists may be symptomatic of some underlying emotional disturbance. To put it another way, what is your body trying to tell you?

Introducing the Three Brains and EFT

Your brain and your emotions are intrinsically linked. Different areas of the brain have specific functions, but the brain is basically divided into three parts: the reptilian brain, the limbic brain, and the cerebral cortex. Figure 2-1 shows you how they are positioned.

Reptilian brain

In evolutionary terms, your oldest brain is called the *reptilian brain*. This brain keeps your circulation, respiration, and digestion going even when you're asleep. Its primary focus is on self-preservation and survival, but it's also where aggression stems from. Your very first experiences as a child are strongly imprinted in the reptilian brain because it's the only part of the brain that's really active at the time.

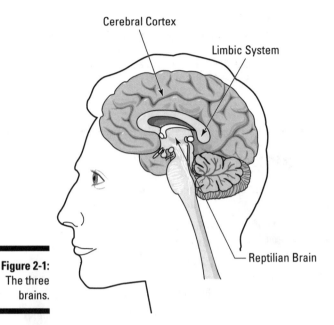

Cerebral Cortex

Limbic System

Reptilian Brain

Figure 2-1:
The three
brains.

Limbic brain

Wrapped around the reptilian brain is the limbic brain, where you process
emotions – both positive and negative – and reactions to certain words.
This brain is where your nurturing, loving, and caring feelings come from,
and it also regulates emotions and transmits them along neural pathways
to the cortex. The reptilian and limbic brains then influence the hypothalamus, which transmits a message that triggers appropriate physical
responses. Pleasure may link to chemical signals produced by the release
of noradrenalin, and pain is associated with many neurotransmitters. Mood
appears to link to serotonin and dopamine.

Cerebral cortex

Humans have not only a reptilian and limbic brain, but also a third brain
called the cerebral cortex, which wraps around the outside of the other two.
This third brain makes humans more sophisticated than reptiles or animals.
As a result, humans can react to words, handle and show emotion, think
logically and rationally, communicate verbally, tell the time, drive a car, and
do a host of other things that reptiles or animals can't.

Applying EFT as I describe in Chapters 3 and 4 while bringing to mind a disturbing memory or anxiety-provoking image causes changes in the neurological connections to the amygdala in the brain (see the nearby sidebar 'Explaining the brain'). These changes reduce the anxious response to that memory or image. In Chapters 3, 4, and 5 you have an opportunity to see how this works when you try the exercises.

Explaining the brain

Different parts of the brain have different functions. Some of the most important are:

- **Amygdala:** Involved in signalling the cortex of motivationally significant stimuli such as those that are reward and fear related.

- **Hypocampus:** Required for the formation of long-term memories.

- **Hypothalamus:** Affects and regulates blood pressure, heart rate, hunger, thirst, sexual arousal, and the sleep/wake cycle.

- **Mammillary body:** Important for the formation of memory.

- **Nucleus accumbens:** Involved in reward, pleasure, and addiction.

- **Orbitofrontal cortex:** Required for decision making.

- **Parahippocampal gyrus:** Plays a role in the formation of spatial memory and is part of the hippocampus.

- **Thalamus:** The 'relay station' to the cerebral cortex.

Chapter 3

The Basic EFT Tapping Routine

. . . .

. . . .

*T*he EFT tapping routine consists of four basic steps, two of which are identical. You must carry out these four steps in a set order. Trying the routine on yourself for the first time may seem a little confusing, but don't worry: after a couple of goes you soon get used to it. Although the technique isn't complicated, I advise you to read to the end of this chapter in order to familiarise yourself with the location of the tapping points on your body and find out how to measure your level of emotion. I often say that it's like a song and dance routine – get to grips with the steps before introducing the song.

This chapter illustrates the meridian points you tap on and offers some practical advice before taking you through the four basic steps. Don't worry: EFT is extremely gracious, and you'd have to try very, very hard to get it so wrong that you don't get a result.

Familiarising Yourself with the Points

During EFT you rub or tap on certain meridian points on your body while saying a phrase. Before you introduce the words, you'll find it helpful to get a feel for where the points are on your body. EFT uses these points because they're the end points of the major meridians that, when tapped on, stimulate the energy around your system and, more importantly, because they tend to work. If you want more information on meridians, look at Chapter 1. Further on in this chapter, I introduce you to these points again as you incorporate them into the EFT routine.

The Sore Spot

The Sore Spot is an acupuncture meridian that relates to the lymphatic system. The spot feels tender (sore) when you rub it because lymphatic congestion tends to occur here. This meridian initially stores and controls all chi (energy).

You can find the Sore Spot (see Figure 3-1) halfway between your nipple and your collarbone (where you'd place your hand when giving a pledge). It's a soft area that feels a little tender if you press into it. Unlike other points on your body, you always rub the Sore Spot gently instead of tapping it. If it doesn't feel tender, don't worry: the technique still works.

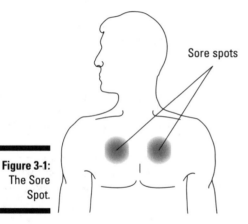

Sore spots

Figure 3-1:
The Sore
Spot.

The Karate Chop

The Karate Chop, shown in Figure 3-2, is in the middle of the fleshy part on the side of your hand. When tapping here you can either use the fingers of one hand to tap firmly on the fleshy part of the other hand or tap both fleshy parts together as Figure 3-3 shows.

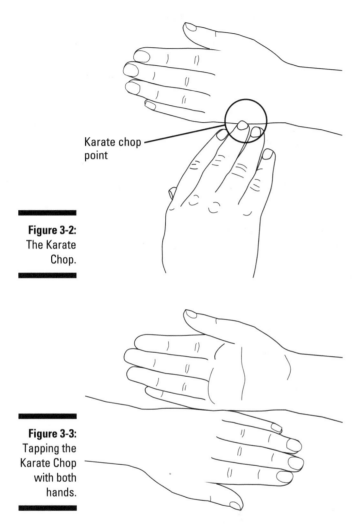

Figure 3-2:
The Karate
Chop.

Karate chop
point

Figure 3-3:
Tapping the
Karate Chop
with both
hands.

Remaining tapping points

The remaining tapping points and their abbreviated names that the EFT routine refers to are as follows. Figure 3-4 shows them all:

- ✔ **Eyebrow (EB):** Found at the beginning of the eyebrow or where the eyebrow meets the top of the nose.
- ✔ **Side of eye (SE):** This is situated on the bony part alongside the eye, slightly out towards the temple.

✔ **Under the eye (UE):** Underneath the eye in line with the iris, again on the bony part.

✔ **Under the nose (UN):** Beneath the nose but above the top lip.

✔ **Chin (CH):** Not actually on your chin but on the part that indents in. Found between the bottom lip and the protruding part of the chin.

✔ **Collarbone (CB):** If you feel around the area where a man would tie a knot in his tie you find a 'V' shape. Go to the top of that 'V' and you find it connects to your collarbone. Tap just beneath this area.

Don't confuse the collarbone point with the Sore Spot in Figure 3-1.

✔ **Under arm (UA):** Located approximately 4 inches or 4 finger widths below your armpit at the side of your body.

If any of these points are difficult to reach or are uncomfortable to tap on, you can leave them out and see whether you still get results. Alternatively, you can take a look at Chapters 13, 14, and 16 for other ways to use EFT without actually tapping.

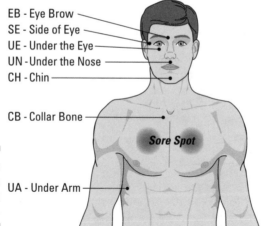

EB - Eye Brow
SE - Side of Eye
UE - Under the Eye
UN - Under the Nose
CH - Chin
CB - Collar Bone
Sore Spot
UA - Under Arm

Figure 3-4: The main tapping points.

The finger points

All the finger points are on the outside edge of the finger where the nail meets the skin, as Figure 3-5 shows.

✔ **Thumb (TH):** Outside edge of thumbnail.

✔ **Index finger (IF):** Outside edge of index fingernail.

✔ **Middle finger (MF):** Outside edge of middle fingernail.

✔ **Little finger (LF):** Outside edge of little or baby fingernail.

✔ **Gamut Point (GP):** In the crease on the back of the hand between the little finger and ring finger.

You may notice that I leave out the ring finger. This is because you tap on the meridian that passes through the ring finger when you do the nine gamut procedure that I describe in the later section 'Step 3: The nine gamut procedure'.

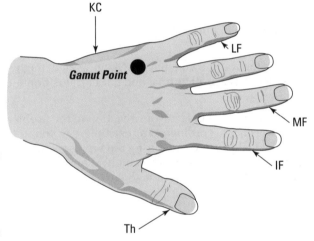

Figure 3-5: Finger and gamut tapping points.

Th - Thumb
IF - Index Finger
MF - Middle Finger
LF - Little Finger
KC - Karate Chop

Putting EFT into Action

Here are some practical hints and tips to note before you begin. The method of tapping that I describe here is only a suggestion, by the way; please feel free to use whatever works for you.

✔ Practise finding the points that Figures 3-1 to 3-5 show before moving on to the four basic steps I list later in this chapter.

✔ Although it doesn't matter, you may prefer to use your dominant hand to tap.

✔ Most people use their index and middle finger to tap, but you can use the pads or tips of any number of fingers from either hand while you tap firmly – but not hard enough to hurt yourself. Alternatively, you can tap with the flat of your hand. Use whichever is comfortable for you.

✔ Tap rhythmically and approximately (and I mean approximately) seven or eight times on each point – neither too fast nor too slow. Try tapping to the tune of 'Jingle Bells' to begin with to get an idea.

✔ You can tap on either your right side or left side, and you can switch sides during the tapping sequence if you like. For instance, you can tap under your left eye and then under your right arm.

✔ To avoid any interferences, and to get the most out of EFT, I suggest you ensure that you're well hydrated by drinking a glass of water before you begin, remove your glasses and watch, and switch off your mobile phone. (Refer to Chapter 6 for more information on what can interfere with EFT working.)

✔ Don't worry about tapping on the exact meridian points that Figures 3-1 to 3-5 illustrate. You're not looking for a bulls-eye here – somewhere in the vicinity will do.

✔ During the tapping routine you may feel light-headed, tingly, or emotional. These feelings are all normal and not harmful. Continue tapping if you can.

✔ You may also notice a change in your reaction to the problem, so change your wording accordingly. For example, say you're tapping on your feelings of being angry and during the tapping you notice that your feelings have changed to being more mildly annoyed. You can easily adjust your wording from 'Even though I'm angry . . .' to 'Even though I'm annoyed . . .'.

✔ Preferably, tap every day and as often as you can.

Using EFT: The Four Basic Steps

Before carrying out the four basic steps, give yourself sufficient time to get the hang of which points to tap on, as Figures 3-1 to 3-5 show. You'll find, with practice, the whole process takes you no more than two minutes to complete. Even if you're a beginner to EFT, without any experience whatsoever, you should still see results using this basic routine.

As you become more experienced and successful with the full tapping routine, you can move to the shortened version in Chapter 4 that works just as well but is quicker and less mechanical. If you're a beginner, I advise using the full routine that I show here, so you have a better chance of it working.

Step 1: Performing the Set-Up

The Set-Up consists of:

1. **Identifying the problem and focusing on it to disrupt your energy system.**

2. **Rating the level of intensity using the Subjective Units of Distress Scale in Figure 3-6.**

3. **Formulating a phrase for the problem.**

4. **Either rubbing the Sore Spot (Figure 3-1) or tapping on the Karate Chop (Figures 3-2 and 3-3) while repeating the formulated phrase three times. This helps to remove blockages to the functioning of EFT.**

Identifying the problem

When deciding which problem you want to work on, I suggest that if you're a beginner to start off by experimenting on something small such as a minor annoyance, pain, or fear. Maybe you have a headache or recently received a parking ticket, you're frustrated because you couldn't get through to a call centre, or a scene in a film scares you? As you think of your problem, how does it make you feel and where do you feel it in your body? Perhaps thinking of receiving the parking ticket makes you feel angry in your chest or remembering the scene in the film makes your heart race?

Measuring your SUD

SUD (not the soapy kind) is an acronym that Professor Joseph Wolpe developed in 1969 for Subjective Units of Distress. He used *SUDS*, the Subjective Units of Distress Scale, to measure the intensity of distress in response to a particular stimulus such as a memory. Distress isn't easy to quantify, which is why the technique is described as 'subjective'.

Having focused on the problem you want to work on, first measure the level of distress or intensity you feel now. It may be a good idea to write this down so that you have some indication of how you felt before and after using EFT. Referring to the SUDS in Figure 3-6 as a guideline, you may rate the pain of a headache at 6, for example, or if you feel extreme anxiety, you may rate this at a 9 or even 10.

You must always measure the level of intensity as you feel it at the present time and not what you imagine it may be. If you need some help arriving at a figure, try to remind yourself what caused you to be anxious in order to bring this feeling back. Perhaps you need to imagine hearing a person's voice, visualise a disturbing scene, or imagine yourself in an anxious situation. I'm not asking you to look for anything major here, just something relatively small that stirs up some emotion and disrupts your energy system.

Chapter 5 explains how to use gentle approaches to deal with very painful or unpleasant memories or feelings.

| 10 |
| 9 |
| 8 |
| 7 |
| 6 |
| 5 |
| 4 |
| 3 |
| 2 |
| 1 |
| 0 |

Figure 3-6:
The
Subjective
Units of
Distress
Scale
(SUDS).

Formulating a phrase for the problem

Having identified your problem, you now need to formulate what's known as a *Set-Up Phrase* to use with the tapping routine. As you repeat your Set-Up Phrase three times, at the same time you either rub your Sore Spot (Figure 3-1) or tap your Karate Chop (Figures 3-2 and 3-3).

If you're using the Sore Spot, start by gently rubbing this area in a circular motion using the pads of your index, middle, and ring fingers. Be sure to rub gently but firmly, yet never so hard that you hurt or bruise yourself.

EFT practitioners often refer to the Set-Up Phrase as the 'Affirmation'. Contrary to what you expect from an affirmation, which is normally in the positive, EFT focuses on the negative. Although focusing on the negative may sound odd, it brings the bad, negative memory, or disturbing thought, to the surface. Maintaining that focus on the negative during the whole of the EFT routine is essential because it keeps the disruption going so that EFT can work on it. If it helps, visualise setting up your negative thoughts, emotions, and so on as targets in a firing range so that you can shoot them down with EFT.

Be as specific as you can in describing the problem. Use the name of a person or place, or describe the location where you have the feeling. Saying 'Even though I have this headache over my right eye . . .', for instance, may get better results than saying 'Even though I have this headache . . .'; or say

'Even though Christopher's voice irritates me inside . . .' rather than 'Even though his voice makes me irritable . . .'. Chapter 4 describes specifics in greater detail and you can find language techniques in Chapter 15.

The first part of the Set-Up Phrase acknowledges the problem and how you feel about it right now. The second part of the Set-Up Phrase is your acceptance of how you feel and your willingness to let go of the problem or feeling. Traditionally, the Set-Up Phrase begins with 'Even though . . .' or 'Although . . .' and is usually followed by the generic Acceptance Phrase of 'I deeply and completely accept myself' or 'I forgive myself'. You use these words because they work and because accepting yourself as having the problem is an important feature of EFT, but it can cause some people to feel uncomfortable. If saying the Acceptance Phrase is very uncomfortable for you, try saying 'I'm okay' or 'I'm still a good person'. If you can't bring yourself to say anything positive at all about yourself, Chapter 7 steers you in the right direction.

This book suggests a host of phrases for various problems and issues. Some may not be traditional, but by all means try them out for size and vary them according to your own situation. Here are some examples to give you an idea:

> *'Even though I have this (anger, pain, sadness, memory), I deeply and completely accept myself.'*

> *'Even though I feel bad about not finishing my work on time, I accept that I was doing the best I could.'*

> *'Although I still feel guilty because I wasn't very kind, I accept that I'm not a bad person.'*

> *'Even though I don't like to hear certain words because of what they represent, I accept myself as a vulnerable human being.'*

> *'Although I doubt myself and my abilities, I want to accept myself as I am.'*

You can reverse the negative and positive if you find it easier:

> *'I accept myself without judgement, even though I have this anger.'*

> *'I want to heal, even though I'm holding on to this resentment.'*

> *'I accept that I wasn't a good person then, but this is now and I want to change.'*

> *'I forgive myself for having this (problem) and I forgive anyone that may have contributed to it.'*

Deciding on your Set-Up Phrase is the fun bit because you can use whatever words you like. Just think of how you feel and give it a brief description. Don't ban or censor anything – all you need to remember is to pair the negative with the positive as the examples in this section illustrate, and tune in to the problem at the same time.

Removing blockages to EFT

Rubbing the Sore Spot (Figure 3-1) or tapping the Karate Chop (Figures 3-2 and 3-3) while saying the Set-Up Phrase removes any potential blockages to EFT working. (You can find more information about blockages in Chapter 6.)

Say your Set-Up Phrase out loud if you can and describe your problem as if you're talking to a friend.

Here's an example of a simple Set-Up Phrase for a headache over your right eye. While rubbing the Sore Spot or tapping on the Karate Chop, repeat this Set-Up Phrase three times: 'Even though I have this headache over my right eye, I deeply and completely accept myself.'

Step 2: Applying the sequence

Having repeated your Set-Up Phrase of 'Even though I have this headache over my right eye' three times, you now go on to apply the sequence, which means tapping on the remaining meridian points while saying a shortened *Reminder Phrase*. You decide on this phrase, but in this example you may shorten this to 'this headache' or 'headache over right eye'. It's called a Reminder Phrase because it keeps you focused on or reminded of the problem. Using Figure 3-4 as a guide, tap approximately seven times on each of the meridian points as you say the shortened phrase.

Do try to breathe evenly and deeply as you carry out the tapping routine. The sequence is:

EB	Eyebrow	'Headache over right eye'
SE	Side of eye	'Headache over right eye'
UE	Under eye	'Headache over right eye'
UN	Under nose	'Headache over right eye'
CH	Between lip and chin	'Headache over right eye'
CB	Collarbone	'Headache over right eye'
UA	Under arm	'Headache over right eye'
TH	Outside edge of thumb	'Headache over right eye'
IF	Outside edge of index finger	'Headache over right eye'
MF	Outside edge of middle finger	'Headache over right eye'
LF	Outside edge of little finger	'Headache over right eye'

Visualise the points between the eyebrow and the collarbone as being set out like a question mark, and then move across the body to under the arm before tapping on the finger points.

Now move on to Step 3.

Step 3: The nine gamut procedure

When you complete the sequence finishing with the little finger, you're now ready to tap on the Gamut Point (see Figure 3-5). Still focusing on your problem, you need to roll your eyes, hum a tune, and count, otherwise known as the Nine Gamut Procedure. I can't blame you if you think I've lost it completely and feel like closing the book right now, but please stay with me on this one.

The Nine Gamut Procedure is a very useful brain balancing exercise that works by rolling your eyes, which stimulates certain parts of the brain such as memory, internal dialogue, and imagination. Likewise, humming engages the right-brain activity and counting activates the left brain. These exercises help fine tune the brain to the right frequency for the problem.

You can find the Gamut Point located on the back of the hand and it's approximately 1 centimetre up from the spot between the knuckles of the ring and little fingers (refer to Figure 3-5).

While continually tapping on the Gamut Point, carry out all the following nine steps:

1. **Close your eyes.**

2. **Open your eyes.**

3. **Look hard down to your right (without moving your head).**

4. **Look hard down to your left (without moving your head).**

5. **Roll your eyes in a full circle clockwise.**

For some people, rolling eyes can cause dizziness or can be difficult, but an alternative is the *Floor to Ceiling Eye Roll*. Instead of imagining following the hands of a clock, try very slowly raising your eyes up to the ceiling, hold for approximately 8 seconds, and then very slowly lower your eyes to the floor.

6. **Roll your eyes in a full circle anti-clockwise.**

7. **Hum approximately 5 seconds of any song ('Happy Birthday', the 'National Anthem', or anything you know).**

8. Count out loud and fast, 'one, two, three, four, five.'

9. Hum another 5 seconds of the song.

10. Now move on to Step 4.

Step 4: Repeating the sequence

Having completed the Nine Gamut Procedure, you now repeat the sequence again on each of the following meridians, again while saying the shortened version of your Set-Up Phrase, the Reminder Phrase:

EB	Eyebrow	'Headache over right eye'
SE	Side of eye	'Headache over right eye'
UE	Under eye	'Headache over right eye'
UN	Under nose	'Headache over right eye'
CH	Between lip and chin	'Headache over right eye'
CB	Collarbone	'Headache over right eye'
UA	Under arm	'Headache over right eye'
TH	Outside edge of thumb	'Headache over right eye'
IF	Outside edge of index finger	'Headache over right eye'
MF	Outside edge of middle finger	'Headache over right eye'
LF	Outside edge of little finger	'Headache over right eye'

After you complete each round of EFT, take a deep breath in, and gently breathe out. Now take a moment to check yourself. Using the Subjective Units of Distress Scale (see Figure 3-6), check whether your SUD level has come down to zero. Well done if it has! If not, don't despair: you just need to do one or more rounds until the level goes down, that's all, using a Remaining Phrase (see 'Dealing with Any Remaining Problems', later in this chapter).

The flowchart in Figure 3-7 helps you navigate your way around.

When you're tapping for yourself, or on someone else, you may come across a certain tapping point that acts like a pressure valve in releasing the negative emotion or pain. You can use this one particular point whenever you need a quick fix of EFT, such as at the traffic lights or in a waiting room. I often use the collarbone in times of need when in public, and who'd notice you doing something that's so discreet? Go ahead and experiment until you find the one point, or more, that works for you.

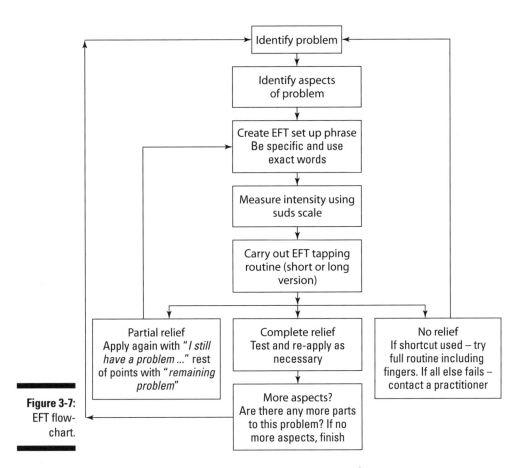

Figure 3-7:
EFT flow-
chart.

 Try not to become confused with the 'Reminder' and 'Remaining' phrases. The Reminder Phrase is a shortened version of the Set-Up Phrase that helps you stay focused on the problem. You use the Remaining Phrase when the first round of tapping doesn't resolve the problem and you have to repeat it with 'This remaining . . .' or 'I still have some . . .' (see the following section).

Dealing with Any Remaining Problems

Sometimes one round of EFT is all you need to obtain complete relief. Other times you may only get partial relief, and in this instance you need to do one or more rounds of Steps 1 and 2 again to bring the intensity down, which is where persistence is the key. The difference this time is that you need to change the Set-Up Phrase slightly in Step 1 and Step 2 to a Remaining Phrase. The *Remaining Phrase* acknowledges that you still have something left to work on, and you need to insert words such as 'remaining' or 'still'.

For instance, while tapping on the Karate Chop point or rubbing the Sore Spot, the Remaining Phrase in Step 1 for 'headache over right eye' may be something like 'Even though I still have some of this headache over my right eye, I deeply and completely accept myself' or 'Even though I have some remaining headache over my right eye, I deeply and completely accept myself'.

The sequence in Step 2 involves using a shortened Remaining Phrase such as 'remaining headache', 'still have a headache over right eye' or 'there's some headache left'. Tapping on the remaining meridian points, you may say:

EB	Eyebrow	'Remaining headache over right eye'
SE	Side of eye	'Remaining headache over right eye'
UE	Under eye	'Remaining headache over right eye'
UN	Under nose	'Remaining headache over right eye'
CH	Between lip and chin	'Remaining headache over right eye'
CB	Collarbone	'Remaining headache over right eye'
UA	Under arm	'Remaining headache over right eye'
TH	Outside edge of thumb	'Remaining headache over right eye'
IF	Outside edge of index finger	'Remaining headache over right eye'
MF	Outside edge of middle finger	'Remaining headache over right eye'
LF	Outside edge of little finger	'Remaining headache over right eye'

Check out your Subjective Units of Distress Scale again and see whether the problem has reduced. If the problem is still there, repeat Steps 1 and 2 with the Remaining Phrase again.

You don't need to carry out the Nine Gamut Procedure on any remaining problem; just carry out Steps 1 and 2.

Also notice how you're feeling now, both physically and emotionally, and notice whether any thoughts or memories are coming to the surface. You may discover some emotional feelings, a new understanding, or a logical explanation of the problem.

You may also notice that, even if the intensity level on this issue is lower, a new issue or emotion or memory may come up now. These are known as *aspects* of the problem (refer to Chapter 4) and you need to address them with a separate round of EFT.

If you're not getting complete relief after numerous rounds of EFT, there may be some underlying problems or interferences. You can find out more about these in Chapter 6, which also acts as a troubleshooting guide.

Looking for a Sign

So you're doing all the tapping and saying the words, but how do you know that EFT is working for you? Obviously, the major sign that EFT has worked is when you can think of the problem or issue again without having the negative emotion attached to it, or that your pain has lessened or gone.

During the application of EFT you may experience physical signs or sensations. The sensation may be a sigh like the 'Ahhhh!' when you sit down at the end of the day, or just a yawn. Muscle tension and tightness often releases because EFT helps relax your energy system. Energy moving and shifting in your physical body also gives you the sensation of warmth or tingling, either in certain areas or throughout your body. Chapter 4 has more information on what to look for when EFT starts to work.

People experience different signs and sensations when using EFT. Some of these are tingling around the mouth, feeling light-headed, tightness in the chest or shoulder, warmth, feeling emotional, and feeling very sleepy and relaxed. When I use EFT on myself and it starts to work, I find I get a slight tightness in my throat and I sigh a lot. I don't know if anyone else experiences what I do. Perhaps everyone has their own unique way of shifting their energy system. When using EFT, notice what your sign is. All these signs, by the way, are very normal and in no way harmful; they just demonstrate that a shift is taking place, which is very good news indeed.

Part II
Venturing Further with EFT

The 5th Wave   By Rich Tennant

"That's amazing. I knew EFT kept your blood flowing smoothly, but who knew it would work on clogged drains?"

In this part . . .

In this part you develop your EFT skills, and the confidence to try EFT out on yourself and others. I also lead you through the tricky business of using EFT to dig up and confront the causes of anxieties, employing sensitivity and humour along the way.

Not everything works smoothly all the time. Sometimes you find that you can't work out why something isn't working, so I include some hints and tips for when EFT doesn't seem to be doing the trick.

Chapter 4

Advancing Forwards with EFT

Sometimes the basic tapping routine I describe in Chapter 3 doesn't seem to work and then you need to identify what may be getting in the way. In this chapter, I offer ways to identify your Emotional Freedom Technique (EFT) roadblocks, as well as providing ideas on how you can overcome them. I also illustrate how to perform an even shorter version of the technique (as if it weren't quick enough already!).

If you're new to EFT, this chapter shows you where to begin, what tapping points to use, and what words to say. If you're experienced, then you may need to do a little detective work to get to the root of the problem, especially if you're not seeing any improvement. Whatever your level of experience, by all means feel free to use the following sections as your guide, but please trust and use your own intuition.

EFT complements qualified medical advice or treatment and is not a replacement.

Getting to the Root of the Problem

EFT is not a 'one-size-fits-all' therapy. Without knowing what the root of the problem is, or the strongest emotional driver behind the problem, you won't be able to aim the EFT treatment in the right direction. When you do, however, you dramatically improve your success rate, and get faster results.

Sometimes you find that the problem has several aspects to it or that you need more details in order for EFT to work effectively. Examining techniques shows you how to identify the different aspects of a problem and how to get to the root cause.

Aspects of the problem

A problem is a problem is a problem. . . . Every problem, though, usually has more than one part to it, and EFT practitioners call these different parts 'aspects'. Often you must treat each aspect with EFT in order to obtain complete relief. For instance, in your mind your fear of heights is just that. You won't necessarily see the many parts that make up that fear, or where it originated from, especially if you've had the problem for a long time. Sometimes you need to remove only one aspect with EFT for the rest to collapse.

Another way to describe aspects is to compare them to the game of Jenga, which is based on the principle of building a tower with blocks of wood. After building a tower, each player in the game removes one block of wood at a time from within the tower while trying to keep it intact. At some stage, a player removes a block and the whole tower collapses, so that player loses.

The model in Figure 4-1 illustrates how the game of Jenga can represent someone's memories of an accident. The tower corresponds to a particular problem and each block represents one aspect of that problem. You need to apply EFT to each of these aspects, such as 'Even though I can hear those screams . . .' and so on.

The best bit, though, is that you may not have to remove all the blocks (aspects) in order to bring down the whole tower – you only need to remove the ones supporting the tower.

Some aspects aren't so obvious, though, and no matter how crazy or silly they seem to you, you need to tap for them. See Chapter 3 for more on the basic tapping technique.

Regardless of your experience, you don't know how many aspects are likely to need treating. In a typical session, you may end up tapping for some of the aspects like those in the tower, or you may hit the problem head on first time.

Persistence pays with EFT.

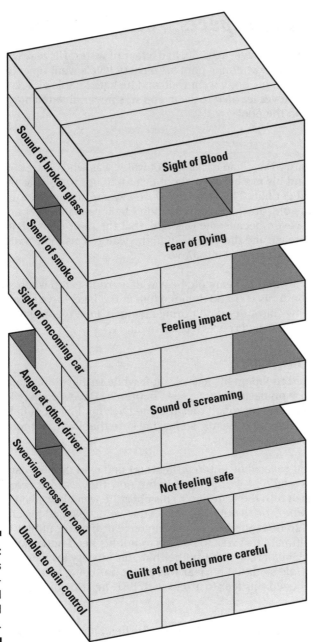

Figure 4-1:
Memories of an accident and its related aspects.

Sound of broken glass

Smell of smoke

Sight of oncoming car

Anger at other driver

Swerving across the road

Unable to gain control

Sight of Blood

Fear of Dying

Feeling impact

Sound of screaming

Not feeling safe

Guilt at not being more careful

Identifying aspects: A real-life example

Since he was young Dave, aged 50, had a fear of water. His fear was so great that if he entered a swimming pool his anxiety levels went up and if the water reached his chest, his body went rigid and he had a panic attack. Because of this fear, Dave never learned to swim and was never able to enjoy playing with his sons in the pool.

Early fears

The first memory Dave had of his fear of water was when, as a boy, he lived near a river and his mother kept shouting at him not to go near the river as the fish would get him. This fear kept Dave away from the river until he was about 11 years old, at which point he didn't believe his mother any more. He did know, however, because he was told, that the river was polluted so he could get a disease and die if he went in the water. This information was enough to put another fear into Dave.

When he was around 13 years old he was at a group camp when some boys teased him about his fear and dumped him in the lake. Dave scrambled to the side but relating this story didn't bring up much anxiety. (This was most likely because Dave had repressed the memory.)

Eliminating the fears

Dave was asked to tap on his fear of water while within view of a swimming pool. (For more on basic tapping, see Chapter 3.) Dave's anxiety levels went down to zero but he reckoned they'd come back up if he went in the pool. EFT is not about forcing events, so making sure that Dave felt comfortable within himself was important.

When Dave felt relaxed he entered the water and said that his usual anxiety levels would be 4 or 5 out of 10 but now they were at zero. When he lowered himself into the water up to his chest he was okay, even though he'd normally be 9 or 10 out of 10. When the water reached his chin he felt anxiety again so he tapped on his remaining fear of water until it went down to zero. His ultimate test was to be able to put his head under water and, although thinking of this didn't bother him, his anxiety levels rose when he tried it out. He said that his fear was about not being able to breathe. After Dave reduced this fear to a zero with EFT, he still couldn't put his head under.

So what was it specifically about putting his head under water that caused anxiety? Dave remembered the boys at camp dunked his head under water when they threw him in and this brought up his anxiety levels again. Dave used EFT on having his head dunked and eventually reduced his fear down to zero. He tried putting his head under again and after a while he was able to put his head under water and sit on the bottom of the pool. He felt so good that he kept on trying it out. All this took 45 minutes from beginning to end. Weeks later, Dave still felt comfortable putting his head under water.

Dave's fear may come back if he immersed himself in a river, because other aspects may come up such as the dark water, muddy river bottom, and so on. For now, Dave is content to be able to use the swimming pool.

Looking into the future

Knowing what questions to ask to get results, and when to ask them, comes with time and practice. With Dave, however, it was necessary to bring all these aspects up during the EFT session in order to eliminate each one to zero so that Dave could obtain complete relief from his fear. If he hadn't knocked down each aspect of the problem with EFT, Dave may have tried, at a later date, to put his head under water and his anxiety levels may have risen again. Dave's anxiety may come back if he ever went into a river but he knows he can use EFT to deal with his anxiety.

You may be interested to know that Dave has three brothers and none of them had the same fear of being in water as Dave had, even though they'd all been warned the same way about going near the river. What was interesting with Dave is that he experienced the energy disruption as a child when he thought the fishes would get him and his energy system was further disrupted when the boys at the group camp dunked his head in the river. Energy disruption in childhood may go some way to explaining why some people have irrational fears when others don't.

If EFT isn't working, it's not a fault in EFT but may be because you aren't addressing all aspects. If you don't treat all aspects, the problem may come back again at a later date.

Don't forget to keep in mind that an aspect can also be an emotion. You may find that the anger you had regarding an event shifts to sadness, which you need to use EFT on. Being aware of these different emotional aspects can take you deeper into the problem.

Being specific

Do you want quick and effective results? Then the best way is to make sure that the global problem is *chunked* or broken down into specifics. Examples are:

✔ Rather than saying 'Even though I'm afraid of heights. . .', try changing to 'Even though I was stuck on the fairground ride at 13 . . .'.

✔ Rather than saying 'Even though I feel rejected . . .', try changing to 'Even though I was rejected by my boyfriend, Alan . . .'.

Even when you identify and deal with the aspects, sometimes you need to describe those aspects in specific terms before you can achieve complete relief.

What you're looking for is the trigger that causes the emotional intensity associated with the memory or event. Asking the right questions, such as the ones in the following section 'Identifying the core issue', can be the key to bringing up to the surface those specifics that trigger the reaction.

Being specific helps you narrow down the problem and greatly increases your chances of success. I can't emphasise enough the importance of being specific when using EFT.

Listen to what words you use to describe the anxiety and use those exact words, no matter how silly or meaningless they may seem. If necessary, write words down.

Identifying the core issue

Discovering core issues is a fundamental part of EFT. The procedure is similar to peeling the layers off an onion to get to the core. Just like peeling onions, the process may involve some crying. The top layer is the problem you have right now, and by peeling off a layer at a time you can discover the real problem somewhere underneath. A problem with sleeping at night may eventually lead to having a fear of being alone. Similarly, a problem with trusting people may stem from being abandoned as a child.

Discovering core issues is what an EFT practitioner is good at, but you can be just as successful discovering and working on your own core issues. Just listen to what memories, thoughts, or feelings come up as you apply EFT on yourself and use EFT on each of the negative ones. Sometimes there can be a *daisy chain effect* where one problem clears up but another comes up to the surface. This is all a natural part of EFT.

If you're using EFT on yourself and you're still left with a feeling of confusion or some outstanding emotion, consult a qualified EFT practitioner for help and advice.

When looking for core issues remember that people have a tendency to push bad or unpleasant memories to the back of their minds so that the memory becomes repressed (refer to Chapter 2 if you want to know more). Just because someone shows little emotion when they're telling a story doesn't mean that they're not bothered. If you're having difficulty getting to the core issue, which may happen at some point, here are some questions that may help you:

- ✔ What does this (problem or issue) remind you of?
- ✔ How long have you had it?
- ✔ What was going on in your life at the time?
- ✔ When was the first or last time that you remember having this feeling?
- ✔ Name one person or event that has had a negative effect on you.
- ✔ What's your biggest regret?
- ✔ When did you last cry, and why?
- ✔ Is there a positive side to having this problem?
- ✔ Is there a remembered sound, voice, smell, or vision that may bring this feeling back?

If you're suffering from losing a loved one, the answer to the last question may be 'the look in their eyes'. The answer is a good place to start and maybe you can then go on to ask yourself, 'Where do I get that feeling in my body?' At that point you can use EFT on that sensation.

One suggested Set-up Phrase that you can use in this instance is 'Even though that look in their eyes hurts in my chest, I deeply and completely accept myself'. For more information on phrases see Chapter 3 and 'Selecting the Right Phrases', later in this chapter.

EFT doesn't have to be complicated. Common sense approaches are usually the most effective.

Generalisation effect

A feature of EFT is its ability to address many related problems at the same time. For instance, if you had 20 traumatic memories of being attacked, you may only need to remove 2 or 3 of those memories for the remaining ones to vanish too. While you treat one problem with EFT, the unrelated problems can also clear up.

Frequently, I've had reports from clients who, when EFT has eradicated a problem such as fear of flying, have also noticed other positive changes in their life. I don't mean they suddenly became concert pianists, or anything like that, but they felt confident enough to apply for job interviews or were able to take driving lessons – things they hadn't generally contemplated doing before their flying fear was removed. This *generalisation effect* is well known amongst EFT practitioners. You may be interested to recognise how other problem areas in your life improve as a consequence of clearing one with EFT.

Selecting the Right Phrases

I wish I had a penny for every time I'm asked, 'What words do I use during the Set-up Phrase or the Reminder Phrase?' (for more on these phrases, see Chapter 3). I understand why people ask this question, because choosing a suitable phrase was a source of concern for me in the early days of learning EFT. My answer is always the same: 'The choice of words doesn't matter as long as you tune into the negative emotion or the words help you tune into the negative emotion.' EFT isn't a psychological therapy but an energy therapy. The words surface to the top as you stir the pot of emotions.

Unless the memory is very painful or distressing, tuning in to the problem isn't that difficult. (For memories that are too painful to recall, see Chapter 6.) Suppose that your father often said to you as a child, 'You're good for nothing.' What brings those emotions to the surface in this instance is remembering those words, hearing his voice, or visualising his facial expression. Anything that gets the energy fired up helps. After the emotion is fired up you can then introduce the Set-up Phrase, which you repeat three times and can vary as in this example:

> *Set-up Phrase 1: 'Even though I'm good for nothing . . . I completely accept myself.'*
>
> *Set-up Phrase 2: 'Even though I'm good for nothing because my father says so . . . I completely accept myself as I am.'*
>
> *Set-up Phrase 3: 'Even though I have this good-for-nothing emotion . . . I deeply and completely accept myself.'*

When moving on to the Reminder Phrase you can again vary the words instead of being too mechanical and rote. As you tap on each of the points, use any words that come into your mind. After using the Set-up Phrase 'Even though I'm good for nothing', you can vary the wording in the Reminder Phrase. These are only examples and you must use whatever words are right for you:

'I'm good for nothing.'

'If my father says I'm good for nothing then it must be true.'

'His face as he says I'm good for nothing.'

'I can hear his voice saying I'm good for nothing.'

'He couldn't recognise my good qualities.'

'I only wanted to please him.'

'This good-for-nothing emotion.'

You can keep tapping on any of the tapping points I refer to in Chapter 3, varying the words as you go along. When you find any particular words that 'hit the button', keep tapping on them. Imitating the voice, expression, or stance of the person who caused you to feel shame, humiliation, hurt, anger, or any other negative emotion can all add to the tuning in process. Even picturing the person right in front of you can bring up the intense feelings that you can then apply EFT to.

Keep using EFT on each of the associated parts of the memory until they've reduced to a zero on the Subjective Units of Distress Scale (see Chapter 3) before moving on.

You don't always have to use a Set-up Phrase (in an emergency situation, for example) but when EFT doesn't appear to work, using a phrase can be very important. (You can find more on this topic in Chapter 6.)

Here are some other useful guidelines when creating your Set-up Phrase:

- ✔ Where possible, use strong positive words such as 'will' and 'want', and avoid weak words such as 'try', 'if', 'don't', 'can't', and 'but'.

- ✔ State what you want and not what you don't want.

- ✔ Your goal must be realistically possible.

- ✔ Your goal must be a 'stretch'. It must be big enough to be exciting.

- ✔ As long as you tune into what causes the upset about the memory, EFT works effectively.

- ✔ Try augmenting your goal with daydreams. Present tense daydreams can be the most powerful tool for establishing new consistent thoughts.

- ✔ To eliminate boredom, adjust your daydreams from time to time. Aim them at different aspects of your goal.

- ✔ Don't affirm the actions of other people. For example, say 'I attract others because I am a warm, loving person', rather than 'David loves me'.

- ✔ Don't hold back with your words and don't clean them up. If necessary, use expletives if you want.

Essentially, listen to what's going on in your body and use the words that best describe what's going on. If you need some help, refer to Chapters 2 and 5.

Using EFT in the Past, Present, and Future

You can use EFT to help with issues from any part of your life, not just the here and now. Try using the technique to deal with problems:

- ✔ **In the past:** If you believe you were here in an earlier life you may have some good or bad memories from that time. You can use EFT to tap on the unwanted memories, whether they're sad, angry, or upsetting.

- ✔ **In the present:** Because your subconscious mind takes commands very literally, use the present tense in your Acceptance Phrase. For instance, saying 'I love and accept myself as I am' is preferable to saying 'I'm going to love and accept myself as I am'. If you don't put the positive in the present tense you may not get what you want.

- ✔ **In the future:** When you've overcome your problem or issue with EFT you can further test this out by visualising yourself in the future without the problem or issue. Try to imagine doing whatever it is you can't do now: Flying on a plane, achieving your goal weight, or being pain-free.

Becoming Acquainted with Reactions

As with most other therapies, recalling an emotional memory may cause a tearful or other emotional reaction, which is a perfectly normal response. You may experience a negative reaction after (or during) an EFT session, especially if you're tapping for yourself. Feelings such as anger, anxiety, uneasiness, and sadness or even temporary worsening of the issue(s) may emerge.

These reactions aren't side-effects of EFT, nor are they an indication that something's wrong with you. These feelings can happen as a result of holding on to emotions that EFT releases. In fact, the release of these feelings shows that EFT is working!

Abreactions in EFT

Researchers conducted an informal study on abreactions in 1997. Of the estimated 10,000 people who used EFT, only 20 cases of abreactions were reported. This equates to approximately 1 per cent. Though relatively insignificant, you still need to take care to avoid or deal with abreactions.

Abnormal response

Some other types of therapies attempt to induce an *abreaction* in clients – a release of unconscious emotional energy. Abreactions can be traumatic events. Fortunately, this methodology isn't a necessary part of EFT's therapy, and techniques exist for painful memories that use the softly, softly approach. (See Chapter 5 for more info on these techniques.)

Abreactions can range from normal (crying, upset, anger) to abnormal (palpitations, sweating, shaking, extreme distress or upset). Occasionally, an EFT session may trigger a memory that's so painful an abnormal reaction occurs.

See an experienced therapist if you've suffered severe trauma or abuse, where abreactions can be more extreme.

If you're unfortunate enough to experience an abreaction when working on someone else, the important thing is to:

- ✔ Keep calm.
- ✔ With the client's permission, tap continually on all the hand points then (again with permission) continually tap on all the body points – with both hands if necessary.
- ✔ Tap for the physical sensations (shaking or sweating, for example).
- ✔ Ask the client to breathe slowly and deeply.
- ✔ All the time, reassure the client that these reactions are there to protect her and that she's perfectly safe.
- ✔ When she's calmed down, ask the client to tap for 'Even though I had a huge reaction just then . . .'.

If you're unsure whether to seek professional advice, see Chapter 1.

Apex effect

Many people find that EFT relieves them of their problems so quickly and effectively that their logical, conscious mind can't accept it as being the reason for their relief. This denial and disbelief syndrome is known as the *Apex effect*. This effect occurs especially when someone's had the problem for many years and suddenly it disappears. Often people attribute the most bizarre reasons for their immediate success: 'You distracted me', 'I'm confused', 'I can't think of my problem now, but I will later', and other explanations. People may even deny they had the problem in the first place.

That's why I advise clients in advance that EFT is often fast-acting and very effective, and that they shouldn't be surprised if they experience almost immediate relief. You may want to remind the person you're helping that she may start imagining reasons for her success other than EFT, but the truth is that EFT can be very effective, very quickly, most of the time.

At the same time, tell clients that persistence is the best way to achieve the best overall results for chronic conditions.

Gary Craig, founder of EFT, has said, 'It isn't a problem in and of itself. It's simply a message that we must change our ways and adapt our delivery to fit within the client's beliefs.' I beg to differ and say that I've tried all ways known to man to change my delivery and some people just won't accept that EFT has caused the positive change. Is this because they're sceptics? One possibility worth bearing in mind is that they're not consciously aware of the problem any more and that such people have a problem in remembering how they felt before the treatment.

My favourite story is about a lady who overcame her anxiety in one EFT session but went on to tell everyone how effective her medication was – truly amazing, even. Only when she next went to see her GP did he confess to her that he'd given her placebo pills. Even though she came to tell me what her GP had given her, she was still hesitant to give the credit to EFT. Personally, I just have a smug satisfaction, knowing what really worked.

Writing down the problem, recording the level of intensity between zero and 10 before treatment, and then comparing it afterwards can provide the evidence. You can find info on the Subjective Units of Distress Scale in Chapter 3.

Cognitive shifts

Reasoning, problem solving, and perception are words that spring to mind when describing cognition. In traditional psychology, a *cognitive shift* occurs when a person experiences a change in how their conscious and unconscious minds communicate with each other and the result can create a wide range of feelings.

'I realise I wasn't to blame', 'I can't wait to get on that plane now', 'I feel sorry for them', or 'I feel it all happened to another person' are the type of comments people make when a cognitive shift takes place during EFT. Why the shift happens during EFT isn't completely understood but it may be that EFT removes the negative thinking and therefore allows the healthier reasoning, or _cognitive change_, to take place. Whatever the reason, do you care as long as it brings about those positive changes?

Judy had a boss called Graham who was piling more responsibility on her and was always complaining of the department not meeting targets. Judy had a sufficient workload as it was, yet felt under pressure to take on more. Eventually, Judy started taking time off because she couldn't face the thought of going into work, and she sought help with EFT.

During the EFT session, the practitioner asked Judy what outcome she wanted and she said she wanted to be able to cope with the workload. After using EFT on the negative aspects of her problem – her inability to cope and how it was her responsibility to share the load – Judy suddenly had a cognitive shift that changed her perception of the problem. Instead of feeling it was her responsibility to share the load, Judy recognised it was her boss who had the problem with work overload, not her. Instead of taking time off, Judy, in her own words, realised she needed to discuss the problem with Graham and explain that it wasn't possible for her to take on more responsibility.

Judy's EFT session left her feeling very empowered and relieved, and as a result she was able to discuss her feelings with Graham. She told Graham that if he had too much work then he needed to sort that out with his boss and not just pass it on to her, and she explained how the work was affecting her health. Graham accepted Judy's proposal and agreed to speak with his boss. Judy doesn't know whether Graham did talk with his boss or not, but the outcome was that her workload no longer caused her stress.

Recent research has recognised that emotion is a cognitive process. When you work with EFT, you engage your everyday knowing, thinking, and understanding, and at the same time you access deeper levels of consciousness, usually expressed through the body, as you physically tap into your energy system. Using the tapping sequence I describe in Chapter 3 to access these deeper levels is often what makes the difference.

Time to calibrate

Calibration is the ability to measure changes. During an EFT session you become aware of how your client shows emotion and reacts to the treatment. Changes in a client's behaviour can signal positive or negative changes like those in Table 4-1.

Table 4-1	Changes Resulting from EFT
Negative	*Positive*
Shoulders stooping or slouching	Sitting upright and straight
Frown or sad expression	Smiling or brighter facial expression
Breathing shallow and fast	Breathing slower and deep
Voice soft and passive	Voice strong and meaningful
Skin tone pale	Skin tone with colour
Appearance dark with drab colours	Appearance bright and creative
Grooming neglected	Improvement noticeable
Feeling tense and fidgety	Calm and relaxed

Other noticeable changes to the original memory occur when a positive change takes place. Some responses you may hear include:

✔ 'It all seems like a blur, as if it's happening to someone else.'

✔ 'I can't focus on the problem any more.'

✔ 'The problem now seems in the distance.'

✔ 'The emotion is no longer there.'

✔ 'The colour, the shape, and the size of the problem described have lessened.'

Assessing Whether EFT Worked

Because EFT works so quickly, testing your results isn't only important but, I'd go as far as to say, essential. How else are you to assess whether or not EFT is working and whether you've got rid of the problem? Tapping away and hoping that the technique has worked is one way but not very practical. If you don't test, then the problem may come back – so don't say I didn't warn you!

When you've reduced every aspect or part of the problem to zero, you should be able to remember the unpleasant memory without emotional intensity. If any residual emotion exists, you may have to use EFT until it's gone. If you're unable to reduce the emotional intensity, take a look at Chapter 6.

Testing procedures

Chapter 3 covers the basic testing procedure, but you can also try the methods in the following list.

If any anxiety or discomfort comes up during the test then tap for it until it's gone or disappeared – then test again.

You want to be sure the problem is no longer bothering you and here are some suggestions to help you with that:

- **SUDs:** You can be sure that the problem has gone when your Subjective Units of Distress (see Chapter 3) have gone to zero and you can vividly imagine or actually confront your problem without any anxiety.

- **Sizing up:** If you find using the Subjective Units of Distress Scale to measure how intense your emotions are difficult, then you can use your hands to visualise the size of the problem – much like an angler may demonstrate the size of a fish he's caught. Start with your hands together in front of you and move them apart. This method of measuring feelings and emotions works best with children.

- **Colour and shape:** Another way of measuring feelings is to describe the feeling as a colour, shape, or object. You can describe a negative feeling as black, square, or a big rock. The measure of whether EFT is working or not is if this colour changes to grey or white, the big rock changes to a pebble, or the square to perhaps a soft round shape.

- **Senses:** Use all five senses, if necessary, to bring back the emotion, using a photo, image, or such like. I have a selection of toy rubber spiders, beetles, and snakes that can do the job; otherwise I bring up an image on the Internet (remember to do this gradually). Describe the problem or memory again and in more detail, noticing if any anxiety comes up.

- **Future test:** Try visualising yourself in the future, without the anxiety or distress of the problem or pain. You shouldn't feel any anxiety or discomfort. While you're focusing on your future, if you run into any difficulty, imagine that you have EFT there to help you. This technique can be a great comfort to some people.

- **Make it bolder:** Just to make sure that you have no intensity left, imagine the scene again in bold technicolour – with digital surround-sound if you like.

- **Live test:** If you truly want to find out if the problem has gone, test it out in a real-life situation – if this is possible, of course. Here are some of my suggestions on how to test in real life, but you can be as creative as you like – just make sure that your actions are legal and not harmful!

Table 4-2 lists ways you can test specific problems.

Table 4-2	Testing for Specific Issues
Problem	*Suggestions on How to Test*
Fear of being closed in	Sit in a wardrobe or very small room.
Scared of snakes	Look at an image of a snake or go to the zoo.
Difficulty raising arm	Measure how high you can raise your arm before and after tapping with EFT.
Addicted to chocolate	Unwrap a bar and smell it.
Fear of flying	Visit a travel shop, visualise the scene, or sit on a plane.
Feeling ugly	Look in a mirror.
Scared of heights	Take a ride in a glass elevator.

Only carry out a real-life test if you feel comfortable that the intensity of the problem has reduced to almost zero. Also, don't test severe reactions to allergies or needle phobias unless in a safe, medical environment.

You don't need to confront your fear or be courageous when testing your reaction to a situation or memory. EFT doesn't involve willpower or expect you to 'face the fear'. You mustn't be feeling any anxiety, or at least very, very little, when thinking about undertaking the action that you're afraid of. For instance, suddenly pushing a spider in front of someone who has a phobia about them is unwise. Ask beforehand if the person who has the fear of spiders objects to seeing one and, if she's okay with that, then introduce it slowly. Remember to tap on any anxiety that may come up.

You may be wondering how you can test for motivation, confidence, or writer's block? You can't easily measure some issues or problems on a scale from zero to 10, and this is where you can use the Validity of Cognition scale from Chapter 15.

Diagnostic muscle testing

In addition, *diagnostic muscle testing* acts like a lie detector. This technique is used in *kinesiology*, a therapy involving rebalancing the body's energy system through gentle hand pressure. The technique involves the client extending her arm: The therapist then presses down lightly on it while the client says a statement that's either true or false. If I say 'My name is Helena' (true statement) my arm should be rigid and remain extended when pressed on. If, however, I say 'My name is John' (false statement) my arm should be weak and drop a little when pressed. Your muscles and your nerves work together, so that when you have an upsetting emotion it causes a change in your muscles as well. The muscles tend to become firmer with positive thoughts or emotions and somewhat weaker with negative thoughts or emotions. The muscles aren't really weak at such times, it's just that the electricity moving through the nerves gets interrupted so that the muscle momentarily can't operate at its best.

Some EFT therapists use muscle testing in their practice to determine whether any energy imbalances exist, but I believe it's an art and in the right skilful hands can produce strong guidance. Because I haven't been trained in kinesiology, I wouldn't rely on it to test whether a client is telling the truth or not.

You still get great success with EFT whether you muscle test or not – when used by a professional kinesiologist the technique just shortens the process, that's all. However, you may want to just tap on all the meridian points instead.

Shortening the Tapping Sequence

You can shorten the basic EFT tapping sequence even further. Chapter 3 describes tapping on up to 14 meridian points on the body. The shortcut version reduces this to just eight by omitting tapping on the fingers and the back of the hand, and leaving out the eye-rolling action. Using the shortcut version makes no difference to the treatment, other than to make it quicker.

Experimenting is all part of using EFT, so be creative in your tapping and EFT techniques when you feel proficient. If you feel that tapping on all the points makes the treatment more effective, then continue to do so. After all, you're adding all of another 20 seconds or so. Tap on all the meridian points if you want to; it's entirely up to you. Tap on both sides of the body as well if this tapping gets that energy system going. (For more information on the full tapping routine and points, see Chapter 3.)

My own acronym for the shortcut version of EFT is RATT (Rate, Affirm, Tap, Test), and here's how RATT works. You can use this version to treat a problem or issue in much the same way as in Chapter 3.

1. **Rate the intensity.**

   If you're not sure how, refer to Chapter 3 for information on using the Subjective Units of Distress Scale.

2. **Affirm the problem in the Set-up Phrase (negative and positive) while rubbing the Sore Spot or tapping on the Karate Chop; repeat three times.**

   (For more information on the full tapping routine and points, see Chapter 3.)

   Here's an example: 'Even though I have these butterflies in my stomach, I love and accept myself', 'Even though I have these butterflies in my stomach, I love and accept myself', and 'Even though I have these butterflies in my stomach, I love and accept myself'.

3. **Tap on the following points while saying the shortened phrase on each point:**

Eyebrow	Butterflies in stomach
Side of eye	Butterflies in stomach
Under eye	Butterflies in stomach
Under nose	Butterflies in stomach
Between chin and lip	Butterflies in stomach
Collarbone	Butterflies in stomach
Under arm	Butterflies in stomach

4. **Take a deep breath and relax.**

5. **Test if the levels have gone down.**

6. **If the emotion hasn't gone down to zero, do another round on the remaining feeling that goes something like this:**

   While rubbing Sore Spot or tapping Karate Chop: 'Even though I still have these butterflies in my stomach, I love and accept myself.'

Eyebrow	Remaining butterflies in stomach
Side of eye	Remaining butterflies in stomach
Under eye	Remaining butterflies in stomach
Under nose	Remaining butterflies in stomach
Between chin and lip	Remaining butterflies in stomach
Collarbone	Remaining butterflies in stomach
Under arm	Remaining butterflies in stomach

If the intensity remains, or moves very little after several rounds, either go back to the full tapping routine in Chapter 3 or work out what may be getting in the way in Chapter 6.

With regular tapping on yourself or others you can identify which points can be left out or which ones work better.

Tapping Additional Points

Introducing a shortened version and then talking about additional points you can tap on may sound a little odd. Some EFT practitioners use these additional points because they believe that they quicken the reduction in emotional intensity and are good for difficult issues such as addictions.

You can use additional points with the full EFT routine that I describe in Chapter 3 or with the shortcut version I explain earlier in this chapter. You can introduce them at any point you feel comfortable with. How you use them is up to you, though I often find that finishing at the top of the head helps round off the routine. Because your energy system is connected, the tapping vibrates throughout your system, just like when you tap a pipe at one end and you can feel the vibration at the other end.

What points you tap on are entirely up to you, but I recommend you first become proficient with EFT before experimenting.

✔ **Liver point:** Under breast (on the rib cage approximately 10 centimetres below the nipple). Practitioners often leave this point out because of its proximity to a woman's breasts. This point addresses sadness, cravings, depression, and anger.

✔ **Crown of head:** Tap with the palm of your hand or tips of your fingers towards the back of the head. Some people use all their fingers in a claw-like position; others just use three or four fingers. This point is very powerful because it's the main contact point for every meridian.

✔ **Inside of wrists:** This is where your watch band goes – use two fingers or more to tap on the entire area. Alternatively, tap together by crossing one wrist over the other with the insides facing. This point has three major meridians that are great for stress, grief, and sadness – some very common emotions.

Chapter 5

Refining Your Technique

. . . .

In This Chapter

▶ Minimising distress

▶ Being creative

▶ Using humour

▶ Being resourceful

. . . .

*U*npleasant memories or disturbing events may sometimes be difficult to talk about because of the fear of triggering painful emotions. You may even be suppressing some painful emotions and not be aware that they're still there, although you exhibit the symptoms.

Fortunately, EFT is good for digging up hidden problems if necessary and doesn't require you to confront your painful memory either in order to work on it. The techniques in this chapter help develop your skill in handling these sensitive issues and help minimise distress.

Getting Started with Different Techniques

Most of the techniques in this chapter are suitable for any problem that involves difficulty communicating what the problem is (for instance, because it causes too much distress) or when you need to trigger a response in order to connect with your own or your client's negative emotions. All the techniques are merely suggestions, of course. However, I do have a few suggestions for you as you practise them:

✔ Be as creative as you can.

✔ Preferably, test these techniques on yourself before trying them on others.

✔ First test these techniques out on a 'low grade' problem or issue. After decreasing the sensitivity level to under, say, 5 on the Subjective Units of Distress Scale (see Chapter 3), you can usually be specific without inflicting any unnecessary emotional pain.

✔ If you're a beginner in EFT, I encourage and even implore you to work with the guidance of an experienced EFT practitioner before trying these techniques out on a client with severe trauma or abuse issues.

'Practitioner' or 'therapist' refers to the leader and the 'client' may be a friend, colleague, child, spouse, or anyone you want to help with EFT.

Some people who have suffered trauma or abuse may have difficulty in accepting themselves and struggle with the Set-up Phrase 'I deeply and completely love and accept myself'. More often than not, people who've suffered trauma do not even *like* themselves let alone *love* themselves. In these circumstances you can allow the client to say 'I'm an okay person' or 'I was in the wrong place at the wrong time', and move on to 'I can learn to love and accept myself' or 'I'm open to the possibility that I can love and accept myself', or similar Acceptance Phrases. If you want to know more, Chapter 7 has more useful phrases.

Familiarising yourself with the EFT routine I refer to in Chapter 3 before you carry out these exercises certainly helps towards your understanding of the techniques.

Describing a Movie

This technique is great at tackling specifics, which is a very important part of becoming successful with EFT (see Chapters 4 and 6). The *Movie Technique* utilises specific words, actions, and feelings and has a beginning and an end. The idea is to narrate the unpleasant memory as a movie but stop and apply EFT on the parts of the movie that bring up any emotional intensity or anxiety. After you neutralise the intensity with EFT, you re-wind the movie a little and narrate it again until you can run through the whole movie without any intensity at all.

You'll find that the Movie Technique also forces the direction of the specific event and provides a gentle way of approaching a sensitive problem. You can carry out the exercises yourself on your own issues, or as a practitioner to a client or one person to another.

Practitioner to client:

1. **Ask the client to identify the unpleasant memory and also ask, 'If this memory was a movie, how long would it last?'**

   The answer needs to be in minutes rather than days, otherwise it's too global. If the client has difficulty with the timing, ask him to narrow it down to the most intense part.

2. **Ask the client, 'What would the title be?'**

   The title here needs to be something like 'The Day I Hit the Blue Car', rather than 'The Accident'. Being specific is the key to success with EFT.

3. **Now have the client run the movie in his mind and ask him to evaluate his anxiety now (as imagined) on a scale of zero to 10.**

   If this is too painful to recall, ask him to say 'Even though I'm too anxious to talk about this (movie title), I accept myself or I am safe'. If the client is obviously becoming distressed, use one of the gentler techniques I refer to later in this section.

4. **Have the client verbally narrate the movie, starting with an easy-to-discuss segment. Tell him to let you know as soon as he feels any emotional intensity or anxiety so that you can apply EFT.**

   Sometimes clients don't stop to let you know when they feel this anxiety coming up, but careful monitoring of their facial expressions indicates to you when they feel intense emotion. When you notice a change in expression, ask the client how he feels as he describes this part of the movie.

   Stop at any intense moment, rate it from zero to 10, and then tap on the emotional intensity until it reduces to a zero.

   Stopping when any emotional intensity exists is most important because, unlike some therapies, EFT doesn't expect you to 'brave yourself through the moment' or to stick it out come what may. The idea is to gently guide you through the memory a bit at a time.

5. **Using the EFT routine I describe in Chapter 3, reduce the intensity of emotion or anxiety for that particular part of the movie.**

   For instance, if the client feels scared at the point in the movie where he visualises the oncoming car, use EFT on 'Even though seeing the oncoming car makes me feel scared, I accept myself'. If the client feels this anxiety in his body, include this as well, such as 'Even though seeing the oncoming car makes me feel scared in my stomach, I accept myself'. Keep using EFT until the fear reduces to a zero. To test this out, ask the client to go back to just before this part of the movie and narrate it again. He shouldn't feel scared at this stage.

6. **Have the client 'rewind' a little and describe the segment of the movie that caused the emotion again, to test whether he has any leftover intensity.**

   If intensity still exists, repeat step 5. If there's none, ask the client to continue narrating the movie and repeat step 5 at any point where some emotion surfaces.

7. **When the client reaches the end of the movie, ask him to go through steps 3 and 4 again.**

When the client requires privacy and doesn't want to talk about what happened, you can skip steps 1 and 2 and just ask him to tap on the most intense part of what happened. At step 3, ask the client to give a name to the most intense part and then tap on that until it reduces to a low level. Repeat as necessary.

This technique is complete and successful if the client can narrate the whole unpleasant memory without any emotional intensity. To thoroughly test the result you can ask the client to exaggerate the sounds, colours, or details while narrating.

Engaging in Tearless Trauma

Wherever trauma or abuse is involved, you usually find that the sufferer is fearful of discussing or even merely mentioning an associated word in case he relives the actual event and is re-traumatised. The *Tearless Trauma Technique* encourages the sufferer not to think too much about the experience as he goes through EFT, but to disassociate the experience from his memory until his intensity level comes down. You can use EFT while disassociating from the actual event by guessing what the emotional intensity would be on the Subjective Units of Distress Scale but without actually reliving the event. Don't ask the client to think or re-experience the traumatic event until he feels comfortable.

You can use this technique on a one-to-one basis or in a group setting. If you're interested in working with groups, you can find more information in Chapter 15 .

To use this technique, ask your client or group to do the following:

1. **Identify a specific traumatic incident from the past.**

   Ideally, the incident took place be at least three years ago, to minimise any complications from the dynamics of a current event. Also, the incident needs to be specific. An example may be a wife who was hit many times by her husband over the years. Using the words in the Set-up

Phrase of 'Although my husband beat me . . .' is too general because the beatings took place over a long period of time. What you're looking to find is a trigger, so try to think of one specific time that comes to mind. For instance, this may be 'Although my husband beat me with the chair and I ended up in hospital . . .'. (Chapter 4 covers how to be specific.)

Shifting to other issues can easily happen, but try to stay on your original issue until you resolve it. (Chapter 6 refers to jumping aspects.)

2. **Without actually visualising the incident, guess what your emotional intensity would be *if* you were to vividly imagine the incident.**

   To rate this you can use the Subjective Units of Distress Scale of between zero to 10, with 10 being the highest. Guessing gives a surprisingly useful estimate, and it serves to minimise emotional pain. Write down your guesses.

3. **Develop a Set-up Phrase as Step 1 describes and then proceed with either the full or shortcut version of EFT.**

   You can use whatever words or emotions you feel. This may be 'Even though I have this husband beating me with a chair emotion in my chest . . .'.

4. **After you complete the EFT routine, guess again what the emotional intensity would be and rate it. Generally, the numbers go down.**

5. **Keep using EFT, using the Remaining Phrase of 'Even though I still have this husband beating me with a chair, emotion in my chest . . .' until the guessed number goes down to 3 or below.**

6. **When down to a 3 or below, repeat step 6 again.**

7. **Try, for the first time, to vividly imagine the incident and give it an actual rating and not an imagined rating.**

8. **At this point you can now safely use EFT on the specifics of the incident.**

Practising a Disassociated Technique

The *Disassociated Technique* is based on a neurolinguistic programming (NLP) technique that's suitable for use whenever fear exists that the sufferer may be re-traumatised. With this technique, you can recreate a past experience from the perspective of an observer or onlooker without the need for the client to relive the original emotion. You can use this as an alternative to the Tearless Trauma Technique that I describe in the preceding section. Remember, the same health warning applies if you're using the technique on sufferers with severe trauma or abuse issues.

I used this technique on Pat, whose mother walked out on her when she was 8. She had no contact with her mother from that day and had recently discovered that her mother had died. She was very distressed at the memory of the day her mother left, and the fact she never had the chance to say goodbye. She told me she became even more distressed whenever she began to talk about her mother. I asked her what was causing her the most intensity and she told me it was seeing her mother walk out on her when she was 8. I went through the technique like this:

I asked Pat to bring to mind the day her mother walked out and to give that emotion a number from zero to 10, with 10 being the highest. Pat gave this a definite 10.

I asked her to apply EFT on herself while saying, 'You were safe before and you're safe now.' This brought the intensity down to around a 5 and she was a lot calmer. I was then able to continue.

I asked her to imagine she was seated in a big comfortable cinema seat. I then asked her to imagine a black-and-white image on the screen of her most intense memory associated with her mother walking out, and to talk me through what she saw, but Pat was to be only the observer. I also explained I'd stop at any time if I thought Pat was becoming distressed and would ask her to use EFT to reduce the distress.

Pat began by saying, 'The little girl on the screen is playing in her room and hears her mummy and daddy shouting.' This was causing her some anxiety, so I asked Pat to carry out EFT using the words 'Even though that little girl is upset because her mummy and daddy are shouting, she loves and accepts herself'. This reduced Pat's anxiety and she was able to continue. Pat carried out EFT on herself each time she experienced any distress. The most intense emotion for Pat was seeing her mother walk away from the house. I asked Pat what she felt and she used her words 'Even though that little girl is sad because she can see her mother walking down the path, she accepts herself a child'. Pat had a lot of other emotions to deal with, such as feeling abandoned and that she was to blame for her mother walking out. We treated all these with EFT.

When I was satisfied that it was safe to do so, I asked Pat to visualise the whole scene again on the cinema screen but this time as if she were in the scene. I invited her to change it from black-and-white to colour and to add sound if possible. This caused only mild anxiety at some points and Pat used EFT on each emotion until it reduced to a zero.

Eventually, Pat was able to talk about that day her mother walked out without showing any signs of distress. Her attitude had also changed to one of acceptance, because she said her mother obviously had her own problems at that time. Before finishing the session, I got Pat to use EFT to forgive her mother and to say goodbye.

With permission, I could have tapped on Pat, but she used EFT on herself instead. It doesn't matter who taps for EFT to work – it's entirely up to each individual practitioner and client. What's important is that the client is conversant with the technique beforehand.

Sneaking Up on the Problem

Another gentle way of dealing with difficult or highly emotional memories is to 'sneak up' on them. This method is similar to the Tearless Trauma Technique I refer to in the section 'Engaging in Tearless Trauma', earlier in this chapter. Sneaking Up on the Problem is a good way of gradually introducing the memory. With this technique, though, you don't have to be specific – indeed, leave specifics out as much as possible to begin with.

Here's an example of a traumatic incident:

> *Donna was walking home from work on a dark winter's evening when it started to rain. Donna took a shortcut down a quiet road to avoid getting wet and was suddenly aware that she was being followed. She quickened her steps and the person behind her quickened theirs. There were no people around so she reached for her mobile phone to call for help. She was about to call when a hand went over her mouth and her head was yanked back by her hair. Donna tried to scream and kick at her attacker. She could see the glint of steel in his hand when suddenly she heard the sound of a car driving on the road towards them. The car's headlights shone on Donna and her attacker and she was able to identify him as a thick-set man with a moustache. The attacker pushed her to the ground and then ran off. After several weeks Donna was still unable to talk about that night without breaking down and trembling.*

Here's how to apply the technique to this event:

1. **Ask Donna to give a general title to her trauma.**

   She names it 'This Nightmare'.

2. **Now ask Donna to use EFT on 'Even though this nightmare happened, I deeply and completely love and accept myself'.**

3. **Ask Donna to use EFT as she describes what happened leading up to the actual attack.**

   For example: 'Even though this nightmare happened', 'Even though I had this nightmare walking home', 'Even though I heard footsteps behind me', and 'Even though I felt his hand over my mouth'.

4. **At each step, ask Donna to use EFT on any emotional or physical intensity that crops up until each one reduces.**

   The idea is to gradually introduce each scene and move on only when the client is comfortable to do so.

The client doesn't need to be specific or imagine too much detail.

This technique allows the client to start off with the least intense part of the problem and work his way up. It paves the way to eradicate each aspect or piece of the problem one by one, while testing it along the way. (For more on aspects, see Chapter 4.)

Most times, you use EFT to remove negative emotions entirely and quickly, but a step-by-step approach is more suitable for certain conditions where a sudden change may be too dramatic. For instance, you're best treating someone suffering from agoraphobia by applying EFT on, say, first enabling the sufferer to open the front door, then to walk to the end of the garden, then to the nearest shop, and so on. Using EFT in this manner involves going at a pace that encourages gradual change.

Telling the Story

You'll find no better time to apply EFT than when you or your client are actually 'tuned into' the problem. A perfect opportunity may arise during a session when the client is narrating a memory or remembers an associated unpleasant memory or negative feeling. While talking about the memory or feeling, start using EFT by tapping all around the meridian points at the same time. This can reduce some of the anxiety.

Stop at any point when the emotional intensity starts to cause any anxiety or distress, and apply EFT on the intense emotion until it reduces to below a 3 on the Subjective Units of Distress Scale (see Chapter 3). Continue telling the story from a point where it's safe to do so, or earlier in the story if preferred. This method not only minimises the distress but can often uncover deeper issues that may otherwise have gone unnoticed. The client needs to talk through the whole story from beginning to end without showing or feeling any intense emotion.

If the client finds it difficult to even beginning to talk about the memory because it creates some negative emotion, you can use a global approach with EFT as follows:

'Even though I'm afraid to tell the story . . .'

'Even though I may not like what happens when I tell this story . . .'

'Even though just thinking about telling the story makes me anxious/ afraid . . .'

Using Codes and Keywords

It's not unusual to come across problems that are too embarrassing or personal to reveal, or that aren't easy to describe. When this situation arises, and it often does, you can overcome the problem by using a keyword, a colour, or a sound. Whatever you use, or even if it's relevant or not, doesn't matter as long as it helps you 'tune into' the problem or issue. You insert the keyword or code into the Set-up Phrase and also the Reminder Phrase. As different parts of the problem crop up, you can use another keyword or code.

Clare came to see me with a problem she didn't want to reveal for whatever reason. To get around the difficulty, I asked her what code she'd like to use to describe her problem. For Clare there was no hesitation that her problem was with 'Mr X'. I didn't need to know anything about Mr X or what the problem was, she just tapped for 'Even though I have this Mr X problem . . .' with the Reminder Phrase as 'Even though I still have this Mr X problem . . .'. We broke the problem down bit by bit and applied EFT to each part of the problem that cropped up until they each went to zero – all without even having to know who Mr X was or what the problem was.

Another option is to not say anything at all but silently say the words in your head or hum the problem if unable to vocalise it. If this technique isn't enough to produce a reduction in intensity, you may need to reveal a little more information to get to the deeper issue. When I'm working with clients I usually find that they're able to be more open after we remove any perceived barriers and build trust.

Experimenting with Props

An excellent way to help bring up an emotional reaction is to use an item or object that you associate with the person or situation. Items or objects such as a certain perfume, photograph, video, music, or an item of jewellery are just a few suggestions. If you can't locate these items, just use your imagination instead.

While focusing on the item or object, ask yourself, 'What does this remind me of?' or, 'What was happening at the time?' Your question should elicit a response, and when it does you may feel a sensation in your body. Notice where you feel this sensation or emotion and at the same time start to apply EFT as I describe in Chapter 3 or 4.

Here are some suggestions to get you going:

> *'Even though I was angry with my son when this photo was taken, he's grown up now and I can put that anger behind me.'*

> *'Even though smelling this perfume reminds me of the night I smashed it in the fight, I accept myself and let this emotion go.'*

> *'Even though looking at this ring reminds me of the hurt and distrust, I don't need this emotional pain and I choose to let it go.'*

> *'Even though this music reminds me of being rejected, I accept myself and choose to move on.'*

> *'Even though I feel scared watching this disaster on TV, I know that I'm safe.'*

> *'Even though that video was the last time I saw him, I release the pain and let it go.'*

Don't use props to entice memories of severe trauma unless you're confident that you can handle an abreaction (refer to Chapter 4 for more on abreactions).

Tap on the physical sensations as well – the pain in your chest, the tightness in your head, and so on.

Try looking in the mirror when using EFT and observe your body posture and facial expressions. Asking someone else to look in a mirror as they describe what they see can also throw up some surprising results.

When Colin came to me with a lack of confidence issue, I asked him to look in the mirror and describe what he saw. He described himself as not only unconfident but overweight and old. Great! This technique brought up other issues to work on.

Injecting Humour

As the saying goes, 'Laughter is the best medicine.' Joking aside, everyone likes a good laugh because it makes you feel good. When you laugh your brain releases endorphins, the body's natural painkiller, and produces a general sense of wellbeing. Laughter makes you feel good because it changes your mood and puts you in a better frame of mind. Now, I'm not asking you to dress as a clown when treating someone with EFT, but do remember that a little injection of humour – at the appropriate time, of course – can certainly help the other person relax. Humour is also a very useful way to change or break a state of mind (refer to Chapter 6).

Laughter being the best medicine

The best-known exponent of laughter therapy is undoubtedly Dr Hunter 'Patch' Adams. Dr Adams had his own psychiatric problems and had even attempted suicide on one occasion. It was while he was recovering from his suicide attempt that he discovered if he focused on other people's problems, he forgot his own. This led him to train and qualify as a doctor, but his unconventional approach to medicine didn't always go down well with other members of the medical establishment. His philosophy was to treat the patient as well as the disease and try to make them forget their troubles through laughter. Dr Adams dressed outrageously and thought nothing of visiting his seriously ill patients dressed as a clown. Dr Adams went on to establish the Gesundheit (German for 'good health') Institute in Washington DC, a non-paying hospital that incorporates all the healing arts. The aim of the institute was to 'bring fun, friendship, and joy of service into health care'.

Although I deal with people's problems every day, I have to remind myself that for the client to pour out his innermost thoughts to a complete stranger takes courage. To overcome clients' tension and nervousness, I sometimes use humour. Occasionally, humour pops up when you're not expecting it, such as the time I was in the middle of a tapping sequence with a client when I completely mixed up the words I was using. Instead of trying to ignore it, I laughed it off and said that perhaps I ought to use EFT for my twisted tongue before we continued. I've even got a client's name wrong, but they're very forgiving (or so they tell me). Being able to laugh at yourself illustrates humility.

Apart from when you make mistakes, another way to inject humour in your work with EFT is by phrasing the negative but associating it with a positive while adding a bit of humour. An example is 'Even though I have to be right, and this causes arguments, at least I'm right about that', or one I used on a friend of mine who's a letting agent: 'Even though I still have this motorway fear emotion, I refuse to allow it to remain rent-free in my body and I choose to evict it'. (You can find more interesting stuff on this in the section 'Reframing' in Chapter 6.)

Be careful to use humour only where appropriate and to recognise that your sense of humour may not be acceptable to someone else. You need to have a good relationship with whoever you're working with before introducing humour, because you don't want him to feel that you're making fun of either him or his problem.

Anchoring the State of Mind

When you hear the music to *Psycho* or *Jaws*, what do you feel or imagine? Your heart may thump, and you may experience other feelings of fear. In NLP terms, these external stimuli are known as *anchors*. Any or all of your five senses can trigger a response.

Think back to a moment in time when you were happy and carefree. What is it that helps you relive that moment? For me, it's whenever I hear the song 'Dancing Queen' by Abba. Upon hearing this I'm immediately transported back in time to being a happy, carefree 21-year-old at the disco. So that shows my age! Going back to the song, it makes me feel good because I associate it with positive feelings. While in this positive state I couldn't experience, for example, a headache at the same time, because the human body can't process negative and positive feelings simultaneously. It has to be one or the other.

As you revisit that happy memory try to identify what sensations it evokes – a sight, a sound, a smell, touch, or taste. When you've connected with this good feeling, close your eyes and rub your index finger and thumb together at the same time. Repeat this many times and each time make the feeling stronger – the sounds louder, the sight sharper and brighter, and the smell stronger. Now focus on something unpleasant and then try rubbing your finger and thumb together and see whether you can bring back that positive feeling instead. What you've created is a *triggered response*.

Next time you pick up a product in the supermarket, try to remember how and where it was advertised and what made you choose that product instead of another. Did the advert use a catchy tune or your favourite record? Perhaps your favourite actor endorsed it or you liked the effect the scene had on you. You associate all these positive feelings with the product when you see it on the shelf, your emotions are triggered, that good feeling comes flooding back, and, before you know it, you're buying the item.

Improving Your Memory

Do you have trouble remembering someone's name or where you left your keys? Well, welcome to the club. Recently, I was in a shop and couldn't remember the PIN number for my bank card. I asked the assistant to excuse me for a minute and found a quiet corner in the store and began using EFT on 'Even though I can't remember my PIN number, I deeply accept myself'. Then I tapped around, saying, 'I can't remember the number. It won't come into my head. There's no way I'll remember it,' and so on. After a few rounds I was beginning to think EFT hadn't worked and was about to leave the store when the number popped into my head. All was saved – or spent, in my case.

You can use EFT to help unearth why you've established a pattern of behaviour or a particular emotion, or why you're reluctant to remember a specific event.

Sometimes the memory comes back instantly, but at other times it may be delayed or come in flashes. Using EFT on memories can also trigger related memories that connect to the main one. Use EFT as soon as any emotional feelings appear, whether or not you've recovered the full memory, to prevent you feeling the full impact all at once.

You may be embarrassed about forgetting things but you can use EFT on that embarrassment. Eventually, you feel relaxed about forgetting people's names when you meet them in the street.

The best way of using EFT for memory loss is to use phrases such as:

> *'Even though I'm embarrassed that I can't remember things, I accept myself as I am, knowing that I'm not alone.'*

> *'Even though I can't remember people's names, at least I smile at them.'*

> *'Even though I can't remember where I left my keys, I deeply and completely accept myself.'*

> *'Even though I don't know why I feel this painful emotion, I deeply and completely accept myself.'*

> *'Even though I don't remember why I feel sad, I deeply and completely accept myself.'*

> *'Even though I don't want to remember what happened on that night, I love and accept myself anyway.'*

You can also add at the end of your accepting phrase:

> *'. . . and I forgive myself, or anyone else, that may have contributed to it.'*

> *'. . . I accept myself as I am and know the memory will surface when it's ready.'*

> *'. . . I thank my body for bringing up this emotion that I need to deal with.'*

Chapter 6

Overcoming Stumbling Blocks

· ·

· ·

*W*hen you don't get the results you expect from EFT, look at what may be causing a blockage to stop it working as it should. These obstructions, or stumbling blocks, can and do happen, but don't worry, all is not lost. This chapter highlights the main causes of why EFT may not work, provides you with a trouble-shooting guide to the problems, and offers solutions. After all, if your car doesn't work when you start it up first time, you don't just give up on it, do you?

After you identify and deal with any obstructions, you can get on with applying EFT in the usual fashion.

Exploring Common Stumbling Blocks

Proficiency in EFT depends on recognising that blockages exist that can interfere with EFT. Knowing how to deal with them makes you even more proficient. It's worth knowing that these blockages aren't always at a conscious level, and that this can make them harder to find. I discuss the most common blockages to success with EFT in this section.

EFT works quickly compared to most other therapies but, if you're a beginner with EFT, you may not be expecting quick results every time you use it. You need to remind yourself now and then that a little persistence and patience reaps great rewards. Next time that you're working on a problem and you find that moving down the Subjective Units of Distress Scale takes time (refer to Chapter 3), go at it from a different angle or read through this chapter in more detail.

Keep in mind that, during an EFT session, you may uncover new emotional difficulties in your client or run across issues that prevent progress and these sometimes get in the way. They relate to your client's initial problem or may be part of the core issue (see Chapter 4). The best way to overcome this problem is to use the Remaining Phrase 'Even though I still have this (problem), I deeply and completely accept myself'.

The following sections highlight more obvious stumbling blocks.

Psychological reversals

Psychological reversals are present in approximately 20 per cent of cases in which EFT is used. Two types of psychological reversal exist, both of which can have a significant effect on the efficient use of EFT if you don't dealt with them at the time.

General Polarity Reversal

General Polarity Reversal (GPR) is when negative thinking interferes with EFT and causes your body's energy to run the wrong way. Your body's energy field or polarity is like any battery-operated device. If you place the batteries the wrong way – that is, you put the positive and negative polarities in the wrong direction – then the device won't work, just like your body's energy system.

Some days you may feel down, lack energy, or feel that nothing is going right and you can explain these feelings as your body's energy system running the wrong way. In other words, the body's polarity is reversed. Chapter 15 describes how positive forces attract and negative forces repel. A good indication of GPR being present is when no movement occurs in the level of intensity on the Subjective Units of Distress Scale (refer to Chapter 3).

Exploring the causes
Several conditions can cause GPR:

- ✔ **Negativity:** Constant, chronic negative thoughts or behaviours – usually found in people with depression.

- ✔ **Dehydration:** Because water conducts the body's electrical system, the energy system slows down or represses if not hydrated.

- ✔ **Addictions:** Addictive substances in the body or having an addictive personality.

- ✔ **Toxins:** For instance, from food, metals, mobile phones, watches, electrical devices, and so on. EFT can't work if there's a strong toxin, or sensitivity to some substances, in, on, or around you. Energy toxins and substance sensitivities are extremely rare, but be aware of them, just in case.

Correcting reversal

Taking action on the cause of the reversal is one way, but more often than not, you can correct this polarity reversal by simply rubbing the Sore Spot or tapping the Karate Chop point while saying the Set-up Phrase of 'Even though I have this (problem), I deeply and completely love and accept myself'. (Refer to Chapters 3 and 4 for more on Set-up Phrases.)

If, however, the problem still doesn't improve, then you need to do additional work to remedy the situation by checking out any secondary benefits, as I describe in the next section.

In most cases, you still need to deal with the addiction or other interferences in the body and eliminate them in order for EFT to work.

Polarity reversals aren't the same as *energy disruptions*, which cause your negative emotions.

You may need to do the EFT tapping routine daily to overcome some problems (refer to Chapter 3). Doing the EFT tapping routine daily may be necessary to reverse your subconscious.

Secondary Benefit Syndrome

Because secondary gains tend to lie within the subconscious, they can be difficult to identify. However, identifying them is not impossible and asking questions like these should eventually tease out any hidden secondary gains sufficiently for you to deal with them with EFT:

- ✔ What is the downside of letting go of the problem?
- ✔ What would be the upside of keeping the problem?
- ✔ What reason could there be for having this problem?
- ✔ What could you do if you didn't have this problem?
- ✔ What can't you do by having this problem?

Some example phrases are:

'Even though I fear letting go of this problem, I forgive myself.'

'Although having this problem makes me different and I like the attention, I forgive and accept myself.'

'Even though I don't deserve to get over my problem, I accept myself. (If there is difficulty saying 'I accept myself', try saying 'I accept myself with this problem' or 'I'm OK'.)

The problem could also be an emotion.

A more permanent solution to resolving psychological reversal can be achieved by looking more closely at any limiting beliefs that are holding you back, and treating these with EFT. (Chapter 15 has more information on limiting beliefs.)

Resisting change

Denial and resistance are the best forms of defence, so if you're having trouble moving towards your positive goal during an EFT session it could be because you're resisting change. If you've ever repeatedly returned to the same seat on a train, in a restaurant or in a training session, for example, then you'll understand what I mean. Leon Festinger, an American psychologist, observed this behaviour and developed a theory known as *cognitive dissonance*. Generally speaking, when you experience new or unfamiliar environments or situations, such as changing jobs, moving house or stopping a habit, these changes can conflict with your inner thoughts, beliefs or emotions. The resulting feelings can cause you discomfort, and in order to avoid these uncomfortable feelings, your brain attempts to gather and filter as much information as it can in an effort to logically condone or justify your thoughts or actions. Why else would someone continue to smoke when they know smoking can cause cancer and other serious diseases?

You'll be pleased to learn that you can use EFT on the inner dialogue with yourself that's causing you conflict with what you want and don't want. When any conflicting thoughts spring up during an EFT session, try introducing phrases such as these:

> 'Even though part of me wants to stop biting my nails, yet another part of me doesn't, I choose to go with the part that wants to stop.'

> 'Although part of me fears change yet another part of me feels safe enough to change, I accept the part that feels safe.'

> 'Even though there's a part of me that wants to succeed, yet another part that fears succeeding, I am willing to go with the part that wants to succeed.'

This same technique can be applied on any conflict that may arise when addressing limiting beliefs referred to in Chapter 15.

Granting yourself permission

I find it very strange when I am told by people I know who use EFT that they don't have enough time to use it on themselves. Obviously this was true, and when I think about it I realise that although we can be willing to help others, when it comes to helping ourselves we put ourselves to the back of the queue. To counteract this, I ask those people 'When was the last time you gave yourself permission to do something?' The answer is usually 'Can't remember' or 'Never'. I then ask them to try using some of these phrases:

> 'Even though I have this (problem) I give myself permission to use EFT to overcome it.'

> 'Even though I haven't got the time to use EFT, I choose to make time.'

> 'Even though I put others before myself, I accept I need to be healed before I can help them.'

Once the deep emotional issues have been resolved with EFT, forgiveness can often be easier to accept. Occasionally, true forgiveness may be hard to accept, so go gently and accept it may take some time. Alexander Pope may have said 'To err is human – to forgive is divine' but he didn't say how long it would take.

It helps to ask the client beforehand if they're ready to forgive and not introduce it during the tapping sequence.

Overcoming difficulty in forgiving

Being unable to forgive can interfere with EFT working. Forgiving and loving are powerful healing tools. Holding on to anger is counterproductive to emotional and physical health, so what reasons may exist for not letting it go? The Set-Up Phrase is designed to help you accept yourself yet it may not be enough. Something may be buried in the subconscious. You can think of forgiveness as 'giving as you gave before the hurt occurred'. Table 6-1 lists some possible reasons for not wanting to forgive.

Table 6-1	Reasons You May Not Want to Forgive
Even Though . . .	*I Accept Myself and . . .*
If I forgive I'll be hurt again.	What proof is there that I'll be hurt again?
Holding on to this hurt reminds me not to get hurt again.	I recognise that this hurt is hurting me rather than them – isn't it time to let it go?
By holding on to this hurt I'm in control – no one tells me what to do.	I can control whether I choose to forgive or not, and I choose to forgive because it's not doing me any good holding on to this.

(continued)

Table 6-1 *(continued)*

Even Though . . .	I Accept Myself and . .
I don't want to forgive because it means it was okay for them to do what they did.	Forgiving is not condoning. I accept myself and accept that I confuse the two.
To forgive means I'm weak.	Forgiving someone is the most powerful thing I can do. What better way is there to demonstrate my strength and courage?
They (my parents) don't deserve to be forgiven.	I accept that they may not deserve to be forgiven and I also accept that they're fallible human beings with their own problems. They did their best with the resources they had at the time.
I'm not willing to forgive.	I accept that I'm willing to discover how to forgive.

After you resolve the deep emotional issues with EFT, you often find it easier to accept forgiveness. Occasionally, you may find it hard to accept true forgiveness, so go gently and accept that forgiveness may take some time. Alexander Pope may have said 'To err is human – to forgive is divine', but he didn't say how long it takes.

Ask the client beforehand whether she's ready to forgive and don't introduce the concept during the tapping sequence.

Clearing your own issues

During your flight, the attendant tells you in the case of an emergency to make sure you put on your own oxygen mask before helping others. Sound altruistic advice when you think about it. How can you help another person if you're suffocating? I didn't include that analogy to depress you, it was meant to emphasise how important it is for you to be emotionally healthy before you try to help others with their emotional problems. Otherwise, your emotions could come to the surface when you're working on clients, or at the very least they could get in the way of EFT working.

There is a very simple procedure you can use to help you with this. The idea is to systematically clear out your own problems and emotional litter with EFT on a daily basis. Ideally, you need to include how you feel about yourself and others; any health issues; what frightens or upsets you and any memories as a child that still make you upset or scared. Remind yourself that it's okay to let the anger, hurt, humiliation or pain be released. This procedure is also useful if you have so many issues in your life that you don't know where to begin when using EFT. If your issues are severe, you may wish to choose an EFT practitioner to assist you.

It doesn't matter how small or insignificant your problems are and it doesn't matter whether they happened today or when you were very young. If you feel you are still affected by something, or could be in the future, then write it down. A typical list could have anything from the death of a loved one to receiving a parking ticket. As you work through your list, notice if any other *aspects* (refer to Chapter 4) come up and work on these too. Don't be put off. The procedure is very simple and easy to follow. If you do this on a continual basis, you will feel emotionally healed.

1. **Write down the specific events and, unless you've lived as a hermit, there should be at least 50 of these to begin with.**

2. **Build them up until you have approx 100–150. I appreciate this may take some time but you don't have to do them all at once.**

3. **Give each one a number from 0 = nothing there to 10 = big emotion.**

4. **Starting with the ones that have the biggest number, give each a title as you would a book or a film.**

5. **Select one to work on.**

6. **Using either the full tapping technique or the shortened version (referred to in Chapters 3 and 4), try tapping and using the event in your Set Up Phrase. Continue using EFT until the levels have dropped to a 0.**

After working on these problems one by one for around three months on a regular basis, you will notice that you don't react to problems in the same way or things just don't seem to get to you as much as they did in the past.

Create your own 'issues' diary. After a couple of months, by treating one to three entries per day and as well as restoring your emotional health, you may notice you are free from some physical ailments too.

When working on other people, you need to be careful that your own issues don't interfere with the process, which is why it's important to clear your issues first. It would be difficult to work on someone who is suffering from self esteem issues for instance if you have problems in this area yourself that haven't been cleared up with EFT.

Switching aspects

It is worth keeping in mind that whilst working on one particular negative memory during an EFT session, a new one can spring to mind. If this happens, it can be a good sign as it means you, or your client, no longer have any negative emotions attached to the original memory and you are now able to move on to the new memory. It could also mean that this new memory is associated with, and therefore part of, the original one. How to recognise parts of a problem, known as *aspects*, is covered in Chapter 4.

My advice would be to either stay focused on the original problem you were working on and continue to apply EFT on it until the emotional intensity has gone to a zero, or deal with the new memory in the same way. (Chapter 3 refers to how to do this.)

New memories cropping up during an EFT session can interrupt the flow of EFT and can cause some confusion. One way to avoid this would be to write each new memory down to ensure you don't miss out on anything important.

If this switching to different aspects happens when working on a client, it would be helpful to make them aware of what's going on so they are able to understand that progress is being made.

You will need to go back to any memory not worked on with EFT to make sure there is no emotional intensity remaining. You can do this by describing the problem again. If any negative memories remain and are not reduced to a zero with EFT, they could be triggered again in the future and bring back negative emotions.

Steve came to see me because he was having difficulty coping with the loss of his mother, as I was working on his grief, he suddenly switched to the problem he had with his wife not understanding his grief. I dealt with that issue but made sure I went back to his original problem around his grief over his mother. 'Oh that', he said 'that's not the problem'. The best approach is to stay with the original problem but I can say from experience that it's not always that easy. As long as you're aware of jumping aspects, you are more likely to ensure success with EFT.

When the problem comes back

Used correctly, EFT is almost always long lasting. If a problem does come back however, the most likely causes could be:

> ✔ All parts to the problem weren't dealt with because a specific part either didn't appear at the time or wasn't addressed fully.
>
> ✔ The original problem was treated too globally. This can happen as a consequence of not getting to the core issue.

Both of these reasons can be corrected using techniques described in Chapter 4.

When the same physical ailment comes back, often this is as a result of the emotional issue rearing it's ugly head again. If no medical reason is found, the emotional issue can be dealt with using EFT.

Working with Non-believers

Sceptics are out there and you may or not be one of them but if you or someone you know finds it difficult to accept EFT, then try these suggested Set Up Phrases and perhaps incorporate the 'What if' or 'choices' statements referred to in Chapter 15.

'Despite the fact that EFT will not work for me . . . I still love and accept myself.'

'Although I have no belief in EFT working . . .what if I just tap and see what happens.'

'I know this tapping isn't going to work, after all, why should it. . . . I accept myself anyway and will just see what happens.'

'Even though EFT will not help me . . . I still accept myself and choose to keep an open mind for the next hour.'

Persisting pays dividends

If you're a beginner with EFT it is easy to expect quick results every time you use it and forget how quickly EFT works compared to most other therapies. It will do no harm to remind yourself now and then that a little persistence and patience will reap great rewards. Next time you're working on a problem and it takes time to move down the SUDs scale (refer to Chapter 3) go at it from a different angle or read through this Chapter in more detail.

Breaking State

If you have been trying with EFT for some time and are beginning to find it difficult to concentrate or can't think properly, it may be necessary to break state. *Breaking state* is a variety of methods used to get your mind to change direction. How many times have you ever tried to remember something like, say, your computer password but no matter how long or how hard you try you just can't remember it? You eventually give up and later in the day when you're just about to put the dishwasher on, up pops that password! By diverting your mind elsewhere it's enabled your subconscious to bring the information to the surface. There are various ways to 'break state' including

- ✔ Spelling your name backwards
- ✔ Walking around the room
- ✔ Having a glass of water
- ✔ Shaking your body

These tactics should interrupt your one-way thinking so you can start afresh.

Needing someone else

Even if you have only studied the basics of EFT you will get good results most of the time. If you're not getting anywhere with using EFT on yourself, you will most likely benefit from another person tapping on your issues. They can often see things from a different point of view. If you don't know someone trained in EFT you can refer to the professional bodies listed in the Appendix at the back of this book.

A qualified EFT Practitioner will have experience in dealing with many problems and can often help when all else fails.

Building rapport

If you are using EFT on someone else, other than yourself, check none of your own problems are getting in the way as described earlier in this Chapter. If you are still not getting good results, try working with someone else. It may be that you simply do not 'connect' with the other person. Building rapport and trust is paramount as well as having connectivity.

Coming to terms

Unfortunately some people just don't want to help themselves to get better. Brenda came to me wanting help to give up smoking yet no amount of treatment worked. Eventually I gave up and I later found out that it was Brenda's husband who had told her to seek help for her smoking. This fact was never disclosed to me even though I asked the question at her initial session.

If the client doesn't want to give up then nothing can make them. A well-known fact amongst physicians is that some patients go to them for help but don't take the advice or medication given to them. Like the celebrity boxer who refused his medication, there is obviously more benefit to hanging on to their condition. Don't take it personally, that's all.

Constricted breathing

You don't have to believe in EFT for it to work but this is gentle introduction to those who are a bit hesitant to use EFT. This demonstration literally puts breath back into your lungs:

1. Inhale 2 or 3 maximum deep breaths. Take your time and don't hyperventilate. This step will stretch out your lungs so that any EFT improvement in your breathing cannot be attributed to a normal 'stretching effect' of your lungs.

2. Once you have stretched your lungs as far as they will go then take another deep breath. This time assess the deepness of your breath on a 0–10 scale where 10 is your estimate of your maximum capacity. Numbers typically vary from 3 to 9 on this. The occasional person who rates their breath at a 10 (they are usually wrong) may find that, after EFT, they will go way higher.

3. Carry out several rounds of EFT with Set up phrases such as 'Even though I have constricted breathing . . .', 'Even though I can only fill my lungs to an 8 . . .' and so on. In between each round, ask the client to take another deep breath and assess the 0–10 deepness. In the vast majority of cases it will keep improving.

4. During the process ask probing questions such as: 'What does your constricted breath remind you of?', 'When in your past did you feel constricted or smothered?', 'If there was an emotional reason for your constricted breath, what might it be?' Often, they will give a big clue as to an important emotional issue.

Part III
Finding Your Way to Inner Happiness

"I'd like to welcome this meeting of EFT students with some homemade double-fudge brownies. Don't all start tapping your meridians at once."

In this part . . .

We all want to be free from fears, phobias, and stress. This part shows you how to use EFT practically to address specific emotional problems, and how to grasp the importance of loving and accepting yourself.

This part also covers how to use EFT to release the deep-seated emotions attached to trauma, and how to deal with anger, grief, and relationship issues.

Chapter 7

Discovering How to Love Yourself

*A*s the song goes, 'Learning to love yourself is the greatest love of all', and so it is. Before you get the wrong idea, allow me to explain. Loving yourself is not about holding others in contempt or feeling superior and it's not about massaging your ego either. Loving yourself is about more than feeling good; it means knowing your strengths and weaknesses, and accepting yourself for who you are, warts and all. It's about being able to accept compliments or criticism, to be able to turn round and say, 'It may not be perfect, but you know what, I've done a pretty good job there.'

Being able to love yourself leads to healthy self-esteem and allows you to accept yourself even if you make mistakes. If you don't feel good about yourself, or find it hard to accept yourself, you may have issues with low self-esteem that can be extremely damaging to your personal development and relationships.

In this chapter I point out where the contributors to low self-esteem come from and tell you how you can knock out those negative thoughts with Emotional Freedom Technique (EFT). Unlike other self-help techniques, EFT doesn't rely on you changing your thoughts or behaviours; EFT does it for you and for good. Don't forget that you may only need to tackle one particular negative thought or behaviour for the rest to collapse (refer to Chapter 4 on aspects).

Spotting the Signs of Low Self-Esteem

'Esteem' comes from the Latin word meaning 'to estimate', so *self-esteem* is how you estimate or view yourself. You may know someone who outwardly shows signs of assurance and confidence yet they hide a multitude of insecurities such as those listed here:

- Taking on the victim role and blaming others for your problems.
- Not taking responsibility for your own life: turning power over to another to make decisions for you, and then feeling victimised if the results aren't to your liking.
- Excessively over- or underachieving with food, play, work, and so on.
- Blaming or criticising self, or constantly putting others down through guilt, finding fault, blame, or shame.
- Fearing change and reluctance to take risks, or too much change; taking dangerous, unwise risks.
- Being constantly negative, or so optimistic that you deny reality.
- Reacting to others with extreme emotion or no emotion.
- Behaving in a boastful, bossy, or bullying manner.
- Needing to be right or perfect; alternatively, acquiescing to the demands or opinions of others.
- Feeling inferior.
- Thinking rigidly.
- Having pervasive, deep-seated feelings of fear, terror, or panic.
- Behaving in an apologetic or aggressively defensive manner.
- Interpreting the hurtful words or actions of others as proof of your unworthiness.

If you're a parent and you know or suspect that you suffer from low self-esteem, you can find some helpful guidance in Chapter 16.

Recognising the Origins

Abraham Maslow was an eminent psychologist who developed the Hierarchy of Needs Model (see Figure 7-1). Maslow's theory was that unless certain needs are met individuals won't achieve healthy self-esteem or be motivated to progress and reach self-fulfilment. Regarding self-esteem, Maslow observed that a higher and lower version of esteem needs exists:

✔ The lower one is the need for the respect of others, the need for fame, admiration, status, recognition, attention, dignity, appreciation, and even dominance.

✔ The higher form involves the need for self-respect, including such feelings as confidence, competence, achievement, mastery, independence, and freedom.

Observe that the higher form includes self-respect, which, when achieved, is a lot harder to lose than the respect of others.

The negative version of these needs is low self-esteem and inferiority complexes. Maslow agreed that these were at the root of many, if not most, of people's psychological problems. In modern countries, most people have what they need with regard to their physiological and safety needs. More often than not, they have quite a bit of love and belonging too. It's a little respect that often seems to be so very hard to get!

Maslow also discovered that after the first four needs are met, individuals are motivated towards self-actualisation. Figure 7-1 shows the most commonly recognised depiction of Maslow's Hierarchy of Needs.

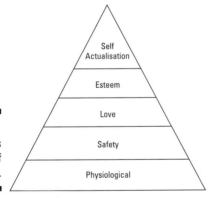

Figure 7-1:
Maslow's
Hierarchy of
Needs.

You can use the model in Figure 7-1 as a framework to help identify your own or your clients' idiosyncrasies.

See whether you can identify the patterns of behaviour in the following scenarios with the unmet needs in Figure 7-1:

✔ **Scenario 1:** Angie was fostered out when she was 5 years old. Around the age of 7 she developed a fear of the dark and had to sleep with the light on. Angie grew out of her fear of the dark as she got older and settled down in married life. However, she always felt scared being left on her own when her husband worked away and would go around checking doors and windows. Sometimes Angie would resort to leaving the light on at night.

✔ **Scenario 2:** Julia is successful in her job and comes across as always happy – nothing gets her down. Julia is also a perfectionist who works long hours to maintain her position in the company and keep up with others. Her position is very important to Julia as she must appear to be as good as her sister, Emma, because Julia's parents always compared Emma's success to Julia's. Emma went to university and left with Honours, going on to study law. Julia struggled at school but eventually found herself a good position in a company with prospects. However, Julia never felt 'entitled' to what she had achieved and couldn't take praise. She would lie awake at night waiting to be 'found out' that she didn't meet expectations.

✔ **Scenario 3:** Geoff had a deprived childhood, and sometimes he didn't know where the next meal was coming from, or when. Geoff grew up to become a very successful and wealthy businessman, yet he found it difficult to throw food away and his cupboards and refrigerator were always stuffed with food. Geoff attributed his behaviour to his love of food.

Are you beginning to get the picture?

Here Comes the Judge

Core beliefs are so called because they're at the very centre of your belief system. Negative core beliefs are the labels you give yourself based on your low self-esteem, which is measured against how you perceive yourself. Experiences in your life, whether early or late, influence how you perceive yourself and your self-worth. Being ridiculed in class, bullied by your boss, or ignored or not praised as a child all contribute to negative core beliefs. They're the judgments you make about yourself based on negative experiences you've had in earlier years.

So if you don't catch the ball and your team loses the game, does that make you a failure or a bad person? If you think about it logically, being what you *do* as opposed to what you *are* is impossible. To be a bad person you'd always behave in a negative manner. To be a good person, you'd need to act in a positive manner towards everyone at all times. Neither of these extremes is possible.

Table 7-1 illustrates common beliefs that people have about themselves. As you look at the table, mark whether you agree or disagree with each statement.

Table 7-1	**What Do You Believe about Yourself?**
Belief	*Agree/Disagree*
I have to be angry to survive.	
People I love leave me.	
I feel left out.	
I don't feel in control.	
In order to be loved I must do as others ask.	
I always draw the short straw.	
I'm . . .	
. . . a failure.	
. . . unlovable.	
. . . dirty.	
. . . weak.	
. . . stupid.	
. . . not good enough.	
. . . bad.	
. . . not to be trusted.	
. . . a disappointment.	
. . . to blame.	

As a practitioner, you can ask clients to complete Table 7-1 if you suspect that they have self-esteem issues. The exercise helps identify any problems around self-worth. After you investigate each of the issues a little further, you can direct EFT on the most troublesome ones. Even without investigation you can try; for example 'Even though I'm not to be trusted, I accept myself anyway'. (You can find more information on negative core beliefs in this chapter and Chapters 8, 10, and 12.) Clients can carry this exercise out at home between sessions.

Also ask the following questions:

- ✔ Where does this belief come from?
- ✔ What evidence exists that supports this belief?

Confronting the inner critic

If you have a poor self-image brought on by an accumulation of negative beliefs, you often find yourself judging others and no doubt putting them down in the process. By putting others down you're *validating* yourself to make yourself feel good, which is why bullies behave as they do. (You can read more on bullies in Chapter 16.)

Getting inside your head and ridding yourself of the inner critic is a job suitable for EFT. You may not even recognise that you have an inner critic until you hear yourself judging yourself or others. If you listen to the voice of your inner critic it's probably that of your parent, teacher, friend, or significant other. If someone judged you as a child, you're more likely to continue to judge yourself as you grow up. You can become really good at telling yourself that you're to blame, that everything is all your fault, and that you messed up again. Before you know it, your inner critic is taking hold of your life.

When you criticise yourself, you contribute to negative changes. When you approve of yourself, you facilitate positive changes.

Finding the Yellow Brick Road

When Dorothy, the Scarecrow, the Tin Man, and the Cowardly Lion mindlessly set off on the Yellow Brick Road they did so in the belief that when they reached the Emerald City and met the Wizard of Oz he would give them answers to their problems. After encountering many catastrophic events, they persevered on their journey until they reached the Emerald City and found the Wizard, only to discover he wasn't a wizard after all but merely a man behind a curtain. However, the man showed each of them how they had the answer to their own problems all the time. Dorothy asked the right question to get back home, and on their journey the Tin Man discovered that he had a heart, the Scarecrow that he had a brain, and the Cowardly Lion found that he had courage.

How many times have you held on to negative beliefs about yourself that simply aren't true? How any times have you searched for help when you have the courage, persistence, and answers within yourself?

In general, people don't like criticism, but if you have healthy self-esteem you either defend yourself against the criticism in an assertive way or hold your hands up and admit that you were wrong or did wrong. You learn from criticism.

If you have low self-esteem, however, when someone criticises you it feels like they're attacking you personally, and you find it hard to admit to being wrong. Criticism to you is further reinforcing your opinion of not being good enough, not lovable enough, or a failure. You most likely act aggressively or defensively towards any criticism you receive, because these are mechanisms for protecting yourself from being found out. If you feel or felt abandoned, you also defend yourself to avoid rejection.

Rather than beating yourself up about any mistakes you make, try working through this simple analysis of the situation to see the problem from a different perspective.

- What was the mistake?
- Why did it happen?
- Could I have prevented it?
- What can I learn from this mistake?

If this exercise doesn't help, then locate in your body the area where you feel the emotion as you replay the critical comment in your head. Use EFT to remove each emotion that you're experiencing until each one reduces to zero. Here are a few examples:

'Even though my dad's voice is telling me that I'm to blame, I deeply and completely accept myself. What did he know? I was only a child – I did the best I could.'

'Even though I messed up again, I accept myself as being a fallible human being. To err is human, as they say.'

'My boss just said that I ruined the whole campaign. I accept that I didn't do a good job, but I also accept myself.'

'Even though I have this hurt feeling in my stomach, I choose to accept myself.'

'Even though I can't take criticism because I feel I'm being rejected, I accept that it's my actions and not me as a person that's being criticised.'

You need to use EFT regularly for a week or two before you start to see results.

Take the 'you' out of any criticism you give. If someone else criticises the 'you', remind yourself that you're unique and don't take it personally. It's the other person who has the problem!

Pleasing people

If you have a need to please people, for whatever reason, remember that this is a pattern of behaviour – it's not who you are. Your past experiences caused this pattern of behaviour, and to overcome it you need to ask yourself the following questions:

✔ What is your motive? Is it love, acceptance, fear of abandonment, or anger?

✔ When this behaviour happens, what feelings do you have in your body?

✔ How do you respond?

Use EFT on each of your fears or motives and also include the feelings that you're experiencing. Remind yourself that you're safe and have nothing to be afraid of. The feelings are just caused by how your past conditioned you.

> *'Even though I can't say no because I fear I'll be rejected, I accept that my behaviour is a consequence of my past experiences.'*

> *'Even though I have to be nice so that people will like me, I recognise that I'm looking for love and approval.'*

These are just a couple of suggestions and you can create many more. Unearth what brought on this pattern of behaviour and use EFT to tackle it.

When you feel you have successfully dealt with your pattern of behaviour, try using EFT to improve on your assertive behaviour:

> *'Even though my needs can't be met, I choose to believe that I'm as important as anyone else.'*

> *'Even though I feel that I can't voice my opinion, I realise that this is just the way I think, not a fact, and I choose to have my voice heard.'*

Perfecting perfection

Along with the inner critic comes its little buddy, the perfectionist. If you're a perfectionist you probably learned early in life that other people valued you because of how much you accomplished or achieved. As a result you may have learned to value yourself only on the basis of other people's approval.

When this happens, your self-esteem may be based primarily on external standards. This situation can leave you vulnerable and excessively sensitive to the opinions and criticism of others. In attempting to protect yourself from such criticism, you may decide that being perfect is your only defence, so up pops that critical voice again. The constant pressure to be perfect leads to a whole host of feelings such as anger, shame, sadness, frustration, humiliation, and guilt.

Try the following phrases to help you with these emotions:

> *'Even though I must be perfect in everything to be acceptable, I accept myself as I am and others can accept me too.'*

> *'Even though everything I do has to be perfect, I deeply accept myself. I accept that no one is perfect at everything – not even, for example, Jamie Oliver, Tiger Woods, or my own parents.'*

> *'Even though I'm humiliated at not getting it right, I understand that it's my inside voice being the judge – no one else.'*

> *'Even though only 100 per cent is good enough, I accept myself and can accept 99 per cent as being satisfactory.'*

Remember what Joe E. Brown said to Tony Curtis at the end of *Some Like it Hot*, when Tony Curtis admitted he was a man, not a woman? 'Nobody's perfect!'

Feeling inferior

As if judging yourself wasn't enough, many people then go on to give themselves rules to live by. As a working wife and mother of two children, the rules I gave myself were that I must:

✔ Balance my work and life.

✔ Look smart for work but not too smart at the school gates.

✔ Have healthy meals prepared each evening.

✔ Be on time for work and school.

✔ Always turn up for school plays and other events, even if I have to miss lunch.

✔ Bake and not buy the birthday cakes.

I desperately tried to live up to these rules, but when I couldn't, boy was I consumed with guilt. In my mind I obviously wasn't as good a working mother as I made out. What made me think I could do both jobs? On reflection, drawing up these rules and then feeling that I must obey them was rather silly. What was I thinking?

Eleanor Roosevelt once said, 'No one can make you feel inferior without your consent.' What a profound insight she had into the workings of human emotions.

If you feel that you're not good enough or inferior, first of all ask yourself how do you know? Where did this opinion come from? Is this feeling based on fact? Have a go at this exercise:

1. **Try naming one major thing that happened or that someone said to you that confirms you're not good enough or inferior.**

   Be specific with the time and event – for instance 'The day of the big game when I was left off the football team', or 'The day my mother left me'.

2. **Use EFT (as I describe in Chapter 3 or 4) on the phrase that best describes the event.**

   'Even though I wasn't good enough for the team, I deeply and completely accept myself anyway.'

   'Even though I obviously wasn't good enough to play, I accept their decision. It doesn't make me a bad person. I can still play a decent game. I'll just try harder, that's all.'

3. **If you weren't good enough for a particular event or team, ask yourself whether you logically believe that that doesn't make you good enough as a person.**

4. **Ask yourself if you can emotionally believe you're not good enough.**

5. **Use EFT on any remaining beliefs about not being good enough until you can talk or think about the event without any emotion.**

Learning to Accept Yourself

Consciously or unconsciously, you may not be able to accept yourself because having low self-esteem makes you feel unworthy. If this is the case, how can you possibly say the generic affirmation 'I deeply and completely accept myself'?

Using the Set-Up Phrase while rubbing the Sore Spot or the Karate Chop, as I describe in Chapters 3 and 4, overrides this psychological reversal (refer to Chapter 6). However, if you cannot believe in yourself to do anything right, even EFT, then this is another matter hiding away in the background that you need to address separately, and here is a humorous suggestion:

'In my opinion I can't do anything right, not even this EFT. However, I accept that my opinion may not be right, so I'll give it a go anyway.'

You need to be as creative as you can, but here are some suggested phrases and tips:

1. **Start a list beginning with 'I cannot accept myself because . . .', and then complete the phrase in a way related to your problem.**

   For example: 'I hurt other people', 'I have . . . problem', 'I was bad in the past', 'I don't know why; I just can't', 'I'm not good enough', 'I'm not pretty enough', 'I'm not clever enough', 'I let people down; I can't live up to their expectations', 'I cheated on my wife', 'I lost my job', and so on.

2. **Use EFT on every reason you can think of as to why you can't accept yourself.**

3. **Check for any emotions (guilt, shame, anger, blame, and so on) that come up and then use EFT on each of them.**

   For example: 'I release this shame and by doing so I accept myself'.

4. **When you feel that you've released all emotions, do a few rounds of EFT using positive phrases.**

   Phrases you can use include 'I'm okay', 'I'm worthy', 'My actions don't make me a bad person', 'I accept my failings', 'I can change', and 'I'm willing to accept myself', and then move on to 'I can accept myself'.

Comforting the Inner Child

Although I'm a qualified and trained hypnotherapist, this technique isn't exactly the same as the inner child work I use in hypnotherapy, but is more of a gentle guiding technique to help clients reach their inner child. Generally, I use this process with clients who have problems stemming from childhood abuse, neglect, or abandonment. Usually, these memories are so unpleasant or so hidden that finding the real problem in order to use EFT can be difficult. At other times, the client can visualise himself as a child. At all times, it's a very relaxing yet powerful and cathartic process. By all means seek the assistance of an experienced EFT practitioner if you need some support.

Here's what you need to do:

1. **Explain to the client what will happen and that the idea is for him to go back to the age he was when the unpleasant memory or event happened.**

2. **Have the client sit in a comfortable chair while holding on to a cushion, pillow, or cuddly bear.**

3. **As he closes his eyes, ask him to focus on his breathing while relaxing every part of his body.**

4. **As the client relaxes, ask him to count down slowly from 20 until he reaches a very relaxed state.**

   I also tap on the client to relax him.

5. **Ask the client to use his imagination to visualise himself as a child.**

6. **When he acknowledges meeting the child, ask a few questions that are appropriate to the situation.**

   The idea is for the client to picture himself at the age when he felt or remembered the unpleasant memory.

   Here are a few questions to get you started:

   • 'What's your name?' Remember that the client may have had a nickname as a child.

   • 'How old are you?'

   • 'Who's with you?'

   • 'What's happening?'

   • 'What are you feeling?'

   • 'Where do you feel this sadness, anger, hurt, fear, or whatever?'

   • 'At what level do you rate this feeling?'

7. **Say that you're now going to tap for the feeling.**

   Examples include:

   'Even though Little Mo is sad because her daddy left her, she is a wanted and loved child, even though it didn't seem like it then.'

   'Even though Little Mo has this sadness in her tummy, she now asks it to go away.'

   'Even though Johnny is scared of riding bikes because he fell off his when he was 5, he knows he's now safe and has nothing more to fear.'

   'Even though Johnny's 5-year-old head hurts from the fall, he's still a good kid, and it's okay to have this fear as a 5-year-old but not as a 35-year-old!'

   'Even though Kitty is angry at her sister, Mary, for ruining her birthday party, she loves and forgives Mary, knowing that she was a child too and too young to know any better.'

   'Even though Kitty's anger is in her chest, she now chooses to let go of this feeling so she can feel better.'

8. **When you're convinced that the client no longer harbours the negative emotion, try a round of positive phrases only.**

9. **Ask the client to see the child again and ask whether the child is happy?**

   Usually, the child is playful and happy.

Injecting humour can be useful at the appropriate time.

When doing inner child work, always remind the client that they're safe and that you're in the room with them to protect them.

Chapter 8

Relating to Relationships

*N*umerous wars have been started and lives lost all in the name of love, yet love has also enriched and created human lives. Although love is universally felt and is the strongest and most powerful of all the emotions, everyone experiences love in their own unique way. The ways in which you love your work, your new coat, your child, your pet, or your best friend serve only to demonstrate how many countless ways exist of expressing the word 'love'.

In this chapter I concentrate on love in personal relationships. I show you how EFT can help you when starting out in a new relationship, and how to overcome those rocky moments. I also demonstrate how you can effectively manage the pain of heartache while leaving the fond memories intact. This chapter helps you understand that by letting go of your own negative emotional baggage, you naturally develop an ability to relate better to others and at the same time improve your relationship with yourself.

Understanding The Laws of Attraction

What is it that attracts you to a person and then makes you want to spend the rest of your life with them? Humans are naturally programmed to seek the company of other humans. People have an intrinsic need to be loved, to connect with others, and to feel a sense of belonging and acceptance. Socialising and engaging with other people enables you to expand upon your own abilities to accomplish things in life, as well as reproduce, of course. When these basic needs aren't met, loneliness ensues as well as depression, low self-esteem, and associated physical illnesses such as heart disease.

Meeting someone for the first time sends all sorts of signals to your brain. At a conscious level, you're probably attracted to their physical features, status, or mannerisms. At a subconscious level, you're probably looking for someone who shares the same qualities and has similar life experiences to you, such as your parents. Yes, you did read right, psychologists support this theory following a study that showed girls who enjoy a good relationship with their father are more likely to choose a prospective partner who looks like him. If their relationship with their father isn't good, girls tend to reject anyone who looks like him. Take a look around you at couples you know and see whether this theory stands up.

The same goes for you, actually. If you hate certain qualities you have, you most likely reject someone else with those same qualities. If you persevere trying to get on with that person despite this, you may be wasting your time and energy because the relationship is most likely to end up in arguments and crumble by the wayside. Which reminds me of the Groucho Marx joke where he quipped that he didn't want to belong to any club that would have him as a member!

The laws of attraction determine that if you like yourself, you like people that you meet naturally, and they, in turn, will like you. If you believe that no one will ever want you or that you'll never find 'Mr or Mrs Right', you're putting up barriers to anyone ever coming into your life. This self-talk is damaging and off-putting for anyone, but you can correct this by reading Chapters 7 and 15.

Taming the Green-eyed Monster

Nothing destroys a relationship faster than jealousy. The jealous partner perceives a threat to their relationship that causes insufferable pain. If you suffer from jealousy, you know the wide range of emotions it creates, including embarrassment, fear, pain, and anger.

Negative thoughts about yourself are often blame, insecurity, self-pity, and resentment. You fear being hurt or disappointed and go to extreme lengths to avoid this by questioning, nagging, or controlling your partner. Feelings of jealousy can lead to aggressive or violent behaviour, which you must never tolerate. You may want to stop being jealous but don't know how to stop the thoughts in your head.

If disagreements in a relationship result in violence, always seek professional help from a domestic violence group. You can always use EFT to help you cope with your feelings in the process.

When I use EFT on a client with symptoms of jealousy, I usually ask her to visualise what the relationship would be like without those negative thoughts. This allows her to see the relationship from a different perspective. I then explain that not feeling safe at some stage in her life is usually the basis of the emotion. By asking the client when she first experienced these same emotions, I can usually find the root cause. I then ask her to write down what situations trigger these jealous feelings and to apply EFT on each of them until no negative emotion remains when she visualises being in that situation again. Before the end of the session, I encourage the client to forgive herself or anyone who may have caused this negative emotion.

Feeling Abandoned: The Root of All Woes?

Frequently falling for the wrong type, or finding yourself attracted to those who are unavailable because they're either married or in a relationship themselves, may indicate that you have abandonment issues. Supposing you were abandoned emotionally or physically (neglected) as a child, it wouldn't be surprising to find that you're fearful of commitment as you grow older.

Feelings of abandonment or isolation can happen at any age to anyone and can be a traumatic experience, similar to grief. You constantly fear being left alone and never really knowing whether those that you love will remain in your life. Different things cause these feelings but they usually stem from:

✔ Feelings of isolation within a relationship.

✔ A mother whose children have grown up and left home.

✔ Break-up of a relationship.

✔ A child given up for adoption.

✔ Loss of job and professional status.

Abandonment issues can also cause reactive attachment or attachment disorder (see Chapter 16).

Making Sense of Your Behaviour

You need to take a critical look at continuing difficulties in forming and sustaining relationships. Search a little into your past and see whether you can establish whether your emotional upbringing or past relationships are responsible. If your family were never demonstrably affectionate or had difficulty in expressing their feelings, this family history may account for the way you show affection towards your partner. If someone treated you badly in a previous relationship, no one can blame you for being cautious about opening your heart to someone else, or believing that you're not good enough.

If, on the other hand, you find yourself repeatedly being drawn towards similar toxic relationships, consider whether this is because you believe it's what you deserve or whether you're staying within your 'comfort zone'. You may not even be aware of what you're doing as you moan about falling for the wrong guy or girl again.

Unresolved feelings of abandonment or not being good enough can result in these negative patterns of behaviour:

- **Relationship addiction:** People may describe you as either being too clingy or jealous, or alternatively acting like a martyr. The need to care for others may mask the fact that this caring is actually meeting your own needs. If you're not interested in nice guys or girls, you may be thinking of yourself as 'broken' like those that you have to care for. This belief means that your partner won't leave you because you're both the same. The need to care becomes almost like an addiction. In fact, you probably feel that's all you deserve. This type of behaviour can result in the carer becoming co-dependent, a situation in which the carer can't say no to anyone's requests. Co-dependent behaviour is often the result of being in an abusive relationship or having a parent who was an alcoholic.

- **Love them and leave them:** You've been hurt or abandoned in the past, so you build up a defensive wall around you. No one is going to hurt or reject you again, so as soon as your partner shows devotion to you, you test his or her love by saying hurtful things or rejecting him or her. You're never convinced that your partner wants you, so you may as well prepare yourself by withdrawing your love. After all, your belief is that your partner will leave you eventually. And you're not surprised when your prophecy comes true.

- **Attracting the wrong sort:** Why is it that some people are attracted to the wrong sort of men/women? Forming relationships with someone who is married, abusive, or treats you dismissively are characteristics of feeling abandoned or not good enough. If you believe that one day your partner will leave you, then you're most likely to be drawn to relationships that are doomed to fail.

- **Conditional love:** Learning from an early age that your love is conditional upon your behaviour results in a pattern of people pleasing. For instance, in order to win others' love and approval you feel that you mustn't do anything that displeases them for fear that they'll reject you. You come across as being timid, but inside you harbour resentment at not being able to express your own needs.

✔ **Fear of intimacy:** This means not letting anyone get too close to you because you needlessly fear that they won't want you when they get to know the 'real you'. You act tough and powerful, which makes you feel good about yourself, but in reality you don't like yourself very much and can't understand why anyone would like you because you're flawed in some way.

If you recognise any of these behaviours in yourself, it's not too late to do something about them. Table 8-1, in the following section, has some suggested phrases to use with EFT before the behaviours start to affect your relationship.

Breaking the Cycle

It's not only fear of abandonment that can interfere with a relationship; if you don't feel good enough about yourself or treat yourself with respect, no relationship is going to work. You may even exhibit some of the behaviours associated with abandonment in the previous section. Chapter 7 has some ideas you can use with EFT if you constantly find you're putting yourself down.

In the meantime, remind yourself that the things that you don't like about your personality are just behaviours, and you can change behaviours with or without EFT. EFT can certainly assist, though, and Table 8-1 provides some speculative phrases you may like to try out.

Following the guidance in Chapters 3 and 4, use any or all the following Set-up Phrases, depending on what applies to you. Remember, they're only suggestions and you can mix them up if you like. To simplify things, this example is from a female's perspective, although the phrases apply to both genders.

Table 8-1	Set-up Phrases for Relationship Issues
Acknowledgment of Problem	*Acceptance of Self*
'Even though I was hurt by (name) and I can't trust any man ever again let alone have sex with him . . .'	'. . . I accept myself as a loving person. (Name)'s behaviour is not my fault.'
Although I can't bear seeing my boyfriend talking to other women . . .'	'. . . I deeply and completely accept myself and choose to feel safe.'
Although I believe once men get to know me they'll reject me or leave me . . .'	'. . . I accept that it's my own insecurities coming into play and I forgive myself.'

(continued)

Table 8-1 *(continued)*

Acknowledgment of Problem	*Acceptance of Self*
Even though I have this fear of letting anyone get close to me . . .'	'. . . I understand that it's my fear of being abandoned and I accept myself.'
Although I'm always attracted to the unavailable ones . . .'	'. . . I accept my fear of becoming emotionally attached.'
Even though I've put my heart on the table in the past and it's been broken so I refuse to let it happen again . . .'	'. . . I understand why I feel this way and I am willing to accept that not all men are the same.'
Although I'm not good enough for anyone to love . . .'	'. . . By loving and accepting myself as I am, I can begin to love and accept those I'm attracted to.'
Even though I don't deserve to be loved because of all my hang-ups . . .'	'. . . I accept myself as a worthy person who deserves to be loved as much as anyone else, and tapping can release my hang ups.'
Although I need constant reassurance from (name) . . .'	'. . . I accept myself as being needy and wanted and that it's an "inside job".'
Even though I've let the hurt from my past relationship(s) affect my present and future relationships and this makes me angry/hurt/ashamed/guilty . . .'	'. . . I'm ready to let those negative emotions go. They're doing me no good and are holding me back.'
Although I really believe I'll never let anyone into my life again . . .'	'. . . I love and forgive myself for feeling this way and I'm willing to put past experiences behind me.'
Even though I fear being found out . . .'	'. . . I accept myself as I am.'

1. For fears of abandonment, try using these suggested Set-up Phrases:

'Even though I have this fear of being rejected, I accept myself with this fear.'

'Even though I believe I'm not good enough to be loved, I can accept myself and that's good enough for me.'

'Even though I have to please people in order to be loved, I accept that my past is causing me to behave this way.'

2. Tap on the remaining points while saying:

Eyebrow: 'I feel rejected.'

Side of eye: 'I feel unwanted.'

> Under eye: 'They always leave me.'
>
> Under nose: 'I'm not good enough.'
>
> Chin: 'I'm frightened of being alone.'
>
> Collarbone: 'I feel this deep sadness.'
>
> Under arm: 'I feel so abandoned.'
>
> Inside of wrist: 'I feel this deep sadness.'

3. **Continuing with the EFT routine that I describe in Chapters 3 and 4, introduce some negative and positive phrases when you begin to feel more positive.** You can find more about positive and negative phrases in Chapter 15.

4. **Finally, end with a round of all positive phrases, tapping on the rest of the points while saying:**

> Eyebrow: 'I'm a good person.'
>
> Side of eye: 'I'm worthy of love.'
>
> Under eye: 'I know I am loved.'
>
> Under nose: 'I choose to feel good enough.'
>
> Chin: 'I have so much love to give.'
>
> Collarbone: 'Deep down I know I'll find love'
>
> Under arm: 'Inside I am kind and lovable.'
>
> Inside of wrist: 'I feel completely safe and secure.'

If some negative emotion remains, use the Reminder Phrase I refer to in Chapters 3 and 4.

Persistent use of EFT on these negative feelings eventually brings about positive changes.

When the Love Starts to Fade: Accepting Differences and Working Together

Remember those early days of being in love? The butterflies in your stomach whenever you met, the way you couldn't bear to be parted from one another? When does this suddenly change into you both bickering, criticising, or arguing with each other?

Understanding that relationships always have differences is helpful, but appreciating those differences in each other is what really matters more than anything. Sitting down together and trying to talk about the differences certainly helps, and shows that you're not taking each other for granted either, which can be a real bone of contention in a relationship. Sometimes, however, talking isn't enough and you still feel those unwanted emotions. When working with couples, my philosophy is that if a couple can connect emotionally, their relationship will withstand most arguments and life's ups and downs.

When I hear the words 'I love my partner but I'm not *in love* with my partner' this indicates to me that a particular characteristic about your other half has changed or is missing. Of course, many other reasons may explain why you feel unfulfilled in a partnership or marriage – too many to include in this book.

The following exercise is a bit of fun, but it brings into the open what may be missing between you and your partner. You can then use EFT on the stubborn differences that you can't agree to change or can't compromise on. Preferably, carry out the exercise when both you and your partner are in a reasonable frame of mind. Before you begin, make sure that you're both familiar with the tapping routine (see Chapters 3 and 4). Decide whether you're going to tap on each other in turn or simultaneously. Tapping for any embarrassment at doing this exercise is also a good idea. Although the exercise is fun, you can also use it for any hurt or upsets between you.

1. **Both you and your partner write down on a piece of paper what qualities you liked about each other when you first met.**

2. **Write down what qualities you now don't like about each other.**

   Interestingly, these may include the qualities that you both initially liked in each other.

3. **Next, you both write down what makes you feel loved.**

   Your partner saying 'I love you', buying a thoughtful present, giving you a hug for no reason, or kissing you goodnight are just some ideas.

4. **When you've completed your lists discuss your answers with your partner and come to some sort of compromise over the differences between you.**

5. **Use EFT as in Chapter 3 or 4 on the differences that you cannot resolve.**

   Start off with the Set-Up Phrase of either 'Even though . . .' or 'Although . . .'. For example:

   'I'm upset because (name) won't buy me flowers to show I'm loved. I accept myself with these feelings and I appreciate that (name) shows me love in other ways.'

'(Name) irritates me when (problem). I accept myself and I accept that I'm not perfect either.'

'(Name) is never going to change the way he eats his food and it annoys me intensely. I completely accept myself anyway and I'll come to accept (name) as he is.'

'Although I'm angry because (name) is so stubborn and never gives in, I accept my anger and I accept our differences. (Name) just needs to do some tapping on her stubbornness, that's all.'

'Even though (name) doesn't do the things I'd like him to do, I accept myself and I love (name) for who he is and not how he makes me feel.'

6. **When tapping on each other you can use a Set-Up Phrase beginning with 'Even though' or 'Although', or you can just tap around the remaining points using whatever words you want. Start off with something trivial at the start.**

   For instance, one of you can tap on the other from eyebrow to under the arm saying phrases such as:

   'I love you but at times I don't like you.'

   'You upset me when you (problem).'

   'I don't like it when you (problem).'

   'I blame you for (problem).'

   'You need to speak up more.'

7. **End up by both tapping on each other simultaneously:**

   'You're still my friend.'

   'We want to resolve this (problem).'

   'We both have our faults.'

   'We respect each other.'

   'We still love each other.'

You can use 'tapping by proxy' as I describe in Chapter 16, to help your partner, but you can't change your partner's behaviour, only your reaction to it. Nor can you use tapping by proxy to make someone else love you or do something for you, by the way.

If you persist in wanting your partner to change, you must face up to the truth that you're struggling to accept your own reactions to what your partner does.

Understanding the Unspoken Rules

Not being aware of your partner's unspoken rules can cause all sorts of misunderstandings and problems, especially in the early years of a relationship. You often carry these rules through life from childhood, and they usually begin with 'I must . . .' or 'I should . . .'. Chapter 7 has more examples. These rules are just like those limiting beliefs that I refer to in Chapter 15. You may have stumbled across them already with beliefs like 'All men are jerks' and 'Women are good for only one thing'. If you believe such things, you need to use EFT on them pretty quickly.

Sometimes, even minor irritations can cause arguments, so you can try EFT on:

> *'Even though my rule is that I control the TV remote, I'm okay with (name) having control.'*

> *'Although it's my rule to have the last word, I accept that this isn't always possible or necessary.'*

Conflicting Emotions: Is It Love or Hate?

One of the worst types of emotions in relationships is being torn between love and hate, anger and forgiveness, fear and longing, and any combination of feelings you can imagine.

You can use EFT to ease the conflict between parts of you that are pulling you in opposite directions by using a conjunction such as 'yet' or 'and':

> *'I realise I need to end this relationship, yet I can't bear to be on my own.'*

> *'I know that being with him/her is destroying me and I can't live without him/her.'*

> *'I love my father and I hate him for what he did, yet I choose to accept these feelings in myself.'*

Regardless of whether your feeling towards the other person is hate, anger, or love, you're emotionally tied to them by your negative emotions. If you don't break the bond, you won't grow or move on emotionally.

Breaking Up Is So Very Hard to Do

At the end of the day sometimes you just have to accept that a relationship has irretrievably broken down. Did you know that psychologists agree that having a relationship break-up is like going through grief? In both cases you lose someone you loved and you're unwilling to psychologically let them go.

By using similar EFT techniques for those used for grief (see the section 'Coping with the Pain of Loss' later in this chapter) you can get over a relationship break-up. Use any of the suggested phrases throughout this chapter, depending upon how you feel.

Regardless of how a relationship ends, you can feel a painful recurrent uncertainty when you wonder if the two of you are actually apart. Following are some suggestions to help you through this period.

Using the routine I describe in Chapter 3, use EFT on:

- ✔ Feelings of anger, sadness, self-pity, loneliness, or hurt.
- ✔ Fears of rejection, failure, seeing them with someone else.
- ✔ Physical pain of heartache, tightness in chest, emptiness inside.
- ✔ Belief that you'll never get over your partner's departure.
- ✔ Disbelief that the relationship is over.

Use your partner's name and exaggerate the feelings or words if necessary to get that emotional charge as you apply EFT. Don't be polite or hesitant: you need to be honest with your emotions.

Without emotions there would have been no relationship.

Coping with the Pain of Loss

Grief is a natural emotion that affects you when someone you love dies, even when you expected their death. To lose a loved one can be absolutely devastating and can leave the survivor wondering how they'll ever cope. The pain of grief seems a constant reminder of the loss. There used to be a recognised 'grief period' of two years during which time you were supposed to come to terms with your loss. But EFT has no timescale, so there's no reason why you can't use EFT immediately.

Carrying a torch

You bump into your ex-boyfriend or ex-girlfriend who dumped you some time ago and you feel that same pain inside. This feeling of pain must surely be some kind of indication that your love was special? Well, no actually.

According to new scientific research that isn't what's going on at all. The pain you experienced when your relationship broke up is etched into your emotional brain and you react whenever you fear your personal being coming under attack.

So in fact those feelings you experience when you accidentally bump into the ex-partner are physical reactions to protect you from danger. These confused feelings can go on for a long time and make you believe your relationship must have been something special when in fact you're being warned not to make the same mistake again.

The hardest part for an EFT practitioner dealing with grief is knowing where to begin. For a start, everyone deals with grief in their own way and how they respond depends on their cultural and religious beliefs as well as their own conceptions about death. Some cultures don't support grieving and can make people afraid of death.

You can also use EFT on preparing yourself or someone else for death.

Many people also believe that if they use EFT for their grief they'll be denied normal human emotion and somehow feel 'disloyal' to the deceased. I can't emphasise enough that this is truly not the case. You can't remove normal human emotion with EFT, any more than removing your fear of heights will make you jump off a tall building. Yes, grief is natural, but EFT only redirects it so at the very least you feel comforted, and everyone needs comforting at times like this. EFT can help you come to terms with bereavement and in Chapter 5 you can find some very elegant and gentle techniques to help with the healing process.

So many variable emotions and situations surround grief, so what I list here is just a very small sample of ways you can use EFT on the generally recognised stages of grief:

  ✔ **Denial:**

   'I can't believe this is happening (or has happened) yet I accept myself.'

   'Although I can't accept the diagnosis, I can come to terms with it and fight on.'

  ✔ **Anger:**

   'Although I'm angry at you for leaving me, I accept myself with these feelings and I choose to feel peace instead.'

'I accept myself even though I'm angry at the doctors, God, and the world.'

✔ **Depression:**

'Although I'm sad thinking of you, I wish us both peace.'

'I deeply accept my human self, although I find it hard to see a future without you.'

✔ **Acceptance:**

'Although I've found it hard to accept you're gone, I accept that life goes on.'

'I'm finding it so hard to accept that you're never going to walk through that door again, but I choose to accept that I can hold on to the happy memories.'

Use EFT for other emotional occasions such as anniversaries, birthdays, and Christmas, for instance.

Some people experience a complete absence of grief and mourning. They may be unable to experience normal grief reactions, or have delayed grief, conflicted grief, or chronic grief. All these factors complicate and hinder the healing process. If you don't deal with unresolved grief it can lead to depression and post-traumatic stress disorder (see Chapter 11.) Chapter 5 has some gentle techniques to help with this problem.

Sexual Healing

Therapists put sexual problems into three basic categories: 'can't get it up', 'can't get it in', and 'can't be bothered'.

Unless there's a medical cause, and I must stress that you should have this checked out first, most sexual problems come from unresolved emotional issues. Get these issues out of the way and you're left with looking at what else may be causing the problems in the bedroom.

The idea of the sex performance gets some people wound up instead of being relaxed about it. Even the word 'performance' can be off-putting. Saying that, if it was as easy as just relaxing then you wouldn't be reading this part of the book, would you? As with the rest of the book, in the Set-Up Phrases you can insert whatever words you like that apply to you and your circumstances.

Before treating any sexual problem with EFT, always check first with your doctor to make sure that no medical reasons are causing the problem.

You can usually treat the following complaints with EFT:

- **Premature ejaculation:** Try to remember the first time this happened. As you relive the memory use EFT on whatever your thoughts or feelings were at the time. How about saying 'Even though I'm under pressure to perform I choose to relax. I choose to hold back. There's no rush'.

- **Inability to maintain an erection:** Maintaining a healthy diet and exercising can help with this problem, but if this doesn't work you need to look at the psychological causes of *erectile dysfunction* (impotence). These include stress, anxiety, depression, and problems in a relationship. Suggested wording here can be something like 'Even though I don't feel like a man, I accept myself', 'Although I can't get it up and I feel a failure, I accept there are reasons for this', or 'Although I can't keep an erection, I accept myself with this problem and this fear'.

- **Difficulty in reaching orgasm:** Look at your beliefs at not being good enough, fear of failure, needing to be perfect, and so on, and then use EFT on the root cause. One way of wording your phrase for EFT can be 'I accept a watched kettle never boils, and I choose to relax and see what the outcome is'.

- **Painful intercourse:** If no physical reason exists for the pain, then you need to look at the emotional issues. Common reasons include sexual abuse, upbringing and beliefs, anxiety, and fear. Establish the cause and then treat it with EFT: 'Even though I was told sex was dirty, I accept myself – it wasn't my fault', or 'Although I fear sex , I can accept making love with someone I love'.

When you're just not interested

For many reasons, couples go through a phase where sex takes a backseat in the relationship. If this situation is becoming a problem for either of you, take a good look at what was happening around the time you started to lose interest in sex. Are you harbouring any resentment towards your partner? Are you jealous or hurt? Have you just given birth or found you were pregnant, so are frightened of sex? Are you unhappy with your body? In your household, was sex regarded as 'dirty'?

Whatever the reasons, you need to use EFT on each and every one of them. The earlier sections in this chapter and other parts in this book can help you, depending on what the issue is.

There is a scene in the film *Annie Hall* where Woody Allen and his wife Diane Keaton are each seeing their own therapist. Each of their therapists asks the same question: 'How often do you have sex?' Woody Allen replies, 'Hardly ever. Three times a week.' His wife answers with, 'Oh, all the time. Three times a week.' Their answers illustrate how important it is to understand what you see as normal or expected in a relationship.

To enhance your desire for sex, you have to use EFT in a very artistic and creative way, and it may go something like this:

1. **Before you start, measure on a scale of zero to 10 your levels of desire.**

   In this instance a rating of 10 means that you really, really don't want sex tonight, so you want this to go down to zero.

2. **Repeat any one of these Set-Up Phrases three times while rubbing the Sore Spot or the 'Karate Chop as I describe in Chapters 3 and 4:**

   'Even though I haven't felt like sex since having our baby, I give myself permission to accept my body as being womanly.'

   'Even though I'm not in the mood for sex, what if I just relax and let those juices flow.'

   'I accept myself even though my sex drive has gone to an all-time low.'

   'Although I have no interest whatsoever in sex, and nothing's going on down there, I accept myself and I'm determined to fix what's not working because I may be missing out on something.'

   'Although I can't see what all the fuss is about with sex, perhaps it's because I've not been allowing myself to relax and enjoy it.'

   'Even though I hold myself back for fear of letting go, I release myself from this fear and open up my desires.'

   'Even though the thought of sex does nothing for me, what if I think of it as a natural way of expressing my love for my partner.'

3. **While tapping on the remaining meridian points from eyebrow to under the arm, say whatever you feel.**

   Here are some examples:

   'I'm not interested.'

   'I have no desire whatsoever.'

   'I don't feel like a woman.'

   'Why should she be interested in me?'

   'I don't like my body.'

   'Lie back and think of England.'

   'I'm not ready.'

   'Sex is a duty.'

'You're not supposed to enjoy it.'

'As long as I keep him happy, that's all that matters.'

'Nothing is stirring.'

'I have no sex hormones.'

4. **When the desire is creeping back and the rating on the Subjective Units of Distress Scale (see Chapter 3) is around a 3 or 4, introduce some positive phrases similar to these as you tap on the meridian points from eyebrow to under the arm:**

'What if I choose to relax and accept my partner making love to me?'

'It's okay to let go.'

'I give myself permission to enjoy myself.'

'I want to give and receive pleasure.'

'Making love is natural and is something I can enjoy.'

'I decide to open up my sexual desires.'

'The feelings are within me, I just need to let them go.'

'I can feel the fires within.'

'I'm not going to miss out on what everyone else is enjoying.'

'Something is stirring down below.'

'My body is ready for love.'

'My body was made for loving.'

'I choose to be free.'

'I can feel some stirrings that haven't been there for a while.'

By all means include more racy thoughts and feelings that are going on that I'm not permitted to use in this book. I think I can leave you to use your imagination on this one.

5. **When you've finished using EFT, project a visualisation of having sex at a future time to see if any problem remains. If so, tap for it.**

Working with or without a practitioner

If working with a therapist or practitioner, you need to feel comfortable and at ease with her. Initially, your therapist needs some details from you, after which she discuss the problem with you and helps you identify if the cause is physical, psychological, or a combination of the two.

If you're in a relationship, your therapist also wants to know if any problems exist that may be causing anxieties or tension. She may give you (and perhaps your partner) some homework. Remember, EFT practitioners aren't trained sex therapists but they are skilled at finding the root cause and treating it with EFT.

A good practitioner doesn't force you to remember or relive painful memories and only goes back as far as is necessary without causing discomfort. Chapter 5 has a range of techniques that you can use.

When you know how to use EFT for yourself (familiarising yourself with Chapters 3 and 4 can help), you can use it in the privacy of your own home without having to disclose your inner thoughts or feelings with a complete stranger. Working on your own in private takes away any shame, guilt, or fear you associate with your problem.

Chapter 9

Fighting Fears, Phobias, and Anxieties

Sometimes it's good to be afraid. Healthy levels of fear and anxiety can be helpful. Fear can protect you from harm and anxiety can push you to meet new challenges in life. In a nutshell, fear can either protect or destroy you.

In this chapter I describe many of the most common types of fears and anxieties, and a few more besides. I also show how you can treat these anxiety disorders using Emotional Freedom Technique (EFT).

Understanding Your Reactions to Fear

You're at home at night relaxing by reading a book when a window opens wide and the curtains blow around. Immediately, you fear something dreadful and imagine perhaps someone breaking in. At the same time your brain has started the fight or flight response experienced as your heart thumping and you feeling startled. You then realise that the catch wasn't on the window properly and it was only the wind that caused the window to open.

For a moment there you felt a real or perceived threat to your safety, which is a natural, healthy fear.

As you've seen in this scenario, fear is an emotion that has everything to do with your mind and your beliefs, but if your belief is unfounded or is exaggerated, then this is an unhealthy type of fear. Fearing that you'll die of a serious disease when you're in perfectly good health or fearing that the world will end tomorrow are examples of unhealthy fears. They're both highly unlikely and no evidence supports them. Unhealthy fear can have a detrimental effect on you emotionally, physically, and psychologically. Illogical fear is really good at holding you back and preventing you from finding fun in life.

Superstitions are based on a belief that something, usually bad, will happen as a consequence of carrying out a particular action. 'Walking under a ladder brings bad luck' and 'Walk on a crack and your mother will break her back' are just two I remember from childhood. Talking of superstitions, would you believe that millions of people in the world have paraskavedekatriaphobia? (A fear of Friday the 13th to you and me.) Where this belief originated from is unclear, but some people avoid getting married, won't change their bed, go to work, or eat out on Friday the 13th. I was brought up with a vanload of superstitions that I know are totally irrational, yet I still won't put new shoes on the table in case bad luck befalls me for the rest of the day. What are your superstitions and do you still believe in them? Can you compare them in any way with any fears you may have?

By treating your fear with EFT, you don't lose common sense and thereby endanger yourself. You can clear your fear of heights, for example, but that doesn't mean that you're tempted to jump off a dangerously high bridge.

When Fear Turns into an Anxiety Disorder

Although anxiety and fear have two different scientific meanings, over the years they have come to be known as one and the same. What defines an anxiety disorder is when your response to fear or anxiety is out of proportion to the situation. It's as if your fears snowball beyond your control and you feel powerless and afraid.

What people fear the most

In a US Gallup poll, people rated their fears as follows:

1. Terrorist attack
2. Spiders
3. Death
4. Failure
5. War
6. Heights
7. Crime/violence
8. Being alone
9. The future
10. Nuclear war

Doggone! That's why!

Beth and Cindy are walking along the road when they both see a friendly looking dog coming towards them. Beth loves dogs and greets it warmly, but Cindy responds by freezing on the spot. Her heart races and her palms are sweaty. She then runs in the opposite direction.

Why did she do this? When Cindy was around 3 years of age she was bitten by a dog and was very emotionally upset by the experience – so much so that she couldn't even look at a photo or a TV screen showing a dog. She never visited her aunt either, because she owned a dog. Because Cindy's unpleasant encounter with the dog who bit her happened so long ago, Cindy had completely forgotten about the experience and accepted her negative reaction to dogs, because in her mind she had always been frightened of them.

What Cindy wasn't aware of was that her subconscious brain had stored the previous negative encounter with the dog in the amygdala. In Chapter 2, I talk about how the amygdala and the hippocampus play distinct roles in the storage of memories associated with emotional events. In Cindy's case, the amygdala saved the sights, sounds, smell, feelings, thoughts, and physical sensations from her previous unpleasant encounter with the dog that bit her. The amygdala saved the information as part of the survival instinct and triggered a negative response so that the body, mind, and emotions immediately reacted as if she was back in the original situation. It pumped blood and adrenalin as a fight or flight response to protect her.

An interesting observation is how the body's energy field came into play here (refer to Chapter 1). Beth's positive emotion *attracted* her to the dog and Cindy's negative emotion *repelled* the dog, just like a magnet.

If your anxiety is affecting you in the following ways, seek professional help:

✔ Your symptoms persist long after the event.

✔ You can't work.

✔ You stop socialising or contacting friends or family.

✔ You avoid situations or stop doing certain activities because of your anxieties.

✔ Personal hygiene or feeding yourself becomes an effort.

✔ Symptoms appear without warning and for no apparent reason.

✔ You feel that you can't control or cope with your anxiety symptoms.

Common symptoms of an anxiety disorder include:

✔ Breathing difficulties

✔ Palpitations or heart racing

✔ Chest pain or discomfort

- Trembling or shaking
- Feeling of choking
- Sweating
- Nausea or stomach distress
- Feeling unsteady, dizzy, light-headed, or faint
- Feelings of unreality or of being detached from yourself
- Fear of losing control or going crazy
- Fear of dying
- Numbness or tingling sensations
- Hot or cold flushes throughout your body
- Fear of fainting

Exploring the Different Types of Anxiety Disorders

An anxiety disorder is a serious mental illness that includes fears, panic attacks, obsessive compulsive behaviour, generalised anxiety, and phobias such as flying, agoraphobia, and many more phobias and fears. If you suffer from any of these disorders you know, like I did, how debilitating they can be.

Childhood fears

Psychologists say that the only fears you have when brought into this world are of heights and loud noises, but please don't test this out with a newborn – just take my word for it. The rest of your fears you gradually acquire along the way.

According to the Child Anxiety Network, 90 per cent of children aged between 2 and 14 have at least one specific fear. Many children share the following fears, which are considered normal:

- **0–2 years:** Loud noises, strangers, separation from parents, and large objects.

- **3–6 years:** Imaginary things such as ghosts and monsters, the dark, sleeping alone, and strange noises.

- **7–16 years:** More realistic fears such as injury, illness, school performance, death, and natural disasters.

With some children, fear can turn to anger when they're too embarrassed to express their emotion in case they're humiliated or ridiculed.

People who actively take part in some form of therapy recover more quickly and have fewer relapses.

Because a disruption to the body's energy system is the cause of all anxieties, you can apply the same basic EFT technique to them all. This chapter specifies the skill and approach you need to apply EFT to each of these anxiety disorders. Being familiar with the symptoms associated with each anxiety disorder helps formulate Set-Up Phrases as I describe in Chapter 3 and get to the core issue (refer to Chapter 4).

This chapter doesn't cover trauma and abuse; check out Chapter 11 for info on these areas.

The sections that follow explain the most common anxiety disorders. Some contain EFT phrases, and others you can address using the guidance later in this chapter in the section 'Managing Your Anxieties with EFT'.

Generalised anxiety disorder

Unlike specific fears or phobias, *generalised anxiety disorder* (or GAD) is experiencing exaggerated worry and a feeling of impending doom and gloom about most common, everyday activities. Physical symptoms come and go but your mind is often in a constant state of anxiety, compounded by you becoming anxious about your anxiety.

If you have GAD you may also suffer from the following:

✔ Feeling restless, tense, or on edge a lot of the time.

✔ Having difficulty concentrating and mind 'going blank'.

✔ Difficulty getting to sleep and staying asleep, resulting in tiredness.

✔ Focusing on the worst outcome.

Factors that can predispose you to GAD are:

✔ Environmental factors (abuse, death of loved one).

✔ Genetics (passed on through family).

✔ Brain chemistry (triggered response to an event even when the 'trigger' has gone).

Some years ago (before I discovered EFT), as a result of past life experiences, I was the type of person who worried if I had nothing to worry about, and this became a joke with people I knew. Even when my life was going well I'd be waiting for something to go wrong. If ever a member of my family or a friend was late, I'd visualise them having been in an accident – planning my route to the hospital, who I'd have to contact, and so on. Of course, they'd always arrive safe and sound, but it didn't stop me thinking the worst again the next time they were late.

A South American study has shown that EFT is as effective in treating GAD as other conventional therapies. The study also showed that EFT requires fewer sessions and the results last longer as opposed to patients who are given conventional therapy, who return to their pre-treatment therapy within a year.

Fears and phobias

A *phobia* is as an excessive or unreasonable fear of a specific object or situation that most people consider to be harmless. In fact, if you have a phobia, you probably realise that your fear is unreasonable, yet you still can't control it. Simple phobias are about one particular thing such as spiders or mice, and are usually accompanied by mild anxiety. Complex phobias include more than one aspect, such as claustrophobia. Some of the most common phobias include:

- **Arachnophobia:** Fear of spiders.
- **Social phobia:** Fear of being judged negatively in social situations.
- **Aerophobia:** Fear of flying.
- **Ophidiophobia:** Fear of snakes.
- **Agoraphobia:** Fear of open spaces.
- **Claustrophobia:** Fear of enclosed places.
- **Acrophobia:** Fear of heights.

Phobias often have the following symptoms associated with them:

- You suffer from intense and unreasonable fear triggered by the presence or anticipation of a specific object or situation.
- Exposure to the feared situation or thing causes immediate feelings of anxiety or panic.
- You recognise that your fear is excessive and unreasonable.
- You avoid the feared stimulus, or endure it with intense anxiety.
- Your avoidance of the object or situation you fear interferes significantly with your normal routine or causes significant distress.

People with phobias do everything they can to avoid their phobic stimulus. If you have a phobia, your avoidance of the feared situation can disrupt your life and become a source of tremendous stress and anxiety.

Social phobia

I've included social phobia here because it's a very common type of phobia and, if you're a practitioner, you'll probably be asked to help someone with this one day.

Social phobia is the fear and anxiety about other people negatively evaluating or judging you. Although many people feel uncomfortable about being in a room full of people – like at a party, for instance, with people they don't know – someone with a social phobia may be physically sick at the very thought. Even though in today's society many people appear to be more confident and outgoing, the very thought of being the centre of attention, engaging in social interactions, or eating in public can set off intense feelings of anxiety in some people.

Associated emotions are usually, humiliation, and embarrassment at your own actions or behaviour. Symptoms can include blushing, stuttering, muscle twitching, or even a panic attack. To counteract these symptoms, sufferers sometimes resort to drinking too much, or taking medication or illicit drugs. Chapters 7, 11, and 15 also contain guidance to help you overcome this type of phobia where it stems from beliefs about yourself.

EFT won't turn you into the most popular or entertaining person on the planet, but it treats the fears and anxieties that go with the thoughts and enables you to relax more.

Again, trying to remember the first time you experienced humiliation in front of people or when you first noticed your fear certainly helps, so that you can use EFT on that first memory. You're also looking at beliefs about yourself and where these came from. Questions to ask may be:

- ✔ When did you first notice this phobia?
- ✔ What's your earliest memory (no matter how long ago) you have that may have caused you to feel this way?
- ✔ At what point do you start to feel anxious?
- ✔ What is it about being in social situations, for example, that cause you to feel anxious? If the phobia is around eating in public, what were eating experiences like at home or school, for instance?

The answers that come up will vary and may be feelings of inferiority; fear of being inadequately dressed, too tall, or too short; having nothing to talk about; or worrying that people won't like you.

Whatever the reason, use EFT on the first memory or emotion you associated with the fear.

Chapter 5 outlines techniques that may also be useful when you prefer to make a gradual change. For instance, use EFT on the negative thoughts or feelings that crop up by just visualising a social event, and then next work on entering the room, someone coming up to speak to you, and so on until all anxieties reduce to an acceptable level.

Panic attacks

If you experience a lot of anxiety, you may be prone to panic attacks. *Panic attacks* are characterised by sudden feelings of terror, usually accompanied by a pounding heart, sweatiness, and dizziness. Other sensations are usually chest pain or a feeling of being smothered, producing a sense of losing control or even dying. These symptoms can last for ten minutes or more. No logical explanation exists for why they happen.

If a panic attack happens in a lift, plane, or on a motorway, for example, this may develop into a fear of being in those places, which can result in your world shrinking around you.

The most frightening aspect of panic attacks is that they come on without warning and can occur in your sleep, which is why I recommend EFT as useful first-aid.

Early intervention can avoid panic attacks developing into serious avoidance behaviours such as a fear of open spaces (agoraphobia). Panic attacks can also lead to other serious problems such as depression or dependency on addictive substances.

I first witnessed a panic attack when I was celebrating my friend Anna's birthday. We'd just arrived at the restaurant where we were meeting other friends when suddenly Anna announced she just had to get out of the restaurant. I thought she was about to faint and took her outside, where she sat on the ground telling me she couldn't breathe and she was about to die. She was absolutely terrified and was asking me to tell her children how much she loved them if she were to die. An ambulance arrived and doctors carried out tests at the hospital but couldn't find anything wrong with Anna, so they sent her home. The hospital staff never even mentioned the words 'panic attack' to her, and it was Anna's GP who explained that she may have suffered a panic attack. Not knowing what caused the attack made her anxiety worse until it spread to her not being able to drive on the motorway. Gradually, her world began to close in until she finally found help with cognitive therapy and then EFT. With this help and daily use of EFT, Anna is almost over all her anxieties.

Sadly, most people don't seek medical help with panic attacks, and when they do, often the doctor doesn't explain panic attacks to the patient and doesn't give a referral for therapy.

Here are some ideas on how to use EFT on panic attacks. Dig around and use EFT on anything that happened in your past or present that may have contributed to the panic attack. Use EFT when you anticipate an attack, when you're having one, and after you've had one. I've separated the phrases you may use between your beliefs, your physical symptoms, and your behaviours. You can work on either or all three, depending on what's going on at the time, and change the tense to fit.

- ✔ **Beliefs:**
    - 'Even though I have this fear that I'll have a panic attack, I choose to remain calm.'
    - 'Although I have a fear of the fear, I accept and forgive myself.'
    - 'I choose to feel safe, even though I fear I'm losing control.'

- ✔ **Physical symptoms:**
    - 'Even though I feel tense as I wait for an attack to happen, I choose to relax.'
    - 'Although my heart is pounding and I fear I'll die, I know that I have nothing to fear and I'm safe.'
    - 'Even though I can feel this tingling up my arm, I'm safe, I'm calm, and I'm in control.'
    - 'Even though I feel like I'm choking, I choose to breathe deeply and evenly.'

- ✔ **Behaviours:**
    - 'Even though I want to run away, I choose instead to remain calm.'
    - 'Although I want to escape, I accept myself, knowing that I'll be okay.'

Panic attacks tend to come on when you least expect them – out of the blue, so to speak. Try using EFT as many times a day as you can with 'Even though I'm going to have a panic attack, I'm ready for it with EFT'.

You may notice that while releasing the emotional issues around panic attacks, physical issues often reduce or disappear at the same time.

If you want some words of reassurance, be aware that no evidence proves that anyone has ever died of a panic attack.

Fearing the needle

A *needle phobia* is a fear of needles, a fear of pointed objects, a fear of pain, and a fear of injections. Most children have a fear of needles but they usually grow out of it.

You may have a phobia of needles because of the following:

- ✔ Fear of objects being stuck into or through the body.
- ✔ Fear of objects being inside a blood vessel.
- ✔ A painful and/or traumatic experience.
- ✔ A family member who has a fear of needles.
- ✔ Fear of pain.

Most people with a fear of needles avoid dentists, giving blood, and minor medical or surgical procedures. You can overcome this fear with EFT, and I'd like to share with you one such case:

Gerry had an intense fear of hypodermic needles, so much so that he often fainted at the sight of one. Unfortunately, Gerry had an illness that required him to have an injection four times a year. He knew what had caused his fear but there was nothing that he could do to prevent his heart racing, palms sweating, and the sheer panic rushing through his body at the thought of the injections.

When Gerry was 12 years of age he was playing with his friend and they tried to climb over a high wall. Gerry fell off this wall and landed on a spike on a rail below. An ambulance rushed him to hospital. He wasn't that badly injured but he had to have a tetanus injection in his buttock. The nurse giving him the injection wasn't very sympathetic and told Gerry that nurses had enough to do without dealing with boys who get up to mischief. The nurse stuck the needle in very hard and made Gerry jump with pain. He not only suffered pain, but also humiliation. The next time Gerry needed an injection was when he developed diabetes many years later but the fear was still with him. When he came to see me he didn't think anyone could help him because he'd been scared of needles for so long.

I asked Gerry to repeat his fears in his Set-up Phrase as I tapped on him:

> *'Even though it's the thought of that needle hurting me as it goes in that gives me palpitations, I forgive myself and accept myself as I am.'*

> *'Even though thinking of this needle phobia is making me shake, I deeply accept and forgive myself.'*

When his physical sensations had gone down to zero I moved on to his feelings of guilt about the incident:

> *'Although I caused a lot of fuss that day, I accept and forgive myself.'*

Lastly, I worked on his humiliation and embarrassment:

> *'Even though I felt embarrassment at having to be taken to hospital and exposing my bottom to a nurse, I deeply and completely accept myself then as a 12-year-old boy and now as a man.'*

I continued to tap on Gerry's physical sensations and psychological emotions until they too were at a zero and he reported 'feeling silly about the whole thing'. I asked Gerry to use EFT each day and whenever he began to feel anxious. When he reported back to me following his next hospital appointment, he said that he was a little anxious but absolutely nothing like he'd been before. He couldn't believe the difference.

 Trypanophobia is the extreme and irrational fear of medical procedures involving injections or hypodermic needles. It's the only phobia where, very rarely, extreme reactions can cause a fatality. Don't test on this fear with an actual needle until in a safe medical environment.

Spiders and mice and other wee beasties

When applying EFT on the fear of spiders, beetles, mice, bees, birds, or the like, you may get instantaneous results there and then, or you may have to work on the specifics before the whole fear disappears (refer to Chapter 4 for more information on specifics).

For instance, if you have a fear of spiders, follow the EFT technique in Chapter 3 but be clear in your mind what your fear relates to. The fear may be of the little legs, hairy legs, long legs, or the speed at which they run. It may be that one was put down your back as a child. It may be all these things, so you need to work your way through by tapping first on the most intense feelings and/or memories of the spider.

Here's an example:

> *'Even though I hate the thought of those spiders with their little hairy legs, I deeply and completely accept myself.'*
>
> *'Even though I can't stand big spiders that run fast, I deeply and completely accept myself.'*
>
> *'Although the memory of that spider in my bedroom makes me feel "uurgh" (yes, you can use this type of description), I accept myself.'*

When you feel all your emotions reduce in intensity, try picturing in your mind that spider and notice what emotion you attach to it now. If you have no emotion, perhaps you can test yourself either on a photo, a toy spider, or even the real thing. If the intensity comes back when you're confronted with the spider, you may need to tap on its proximity: 'Even though that spider is too close to me, I choose to remain calm'.

Dreading the dentist

You may have a fear or phobia of visiting the dentist and if so you're one of the estimated one in three people who have some form of anxiety at the mere thought of booking an appointment for a dental examination.

You may not even be aware of where this fear came from. It may have come from your own traumatic experience at the hands of dentist if he or she was too rough or insensitive. Or you may have heard other people's horror stories which, for some reason, they're only too happy to share with you.

You know that the longer you wait for treatment, the more your fear increases, and the situation turns into a vicious circle. By not visiting the dentist you horde up a number of health problems and many people can be emotionally and psychologically affected. They may be embarrassed to smile or they don't like being close to someone because of their bad breath or teeth. Bad dental hygiene can also lead to feelings of shame or inferiority. Like all fears, dental fear is a learned response.

Write down everything that you can think of that frightens you about the dentist. After writing your fears down, use the EFT Set-Up Phrase of 'Even though I have this (fear) . . .' on each one of them until you find your anxiety is no longer there.

Here are some examples of what you may be afraid of:

- ✔ The unknown
- ✔ Personal experience
- ✔ Negative story heard from family or friends

✔ Perceived pain

✔ Injections or fear that the injection won't work

✔ Side-effects of the anaesthetic

✔ A particular sound or smell

✔ The white coat, mask or gloves

✔ Feeling helplessness and out of control

✔ Embarrassment about dental hygiene

If you need to refresh your memory on how to be specific with your wording, then flick back to Chapter 4.

Extracting the fear of dentists

A study conducted by Dr Graham Temple, an English dentist, shows that patients using EFT experienced a significant reduction in anxiety regarding necessary dental work.

In the study, Dr Temple asked patients whose examinations showed that they required treatment such as fillings, extractions, or crown and bridgework whether the thought of the proposed treatment caused them any anxiety. He then asked patients who stated that they felt anxious whether they would like to try EFT, which he explained as a form of 'psychological acupressure'.

All the patients who agreed to try EFT had appointments that included an extra ten minutes for EFT. When they arrived for treatment, patients rated their anxiety on a scale of zero (completely calm) to 10 (most anxious). The study only used patients who reported an anxiety rating of 6 or more – a

total of 30 patients. After six minutes of acupressure tapping, patients again rated their anxiety. The dental treatment immediately followed the EFT treatment. Dr Temple told patients that they could tap on points on their hands, if necessary, during the dental procedure.

Following treatment, Dr Graham Temple asked the patients to comment on their experience. All (100 per cent) of the participants reported reduced anxiety, with over 72 per cent experiencing a level of comfort and feeling of control that allowed them to cope well with the dental work.

The study showed that even very brief (six minute) tapping sessions can significantly improve the experience of dental visits not only for patients – who may otherwise postpone or avoid necessary dental work – but for dentists and their staff as well.

Managing Your Anxieties with EFT

If you're suffering from any fears, phobias, or anxieties and conventional techniques haven't been helpful, then you'll be pleased to know that they all respond effectively to EFT. The technique works by breaking the connection between the stimulus and the reaction in your unconscious mind. In the process, EFT removes the unwanted emotions. It may cheer you up to know that you don't have to face your fear with EFT.

How you apply EFT and what words you use varies, depending on the type and level of anxiety. You can adapt the examples that I describe in this chapter to suit the situation.

EFT can't make the circumstances that are causing your anxiety to disappear, but daily application can certainly reduce your anxiety levels. Unlike most conventional therapies, you don't need to confront, conquer, or expose yourself to your fears or anxieties.

Applying the EFT technique (refer to Chapter 3) or even the shortened technique (refer to Chapter 4) while experiencing these unpleasant feelings allows you to focus on the negative emotion or physical sensation, and at the same time tapping your meridians rebalances your energy system. The outcome leaves you feeling calm with a healthy fear while removing the negative symptoms and unhealthy fear.

Although you apply the same EFT technique that I describe in Chapters 3 and 4, the following pointers may help you when using EFT on fears, anxieties, and phobias.

1. **Rate the anxiety on the SUDS scale.**

2. **Establish when your fear or anxiety first started. Try thinking back to what was going on in your life around the time you started suffering these feelings of anxiety.**

   Were you in a car where the driver was racing at a high speed? Were you made redundant? Did your children leave home? If you're having difficult associating an event, ask a friend or member of your family when they noticed the changes in you.

3. **If you can't think of anything from the past, you can tap for 'Even though I don't know what has caused this fear, I deeply accept myself'.**

   If that doesn't bring any memory up, try to visualise yourself in the present, confronting your fear or whatever it is that causes you anxiety.

4. **Slowly recreate the situation or thing as best you can. Make the colours brighter and the sounds louder if doing this helps your recall.**

5. **Use words that are meaningful to you.**

6. **Use EFT on any emotions, beliefs, physical symptoms, or behaviours you associate with the anxiety.**

7. **If your anxiety levels are quite high, use the shortened version of EFT (see Chapter 4 for more detail).**

   You don't need to carry out the Set-up Phrase of 'Even though . . . '. You're already tuned into the problem so you can start tapping on the meridian points while saying, for example, 'This fear of dogs', 'My heart is racing', or 'I want to run'. Include the extra tapping points of the top of the head and wrist (see Chapter 4 for more on these).

8. **After you apply EFT to your anxieties and any associated memories, close your eyes and try to remember whatever caused you the anxiety in the first place.**

   If necessary, make the image bolder, brighter, and louder.

9. **Compare what number on the Subjective Units of Distress Scale you have now with what it was at the beginning.**

   (Check out Chapter 3 for more on the Subjective Units of Distress Scale.)

10. **If any emotion remains, just tap on that remaining anxiety again until the intensity goes to zero.**

You may wonder how long this process takes. It can sometimes take just minutes for you to see a noticeable difference, or longer depending on the problem. With all anxiety-based problems I recommend that you tap up to ten times on a daily basis, because many people find that the tapping in itself provides comfort as well as reducing the anxiety symptoms.

You can deal with the majority of the anxiety disorders I mention in this chapter with the simple technique of EFT. However, if just thinking of the anxiety such as flying on an airplane causes extreme discomfort, use another approach. Chapter 5 describes a number of methods, such as 'Sneaking Up on the Problem', 'Telling the Story', or the 'Movie Technique'. If your anxiety is very severe or complex, you may want to consider seeking advice from a trained EFT practitioner.

Chapter 10

Beating Anger

*R*age, fury, temper, or hate – whatever you want to call it, anger is a human emotion and a very complex one at that. Anger manifests itself in many different ways. Although anger is a necessary emotion designed to protect people, inappropriate anger can be destructive and many psychologists blame depression on anger turned inwards. When you can't control or handle your anger, you're at the mercy of a host of other emotions that go with it.

Recently, I've seen an alarming increase in clients coming to me for anger issues and, more alarmingly, they're getting younger. This chapter defines for you what anger is and guides you through the most common underlying types. The chapter also provides some examples of self-help solutions you can integrate with, or use during, your EFT therapy.

Defining Anger

Anger is one letter away from 'danger'. Although anger has many facets, fundamentally two types of anger exist – healthy and unhealthy.

Anger is *healthy* when you:

✔ Can talk about your feelings; for instance, when you say something like 'When you do that it makes me angry'.

✔ Don't use it to punish, intimidate, control, or manipulate another person.

> ✔ Can recognise and address it.
>
> ✔ Are able to control or let go of it.
>
> ✔ Can see the other person's point of view and respect their opinion, even though you may not necessarily agree with it.

Conversely, anger is *unhealthy* when you:

> ✔ Push down your emotions because you believe 'big boys don't cry' or 'I mustn't show my feelings because that means I'm weak'.
>
> ✔ Feel angry at yourself, at others, or the world, because you believe you're bad, guilty, or shameful.
>
> ✔ Blame others for your mistakes.
>
> ✔ Begin to lose trust and respect in others.
>
> ✔ Choose to be with others who are aggressive or angry.
>
> ✔ Hold on to your anger for no reason.

Of all the emotions, unhealthy anger has to be most destructive and contagious of all. Because it affects your mind and body, it can also have a negative impact on your emotional and physical health. Healthy anger, however, is a natural response to a threat and the feelings of aggression that go with it are necessary to your survival.

Discovering how to deal with your anger is far preferable to keeping it hidden, because this suppressed anger can be explosive when it erupts.

For obvious reasons, don't use EFT when either you or someone else is in the middle of a rage. Use it after the anger subsides.

Anger is a survival instinct and people used it in the past to protect themselves. Therefore, some people with deep anger issues sometimes also have an unhealthy interest in weapons or fire. Anger also affects your emotional security and when this is affected it creates more anxiety and more anger.

Recognising Where Your Unhealthy Anger Comes From

Who or what makes you angry or 'pushes your buttons'? Actually, no one or nothing makes you react with anger, it's your defensive reaction to a perceived threat, loss, or stressor. To put it another way, there's an underlying trigger to your anger, either external or internal. An external trigger may be someone lying to you or letting you down. The internal trigger is made up of your beliefs and you can usually justify these. Some examples include:

- ✔ The man who hits his wife and claims she made him angry.

- ✔ The road rager who believes all drivers on the road are idiots except her.

- ✔ As a child you were badly let down by your parents and others close to you. Anyone else who lets you down deserves your anger.

- ✔ Being sarcastic or critical of others prevents you from being exposed to your weaknesses.

Take a careful look at your anger and see whether you can identify where it comes from and what triggers it.

Understanding your triggers is a move in the right direction. Up until now, though, you may not have considered what fuels your anger and perhaps you have found ways to deal with your own anger that doesn't hurt others. If, however, you think that getting it off your chest now and again or hitting a punch-bag is a good way to deal with your anger, think again. Psychologists agree, thank goodness, that this type of activity only serves to fuel anger even more. If you feel overwhelmed by your anger or are losing control, you need to manage it before it manages you.

Underlying fear

Next time you get angry, try to notice what's happening in your body. You feel your heart racing, have sweaty palms, and feel the adrenalin rush. You feel these same symptoms when you experience fear and this is no coincidence, because anger stems from fear and a sense of not being in control, being found out, ignored, unsafe, or unloved. Recognising the origins of anger helps you when using EFT.

The pleasurable feeling from the adrenalin rush can be addictive, so watch out.

With EFT, you can encourage the release of the fear associated with the anger as the following phrases demonstrate:

- ✔ 'Although I fear that if I release my anger I . . .

  - won't be in control

  - will be admitting to my anger

  - will lose my identity

- won't be safe

- won't be loved

- will let others take advantage and walk all over me

✔ . . . I accept myself anyway.'

You can introduce other Set-up Phrases when moving towards a positive change:

✔ 'Although I refuse to let go of my anger, how does it benefit me to hang on to it?'

✔ 'Although I need this anger to remind me of the hurt I experienced, I accept myself anyway and I don't need this anger as a reminder.'

✔ 'Even though I don't know how to let go of this anger, why don't I just let this tapping take care of it for me?'

The following sections can help you recognise where some of your anger comes from, but be aware that a lot of ingredients go into making anger and more than one source may exist. You can use the Set-up Phrases I give later in this chapter for these situations. Select and use whichever applies.

Mimicking learned behaviour

If you've seen either or both parents use anger inappropriately, you probably respond in the same way. You may also have experienced feelings of not being in control because you were dominated by their anger. These feelings can simmer inside until, as an adult, you find you too can use this anger to gain power and control. You feel this surge of power with your outbursts when everyone sits up and takes notice of you. Unfortunately, you don't know, or may not want to know, how to handle it, and therefore it becomes easier to justify your anger because you can't help it.

Using your mouth before engaging the brain and saying things that you later regret are common. The person who suffers from mimicked anger often comes up close to you and stabs their fingers at you, or shakes their fist.

Feeling ashamed

You aim guilt at yourself so you must punish yourself for it. As a consequence, you suffer from shame and blame. The anger you feel is aimed at you and you feel powerless.

When you blame yourself for not being good enough, unreliable, bad, or unloved, these feelings are as a consequence of your 'negative core beliefs' (see Chapter 7). When others tell you that you can't be trusted or that you're stupid or you let them down, this further reinforces your beliefs about yourself. You don't like these feelings and you become ashamed of them, so you build up a defence mechanism to cope with them and respond the best way you know how – with anger. You may also find that you don't like to see these traits in others because they're a reflection of you. Therefore, falsely blaming or accusing others takes the spotlight off you. This defence mechanism is particularly prevalent in men where anger is more acceptable and preferable than talking about their feelings.

For example, Carl's girlfriend tells him that she'd like to stay in tonight. Carl may interpret this statement as 'She's fed up with me already because I'm a loser. I may as well dump her before she dumps me,' and get angry with her. Or he can choose to think 'Okay, I could do with seeing my mates tonight anyway,' and remain calm.

Next time you have a negative thought, ask yourself what evidence exists to support it. If no evidence exists, challenge the thought in an assertive way, and if you can't think of any then move on – life's too short.

Harbouring hurt and injustices

To some people life doesn't seem fair. The whole world appears to be against them, so they decide that they may as well battle anything that gets in their way. Getting their own back at others and the world by either harming them or their feelings is their way of getting revenge. Stealing, jealousy, and manipulating others with emotional blackmail are other traits.

They cannot possibly forgive others because carrying that grudge reminds them of the hurt. Wrong! If this is you, then by holding on to this anger and hurt you're simply hurting yourself, and most times the other person isn't even aware of your anger, so they can be having a good time totally oblivious of your hurt. (For more information and some Set-up Phrases on forgiving, head to Chapter 6.)

If your anger erupts after drinking too much alcohol, you need to address the alcohol problem first before tackling the anger issues. Chapter 12 can help you with this.

Nailing your anger

The next time you're tempted to say something hurtful to someone just because you're angry, you may want to stop and remember this story:

There once was a little boy who had a bad temper. His father gave him a bag of nails and told him that every time he lost his temper, he must hammer a nail into the back of the fence.

The first day the boy drove 37 nails into the fence. Over the next few weeks, as he learned to control his anger, the number of nails hammered daily gradually dwindled down. He discovered it was easier to keep his temper than to drive those nails into the fence.

Finally, the day came when the boy didn't lose his temper at all. He told his father about it and the father suggested that the boy now pull out one nail for each day that he was able to keep

his temper. The days passed and the young boy was finally able to tell his father that all the nails were gone.

The father took his son by the hand and led him to the fence. He said, 'You have done well, my son, but look at the holes in the fence. The fence will never be the same. When you say things in anger, they leave a scar just like this one. You can put a knife in a man and draw it out. It won't matter how many times you say I'm sorry, the wound is still there.'

The little boy then understood how powerful his words were. He looked up at his father and said, 'I hope you can forgive me, Father, for the holes I put in you.'

'Of course I can,' said the father.

Releasing the Pressure Valve with EFT

EFT can be absolutely amazing when it comes to dealing with anger and can calm you down in an instant. If EFT has no effect on the anger, or the anger actually gets worse, then anger is probably not the primary emotion but is driven by some other underlying emotion or emotions instead, as the earlier section 'Recognising Where Your Unhealthy Anger Comes From' describes. After you discover the underlying emotion or emotions and treat them with EFT, the anger quickly subsides. If you're worried about finding the underlying emotions, see Chapter 4 for some helpful guidance.

The following questions help you to formulate what words to use when applying EFT for anger. You can even ask these questions as you tap around the points, and then use EFT on the answers. For example, if an answer to the first question is 'My dad causes me to be angry', then tap for 'Even though my dad causes my anger, I accept myself'. If the answer to the second question is 'Because I don't like being told what to do', then tap for 'Even though I don't like being told what to do – especially by my dad – I accept myself'. You don't have to go in strict order with these questions or use them all; they're just an illustration of how to get to the bottom of the anger problem.

> ✔ **Who or what causes you to feel anger?** Notice this question isn't asking 'Who makes you angry'. The answer should bring out the belief.

✔ **Why do you think you react this way?** This leaves it open to use EFT on the reasons. You can talk this through as you tap along.

✔ **How would you describe your feelings of anger?** Anger can be too much of a global statement, so try to describe the anger in more detail. Use any words that come up such as 'destructive', 'explosive', 'frustrating', 'fighting back', or 'red mist'. You can incorporate these words into the Set-Up Phrase. For instance: 'Even though I have this explosive feeling . . . '.

✔ **How do you respond to this anger?** Do you lash out? Are you sarcastic or hostile? Do you keep your anger hidden or out of the way, for instance? You can use EFT on hidden anger in the same way.

✔ **Where do you feel the anger?** When your brain thinks of an emotion, it also allows you to feel it in your body. Describing where in the body you feel this anger is helpful at aiming EFT in the right direction. If the anger is felt in the chest for example, you would say something like 'Although I have this explosive feeling in my chest. . .'.

✔ **When do you feel the anger?** Identify when you feel angry, or what reminds you of your anger, helps you with the trigger, as I explain earlier in this section. For example: 'Even though I'm reminded of this anger when I see him in that photo . . .'.

✔ **What is it about the situation that makes you most angry?** This question establishes who or what is causing the anger. Someone forcing you to do something, for instance, can cause you to feel powerless. The Set-Up Phrase can then be 'Even though I feel powerless when . . .'.

✔ **Why do you need to hold on to this anger?** A good way of getting the logical brain into gear is to ask a question like this. This question helps you formulate the Set-Up Phrase of 'Even though I need to hold on to this anger because. . .'.

✔ **What benefits exist to letting go of this anger?** This question highlights the positive effects of letting go, and at the same time steers you towards where you want to be. The Set-Up Phrase can be 'I accept myself and choose to let it go because . . . (insert the benefits here).'

Use this exercise while focusing on a trivial annoyance. It helps if you familiarise yourself first with the tapping routine that I describe in Chapter 3. This exercise shows you how you can find relief from your anger with EFT. When you feel more confident, you can use the exercise for something more annoying or on anything that makes you really angry when you think about it.

1. **Imagine something trivial that annoys you.**

   Examples include receiving a parking ticket, getting through to a call centre, receiving numerous telesales calls, or anything else that 'gets your back up', so to speak, when you think about it.

Other helpful advice

Apart from EFT, it's nice to know other techniques exist that can go with it to help you. Here are a few:

- Take away the 'should' as in 'I should have. . .' and replace with 'could' as in 'I could have . . .'.

- Take away the 'you' as in 'you are stupid' and replace with an 'I' as in 'I don't like your behaviour'.

- Accept that feeling angry at times is normal.

- Try not to take things personally.

- Let go of the past.

- Accept responsibility for your actions.

- Deal with your anger appropriately.

2. **While thinking about the annoyance, notice what thoughts and feelings go with it and give it a number from zero to 10 with 10 being the highest intensity.**

3. **Now give the annoyance a description in your own words and include any feelings that go with it.**

   For example 'Frustration at Sam's loud music'.

4. **Design a Set-Up Phrase (see Chapters 3 and 4) to include your description as follows:**

   'Even though I have this anger with Sam's loud music, I absolutely accept myself.'

5. **Repeat your Set-Up Phrase three times while either rubbing the Sore Spot or tapping the Karate Chop (see Chapter 3 for details on these).**

6. **Tap on the remaining points with the words that come into your head (see Chapter 3 for info on the other tapping points).**

   Examples include 'Sam's loud music', 'She plays it so loud', 'It makes me angry', 'Why can't she stop', 'Why does she never listen', and 'This anger at Sam's music'.

7. **Check what intensity you have now. If it hasn't gone down, do more rounds using 'this remaining anger. . .' and use whatever words come up during the tapping. If the number has gone down to below a 3, then introduce some positive phrases.**

   Positive phrases may be 'Even though Sam's music makes me angry, I accept that she's only 15', 'Although Sam's music makes me angry, I accept her as a teenager', or 'Although I have this anger, I forgive myself.'

8. **(Optional) On the remaining points, include your thoughts or memories:**

   For example 'She's only 15', 'I couldn't play loud music at 15', 'My parents wouldn't let me', 'I'm taking my resentment out on Sam', 'We can come to a compromise', 'Compromises work', and 'Anger doesn't work'.

Other useful phrases for your portfolio include:

   'Even though I have this anger at (insert problem), I choose to find other ways to deal with it.'

   'Although I can't control my anger, I choose to allow my subconscious to help me.'

   'Even though I can't help my anger, I accept that I have choices and I choose to let my anger go instead.'

You must use your own words and you can 'mix and match' any of the phrases used in this chapter.

So, give yourself permission to be angry and to release this anger with EFT. It may just be the one thing you've been waiting your whole life for.

Chapter 11

Releasing the Emotions Attached to Stress, Trauma, and Abuse

. . . .

In This Chapter

▶ Recognising the difference between stress and trauma

▶ Working with complex cases

▶ Showing no emotion

▶ Tackling depression

. . . .

Although EFT is a gentle, safe therapy that works without the need for tears or re-traumatising you again, this chapter contains warning signals for beginners who may be dealing with severe cases of trauma or abuse. These warnings are there for your own good.

With your knowledge of EFT you have more control than you realise over coping with the symptoms of stress and depression. Trauma usually comes with high emotional intensity, so you need to use the full routine, including the additional points I describe in Chapters 3 and 4. If you feel like using the full routine anyhow, I certainly recommend doing so.

Stress and Danger: Affecting You Physically

Imagine if you could see what happens to your body when it perceives stress or danger. You'd see that all those signals are sending hormones, oxygen, and blood whizzing around your body so that it can prepare to act in defence or run a mile – what you may refer to as the *flight or fight* response. When the danger is over, your body usually returns back to its state of equilibrium, or balanced state.

Experiencing stress over a period of time affects your body's ability to return to its original balanced state. You can compare this gradual increase in stress to the old story of the boiled frog. The story goes that if you try putting a live frog into a pan of boiling water he'll jump out. Try putting a frog into a pan of cool water and gradually turn the heat up and he'll be cooked before he's even noticed what's going on.

Appropriate stress is good for stimulating your brain and building up your body's defence systems, but inappropriate stress can actually damage your brain cells while at the same time end up making you very sick. I could fill this chapter alone with stress-related conditions that would include high blood pressure, heart disease, cancers, headaches, arthritis – you name it – and stress is most likely the contributor.

Did you know that the term 'stress' is short for 'distress', a word evolved from Latin meaning 'to draw or pull apart'?

Responding to stress

To a large extent, unlike trauma, stress isn't sudden, so how it affects you depends on how you anticipate it and what you do to avoid the stress in the first place.

Take Fred, for example. Fred retires from work after 50 years' service with the same company. All his colleagues turn up for his retirement party; they wish him well, telling him how jealous they are and how lucky he is. Fred smiles and agrees with them as he joins in the fun. The reality is that Fred is already starting to feel the stress – not only about retiring but about his ability to cope without the structure of work and seeing people, how he'll manage on his pension, and what his future holds.

Knowing that he was about to retire, Fred could have managed things better to avoid the stress. He could have found a little part-time job that would not only boost his pension but would give him the opportunity to meet people again. He could use his new-found freedom to catch up with old friends or family.

Using EFT in the workplace

Much of the time, a person's job contributes greatly to their stress. Consider that, in the UK alone, each case of work-related stress, depression, or anxiety leads to an average of 30.2 lost working days.

During my years as a manager, I went on countless training courses, including some on interpersonal skills, but none of them ever taught me how to manage my emotions or how emotions influenced and controlled the behaviour within my team. I didn't recognise barriers to success were my team's own limiting beliefs or feelings of low self-worth. I saw staff going off with stress following perceived negative feedback from their manager. During periods of change, sick absences would increase, possibly because staff couldn't or didn't know how to handle change.

Just imagine the potential benefits of using EFT in the workplace. Some of the benefits include:

✔ Removing the fear of giving presentations, making phone calls, and holding meetings.

✔ Overcoming emotional barriers to success.

✔ Empowering the sales staff to achieve their targets.

✔ Creating positivity.

✔ Reducing anxiety when dealing with angry customers.

✔ Reducing sickness absence due to stress, anxiety, or personal emotional problems.

✔ Increasing motivation.

✔ Overcoming your own anger issues.

✔ Feeling able to receive and give criticism in a constructive way.

✔ Accepting change more easily and readily.

The added bonus with EFT is that it's a self-help tool so managers can teach the staff how to use it on themselves whenever they feel the need. Chapter 15 also has some help and advice on how to empower yourself and others, including removing limiting beliefs, and Chapter 7 can help with any feelings of low self-worth.

Employers in the UK are legally bound to assess the risk of stress-related ill health arising from work activities and to control that risk.

Dealing with Trauma and the Aftermath

Some people are able to recover quite quickly from a severe stressful event, but other people are badly affected. How quickly you recover depends upon your subjective emotional experience – in other words, how traumatic the incident is, whether you've experienced something like it in the past, and whether you have a supportive network of friends and family around you. If the stressful symptoms don't go away, you may be suffering from *trauma*.

Even if you recover quite quickly from a trauma, at some future time painful memories or emotions arising from the trauma may affect your mind or body. Memories that you store in your mind, such as when you can remember where you were when the trauma occurred, are called *explicit* memories. Memories that you store in your body are *implicit* memories, and they can trigger an emotion without you even knowing why. Sometimes you have both explicit and implicit memories of the incident; at other times you have either one or the other.

Speaking in public

If the thought of giving a speech in public fills you with stressful thoughts, you're not on your own. A recent poll carried out revealed that public speaking is high on the list of fears and phobias. It doesn't have to be at work either; you may be giving a speech at a wedding or other special occasion.

If you want to overcome your problem of speaking in public then you need to identify the culprit so you can aim EFT at it to shoot it down. You need to consult Chapter 4 for how to perform EFT first.

Have a go at these questions either with yourself or a friend and use EFT as instructed. As you do so, observe any changes in confidence levels.

✔ What has caused this problem with speaking in front of people? (Early experience, belief, hereditary, always been there, other reasons?)

✔ What do you feel as you visualise standing in front of an audience? (Heart pounding, sweaty palms, mind goes blank, mouth like a plank of wood, other feelings?)

✔ What exactly are you afraid of? (Making a fool of myself, may make mistakes, stuttering, I'm not as good as others, other factors?)

✔ What do you need to overcome this? (Strength, courage, voice technique, charisma, belief, confidence, calm, other characteristics?)

Use your answers to the first three questions to form the first part of your Set-Up Phrase and then use the answer to question 4 to complete it. Here's an example:

'Even though I have a belief that I can't speak in front of people, I choose to find the confidence to overcome this.'

'Even though my mouth goes dry like a plank of wood at the thought of speaking in public, I deeply accept myself and want to remain calm.'

'Although I'm afraid I'll make a mistake when I speak in front of people, I choose to believe that I'll remain calm and confident even if I do make a mistake. I'm only human, after all.'

You should notice some changes in feelings of confidence as you use EFT. If no noticeable changes happen, look at anything that may have contributed to this problem, whether in your past or recent present. Note any memories or feelings that come up during the EFT process.

You can always test your confidence by visualising yourself in front of an audience or do the real thing if you feel confident enough.

Emotional or psychological

At one time people thought that only psychological trauma existed and affected men who served during catastrophic wars. During the '60s, researchers found that people can also suffer emotional trauma as a consequence of the following, for example:

- ✔ Physical or sexual abuse as a child or adult
- ✔ Bullying
- ✔ Violence
- ✔ Torture
- ✔ Loss of a loved one
- ✔ Car accident
- ✔ World disaster
- ✔ Break-up of a significant relationship

Trauma can briefly be defined as stress gone haywire and is usually:

- ✔ Dramatic
- ✔ Unexpected
- ✔ Unpreventable

Small 't' or big 'T' trauma?

If you're an EFT beginner, how can you tell what you can and can't deal with? The EFT community refers to small 't' trauma and big 'T' trauma. A *small 't' trauma* is a trauma that happened at least three years ago and causes mild to moderate emotional or physical anxiety when you think about the incident. A *big 'T' trauma* is generally associated with recent or more severe trauma that creates moderate to high emotional or physical anxiety when you recall the memory. As a therapist, you ask your client questions to determine how major his trauma is and from this information you can determine the type of technique to apply. This chapter, or Chapter 5, helps you here. If you aren't a therapist and have little knowledge of EFT, you need to consider whether you feel competent enough to deal with another person's trauma. Chapter 19 has a list of frequently asked questions to help you out.

If you do decide to deal with any type of trauma, keep the following pointers in mind:

- Don't rush a client to work on the trauma even if you feel that he's making good progress. Always take the slow approach.

- If you're working on a trauma of your own that you define as a big 'T', work with a professional who'll ensure that you can handle resolving the trauma.

Post-traumatic stress disorder

Imagine what it must be like to relive being in a car crash several times a day, feeling the emotions and visualising the scene, or being in a state of constant vigilance. In addition, you may also be experiencing nightmares about the crash, depression, and panic attacks. Not very pleasant, is it? And for some people this is what *post-traumatic stress disorder* (or PTSD for short) can feel like on a daily basis, and it can last for months or even years. Almost everyone suffers the effects of severe trauma to some degree but not everyone suffers from PTSD.

Psychologists think that PTSD is a result of the trauma becoming 'stuck' in the memory part of your brain, which causes the 'flashbacks'. EFT can unblock and release the stuck energy and at the same time remove the negative emotion.

Treating veterans of war

In 1994, Gary Craig, the founder of EFT, and a colleague visited a Veterans Administration hospital in California, where they worked on-camera with Vietnam War veterans.

'These men hadn't had a moment's peace in 20 years,' says Craig. 'Their lives revolved around their terrifying memories.' But after just a few minutes of tapping, all the men experienced profound release.

Despite the dramatic results that the patients at the VA hospital achieved, says Craig, none of the staff were interested in find out more about EFT.

Today, the Department of Veterans Affairs pays compensation for PTSD to nearly twice as many veterans as it did six years ago, at an annual cost of $4.3 billion.

Many, many thousands of veterans of war are still suffering from PTSD because, unfortunately, medical funding doesn't always stretch to treat the suffering of the symptoms that often lead them to resort to substance abuse to obliterate the horrifying images and emotions. What funding is available is used on medication or drawn-out talk therapy.

PTSD causes a ripple affect within families because those who suffer find that they don't always recognise the symptoms and their families feel powerless to help. EFT not only prevents post-traumatic memories from causing problems, but it successfully treats memories that are years old.

Healing trauma using conventional therapy is usually painful, but Chapter 5 outlines EFT techniques, such as the 'Movie Technique', which are perfectly suitable for avoiding any unnecessary distress.

Dealing with a trauma usually calls for more sophisticated techniques that come from an EFT practitioner. You may, however, get good results by dealing with the painful emotions a client feels in his body.

Here are some suggested phrases for trauma:

> *'Even though I have these flashbacks of being attacked, I completely love and accept myself.'*
>
> *'Although I have this gunshot emotion in my stomach, I feel completely safe.'*
>
> *'Even though my chest feels tight when I remember those men smashing my car window, now I'm safe. I was just in the wrong place at the wrong time.'*

You know you're over the trauma when:

- ✔ You can think of talk about the trauma without becoming distressed.
- ✔ You no longer suffer any of the symptoms associated with the trauma.

Be specific. Chapter 6 can help you with this one.

Working with Abuse Issues

If a client doesn't disclose to you that he was abused until well into his therapy, don't be concerned. This kind of situation happens and the reasons for this vary. Maybe he's used to keeping the abuse a secret and he's not yet confident in you. Or perhaps he's not ready to let go, face up to what happened, or believe that he'll ever get over his feelings and emotions.

Building trust and rapport is the first and most important requirement when working with those who have suffered abuse. Self-punishment is the key with abuse sufferers and with it often comes with the belief that what happened was somehow their fault.

Watch out for abuse sufferers who frequently blame themselves by saying 'If only I hadn't been there at the time' or 'I shouldn't have allowed it to happen'. These feelings of guilt and shame are common and you can treat them with EFT.

If you aren't qualified, please note that some people may have been so badly traumatised and/or abused in their lifetime that they have developed severe psychological problems such as multiple personalities, paranoia, schizophrenia, and other serious mental disorders. Although EFT may help even in such severe cases, in these instances I strongly recommend you consult a mental health professional or an EFT practitioner experienced in dealing with such cases.

Healing the hurt with EFT

If your client has been subjected to verbal or physical abuse over the years, he may have many, many emotions or memories to deal with, some hidden away, even if he's not showing them.

With serial abuse, one memorable episode always exists that's more distressing than the rest and causes the most emotional intensity. This is the one I usually work on first, using the gentle techniques, if necessary, as I describe in Chapter 5. I go through each significant memory until either very little or no emotional intensity remains. You find as you move through each painful memory that EFT has already reduced the emotional distress as you bring up each one.

Sometimes, it can be difficult to distinguish one memory or emotion from the rest. When this happens, I suggest you use the following approach, which involves asking your client to collectively bring all the unpleasant experiences together. For example:

1. **Ask your client to write down all the negative words, phrases, and actions that were repeatedly thrown at them and label them all under one heading.**

    The heading can be anything the client likes, but generally a short description such as 'school bullying', 'my box of emotions', 'my bag of traumas', 'Dad's drunken nights', 'I was never good enough', or 'I wasn't wanted' is usually sufficient. The words don't matter; it's whatever symbolises their experiences that's important.

2. **Get the client to rate the chosen heading on the Subjective Units of Distress Scale (refer to Chapter 3) on how they felt at that time.**

3. **Because most abuse victims have a tendency to identify with their experiences and be fearful of letting them go, try any one of the following Set-Up Phrases three times or all three to eliminate any resistance:**

   'Even though I don't want to get over this (experience) because I'm afraid to, I do want to be able to accept myself.'

   'Even though I've lived with the memories of this (experience) for so long, it's who I am. I accept that I can release these memories and accept myself for who I am now, which is important.'

   'Although I don't feel I deserve to get over this (experience), I accept that I can't be tied to the past forever and I want to let go and free myself.'

4. **As you, or your client, tap around the remaining points (refer to Chapter 3 for more information on the tapping points), try one of the following:**

   'I'm afraid to let go of (experience).'

   'I identify with (experience).'

   'What will happen if I let go?'

   The Reminder Phrase on the rest of the points can be 'This (experience)'. (See Chapter 3 for information on the Reminder Phrase.)

5. **Then do another round, leaving out the Set-Up Phrase and saying:**

   'Even though I have this (experience), I want to love and accept myself', or 'Although I've had this (experience) for so long, I want to love and accept myself'.

   Include the heading in the remaining points; for instance 'This "I was never wanted" emotion'.

6. **Keep tapping until the distress reduces to below 3.**

   On the subsequent rounds, try introducing specific feelings. Especially encourage your client to use strong words that describe his anger, hatred, or loathing. If you're not too sensitive, even get your client to use swear words. The idea is to release any pent-up feelings. You can tap on your client as he comes up with all his suppressed feelings, such as not feeling wanted, feeling in the way, wanting to be hugged, and so on. Use all the points plus the additional ones I refer to in Chapter 4.

7. **When finished, rate the feelings again and don't be surprised if the rating has gone up because other painful memories sometimes come to the surface. Just do the EFT routine again on that particular memory until it reduces to zero.**

Say something like 'Even though I still have some painful memories such as (example), I accept myself and I want to let them go'. The Remaining Phrase (see Chapter 3) can be 'This remaining . . . memory'.

8. **When emotional intensity appears to reduce significantly, ask your client to carry out a round of positive phrases in his own words on the remaining points. For example:**

   'I choose to let go of this (experience) and free myself.'

   'I decide now to get over this and not have it hanging over me any longer.'

   'I give myself permission to let go.'

   'My new identity lets go of these negative emotions. I am calm.'

At this point, I sometimes ask my client to imagine, as I tap, putting his unpleasant memories into a hot air balloon basket and letting it soar, or putting them into a boat and pushing the boat out to sea.

9. **Finally, when all negative emotions reduce to zero, have your client, or you, carry out one or two rounds on the remaining points without the Set-Up Phrase:**

   For example 'I'm a survivor', 'I'm strong', 'I have it within me to be resourceful', 'I'm a good person', 'I'm caring and supportive', 'I deserve freedom,' and so on, using positive words.

Although I mention ideally you need to 'tune into' the problem for EFT to be successful, it isn't a mandatory requirement. Please don't be put off trying EFT if no emotion or memory exists, because it can still work.

Chapter 5 contains ideas and tips on how to trigger memories, but don't use these triggers on someone who has severe trauma.

To help with the healing process and move on with their life, it's important for abuse sufferers to forgive. Chapter 6 can help with understanding forgiveness and how EFT can help with this.

Positive thoughts and memories tend to flow through your energy system, but negative thoughts or memories tend to get stuck or blocked.

Showing little or no feelings

So how can you treat someone with EFT when no memories exist, or if the person has memories but has no associated feelings? People can lose memories partially or completely when they suffer repeated or prolonged periods of stress or abuse. Parts of the brain where memories are formed can be damaged, which can lead to a memory disorder. By contrast, people are more likely to remember single, brief traumatic episodes. Severe disturbances of memory, and related PTSD, also affects those who have suffered childhood sexual abuse. Whether the trauma was over a period of time or a one-off incident, your energy system has no doubt been disrupted.

Ideally, you get the client to tune in to the problem while carrying out EFT, because it disturbs the energy so you can work on it. But this isn't absolutely necessary for EFT to do its work.

If you do need help to bring up an emotion, you can employ some of the following tactics:

✔ Try asking the client to tell his story or problem from a different angle or perspective.

✔ Ask him to describe the associated sounds, smells, or sights.

✔ Get him to describe in more detail what he means.

✔ Introduce photos or objects linked to the memory.

✔ Write a story about what happened and use EFT on any emotional disturbance you feel as you write. For example 'When I was 12 years of age I was in the school toilets when a gang of boys came in . . .'. If this causes any emotional disturbance, use EFT on it, and then move on. This is similar to the 'Tell the Story' technique in Chapter 5. You can also use this approach after EFT to test out whether you have any negative emotions left.

During the course of your work with abuse sufferers you may hear some pretty horrific stuff that your client can talk about in a very unemotional way. The important thing to remember is not to react alarmingly or express an opinion either way, but to comment in a manner that is very matter of fact.

Suppressed memories

No therapy should entail forced memory recall. Providing you feel that you need to deal with a suppressed memory, you can use EFT on yourself, but if it's complex or very traumatic, I advise seeking an EFT practitioner. If suppressed memories surface during an EFT session, then deal with them if you feel competent enough. You may want to note that, according to psychiatrists, no scientific evidence supports the idea that repressed memories don't exist, that they are always true, or that if you think you were abused then you were.

While using EFT on trauma and abuse, it's common to have feelings of detachment, as if it was happening to someone else. This is quite normal and nothing to worry about, but may sometimes account for why you can't bring up some memories because there's no significance attached to them any longer. If, however, you feel confused or disturbed after working on your own trauma, please consult an experienced EFT practitioner.

'I can get over it'

In America, researchers are conducting a major study, the largest of its kind, on adverse childhood experiences (ACE). The study compares current adult health to childhood experiences decades earlier.

The findings provide remarkable insights into how people develop as individuals and as a nation. The ACE study reveals a powerful relationship between emotional experiences as children and adult emotional health, physical health, and major causes of mortality in the US. Moreover, the time factors in the study make it clear that time doesn't heal some of the adverse experiences found so common in the childhoods of a large population of middle-aged, middle-class Americans. You don't 'just get over' some things.

Lifting the Lid on Depression

Stress, trauma, and abuse can all lead to depression. When treating your client for depression, remember that no single cause exists for depression. Your experiences and your problem-solving abilities all contribute to how bad your depression is.

Recent research has led the medical profession to conclude that the drugs doctors prescribe to suppress the symptoms of depression don't work. They admit that once you come of these mood-enhancing drugs, the problem is still there so that you're in effect no better off. I find it hard not to say 'I told you so' but I've said it now. Although billions have been spent on these drugs, it's worth noting that EFT costs nothing, has been shown to be very successful in treating depression, and results can sometimes be seen immediately.

Take a look at these case scenarios:

- ✔ Charlie was made redundant. He wasn't bothered at first because he knew he'd get another job. However, after a few months of job-hunting and no job, he now sits around most of the day and has started drinking during the day too. He loses his temper a lot as well.

- ✔ Since Louise's divorce 12 months ago, she has managed bringing the children up on her own but finds it hard to cope. She's moved house and feels isolated. Now she can't concentrate enough to do her part-time job properly and has no interest in her looks or her children.

- ✔ Three years ago Freda's husband died after 55 years of married life together. She sits by the window watching people go by but doesn't want to go out. No one comes to visit her and some days she can't be bothered to get up, feed herself, or get dressed.

If you suffer from depression, you experience feelings of helplessness and hopelessness, and the negative thinking that is associated with depression makes seeking help very difficult. You have the feeling that you can't do anything about your illness. When you're depressed, your whole body is depressed, and this depression suppresses and blocks your energy flow, which is why EFT is so good because it gets your energy moving.

While saying that EFT can bring about rapid improvement with depression, you can also use other self-help strategies alongside EFT, such as these recommended by The National Institute for Mental Health in the US:

- ✔ Set realistic goals in light of the depression and assume a reasonable amount of responsibility.

- ✔ Break large tasks into small ones, set some priorities, and do what you can as you can.

- ✔ Try to be with other people and to confide in someone – it's better than being alone and secretive.

- ✔ Participate in activities that make you feel better.

- ✔ Mild exercise, going to a movie or a football match, or participating in religious, social, or other activities may help.

- ✔ Expect your mood to improve gradually, not immediately. Feeling better takes time.

- ✔ Postpone important decisions until the depression lifts. Before deciding to make a significant transition – changing jobs, getting married or divorced – discuss it with others who know you well and have a more objective view of your situation.

- ✔ Remember, positive thinking helps replace the negative thinking that's a central part of your depression. Negative thoughts disappear as your depression responds to treatment.

- ✔ Let your family and friends help you.

- ✔ Use EFT on a regular basis to promote feelings of calm and relaxation.

You need to use EFT on a daily basis on any negative thoughts, feelings, or beliefs you have as soon as you awake, during the day, as you go about your daily routine, and at night before you go to bed – in fact, at any time, whether or not you're feeling down. After approximately one month you should notice a considerable improvement in your symptoms. Also look into what may have caused your depression in the first place and work on that. If you're not getting the results you'd expect, consult an EFT practitioner to help you.

Use some vigour, without hurting yourself of course, when tapping. Use an open hand to slap on the wrist points, or collarbone.

You may not like yourself much with your depression, so how about saying 'Even though I don't like myself with this depression, I accept this isn't who I am, it's just the way I am at the moment'.

Suicidal thoughts are the most serious symptom of depression and you must always take them seriously. If you suspect someone is at risk of doing harm to themselves or others, please seek professional help right away.

Part IV
Applying EFT to Physical Issues

The 5th Wave   By Rich Tennant

"I keep forgetting my Reminder Phrase. Is it, 'chew the furniture,' or 'dump the garbage?'"

In this part . . .

*W*ant to know how EFT can help you with cravings, addictions, and physical problems? This is the part for you.

I don't claim that EFT cures serious disease, but it can certainly help you to relieve the symptoms. If you remove emotional problems, physical symptoms of illness really can reduce in intensity.

I finish up the part by sending you to sleep . . . more interesting than it sounds!

Chapter 12

Controlling Cravings, Addictions, and Bad Habits

. . . .

In This Chapter

▶ Knowing why people do what they do

▶ Taking control

▶ Working on common addictions

▶ Creating EFT phrases for addictions

. . . .

*H*ave you ever wondered why most people rub around the outside of their eyes when stressed, rub the bridge of their nose when confused, tap their chin when trying to think, or put their hand over their collarbone when hearing shocking news? They may also tend to clasp their hands together when tense or wrap their arms around themselves in times of distress. It's no coincidence that all these points are synonymous with the EFT tapping points and are habits people often use without thinking, because they give comfort or relief. Other habits, however, can be irritating or annoying to say the least but, thankfully, you can control them by using the basic routine of EFT that I describe in Chapters 3 and 4.

Recognising an Addiction

If you find that your habit is controlling you and affecting your health, and yet you still carry on regardless, then your habit is as an addiction.

Many years ago an addiction meant a devotion or longing for something or someone, but today it's more likely to refer to food, gambling, the Internet, drugs, alcohol, sex, love, shopping, or even chocolate. Anyone can have an addiction to almost anything.

If you don't have the skills to cope with life's events because of a lack of education, your environment, or the fact you were emotionally deprived, there's an increased risk of you reaching for tranquillising substances at times of stress. There's no doubt that addiction is a global problem and your attitude to addiction is just as much shaped by your cultural attitudes as by medical science.

As to whether addiction is genetic, behavioural or biochemical doesn't matter in the context of applying EFT and getting results. What does matter is that EFT works a treat on cravings and addictions, and in most cases you can see the results immediately. If you know of an EFT practitioner who specialises in addictions, and you need help, I advise you to contact that person.

You need to rewire your brain

Researchers tell us that if you repeat a thought, experience, or action for approximately 21 days, it can become a habit. Each time you form a habits, your brain builds what's known as a *neuropathway* to make it easier for the information to flow through the brain. These pathways are like the grooves on a record, which is why when you form a habits, it can be difficult to change. That's great if you want to develop a new skill, like driving a car or riding a bike, but if you've developed a habit such as biting your nails or smoking, and you'd like to stop, it may not be as easy as you think.

Most bad habits begin because whatever it is you're doing makes you feel better or good about yourself at the time. You then associate the action with that feeling and stopping becomes difficult because stopping the habit causes anxiety. So you not only have the biological resistance to address but you have your underlying emotional issues and, sometimes, beliefs to contend with. (Chapter 15 discusses beliefs in more detail.)

Don't forget that your subconscious is there to protect you and, to make sure it does a good job, your subconscious can even find ways to sabotage any attempts you may make at trying to get onto a different path. Common sense also tells you that treading a well-worn path is easier than creating and getting used to a new one.

If you want to know whether you can change a habit, well, the good news is, yes you can. Without being scientific, it works by using EFT to tap into your subconscious. By doing so, you can effectively move negative thoughts or behaviours onto a new neuropathway, which enables you to change to a new, more positive habit. In effect, you 'rewire your brain'.

If it feels good, you do it

Can you remember the last time you rewarded yourself with a drink, a new dress, or a good meal after a hard day, and can you remember the nice feeling it gave you? That feeling came from a part of your brain known as your *limbic brain* (refer to Chapter 2 for more on the different parts of the brain), which is responsible for the *pleasure or reward centre*. This bit of your brain releases the chemicals dopamine and serotonin. Researchers claim that the chemical dopamine is responsible for the 'must have it' stimulus (like when you see a super sports car or a fantastic pair of shoes). The other chemical, serotonin, accounts for the 'Oh! that feels good' sensation you get from eating certain foods, and other pleasurable pursuits.

Low levels of serotonin are not only associated with anxiety, depression, and addiction, but are responsible for increasing the release of dopamine.

Just in case you wondered, animals also have this reward system associated with dopamine, usually triggered by food or sex. Drugs, including nicotine and alcohol, can affect these dopamine levels. At first, they act in the same way as 'natural' rewards, producing pleasure. But with increased use, reliance on the drug to stop unpleasant withdrawal symptoms becomes more necessary. Even subconscious exposure to the stimulating object, through subliminal messaging, can stimulate the reward centre of the brain. This subliminal stimulation explains why addicts fail to understand what triggers their craving.

Studies using magnetic resonance imaging (MRI) technology demonstrate that stimulating certain meridians with EFT not only changes brain activity to remove levels of fear and pain, but also reinstates the levels of serotonin, providing that comforting, soothing feeling. So not only does EFT rebalance the serotonin and dopamine levels, but it deals with the emotional drivers of the behaviour too.

I don't suppose an addict wakes up one day and decides 'This is a good day to become an addict', so how does it happen? No one knows exactly what causes an addiction but what EFT is best at is removing the anxiety caused by underlying emotional drivers such as fear, guilt, anger, and trauma. Although addictive substances act as tranquillisers by reducing the anxiety, this 'feel good' sensation is short-lived. You need to remove the cause of the anxiety so that you don't need to reach for the tranquilliser.

Applying EFT to Addictions

The following sections guide you through some common addictions and how to get to the root cause of the anxiety so that you can treat it with EFT. As with all other suggestions throughout this book, they're yours to use freely so you can expand on your knowledge when working with clients who have addictions.

All addictive behaviour is the symptom, not the cause. If you want EFT to help you, you need to address the underlying cause. In the meantime, you can, of course, use EFT on the symptoms.

Before you begin, I'd like to alert you to some important information about EFT and the general application to use with all addictions, including those mentioned in this chapter:

- ✔ EFT doesn't allow the addict to 'have a little now and then'.

- ✔ Addictions can be triggered again.

- ✔ Use the full EFT routine as I describe in Chapter 3. Addictions often warrant everything thrown at them so, unless you're pregnant, throw in the additional points in Chapter 4 (top of the head, the wrist point, liver point, and ankle point).

- ✔ Repeated use of EFT weakens the desire.

- ✔ In some instances you may have to use EFT up to 15 times a day.

- ✔ Use EFT before you feel the urge, during giving in to the urge, and after the urge, using a Set-up Phrase that best describes what you're thinking at that time.

- ✔ Visualise as best you can the feelings or situations to bring the desire up as high as possible.

- ✔ Ensure the craving or desire reduces to a zero; don't leave it at a 1 or 2.

   * Preferably, deal with all the symptoms before getting to, and using EFT on, the underlying cause of the addictive behaviour, although this may freely come up during an EFT session. Use EFT liberally on the physical symptoms, the psychological beliefs, and any emotional feelings of pain or distress associated with the addiction before moving on to finding the cause.

- ✔ If you need help in trying to get to the cause (you need to block out unpleasant thoughts or experiences, for example), refer to Chapter 4 on 'Getting to the Root of the Problem' for more help.

✔ Tapping under the eye, the collarbone, and under the arm alone are what I refer to as the 'emergency stop points'. You can tap on these three points for whenever cravings emerge that you need to deal with in a hurry.

✔ Don't try willpower with EFT; it's not necessary. If you rely on willpower and fail, you'll blame EFT. Willpower isn't for long-term use anyhow.

✔ EFT can eliminate both the craving and addiction in one session, but if the craving comes back, you need to identify and address the underlying emotions with EFT.

✔ If you have no joy, check for any psychological reversal (see Chapter 6) and any core or limiting beliefs (see Chapter 15).

✔ If you resolve the addictive behaviour but the behaviour switches to another addiction, this indicates that you haven't dealt with the underlying emotional issues. You need to start again.

Use EFT repeatedly before you feel the urge, when you feel the urge, when you've given in to the urge, and after you've given in to the urge.

Quitting Smoking (and Other Addictions) by Using EFT

If you're a smoker, I have no intention of warning you here of the dangers of smoking, because you have enough information thrust down your throat on a daily basis. You know smoking isn't good for you, but if you're serious about giving up, this section certainly helps you achieve that. If you're a practitioner, you also find some useful tips here to work on clients.

You don't need to suffer terrible withdrawal symptoms because EFT can work on those too and, because it's portable, you can use it wherever and whenever you need to.

Although the advice here is for practitioners to help their clients give up smoking, you can apply these techniques on yourself to help give up your addiction. Whether you believe smoking is a habit or an addiction is irrelevant. I refer to smoking in this chapter as an addiction but you can change the wording to whatever you feel comfortable with.

I always advise clients before they begin using EFT to stop smoking that it's best not to use any support aids such as nicotine patches or gum for up to a week beforehand. This is so that the client knows that EFT is doing the work. It would be a shame to attribute the success to nicotine patches and give up on EFT.

When a client comes to me to give up smoking, the single most important question is 'Why do you want to give up?'. If the client tells me it's because she's been asked to find help, or she feels obliged to give up because her partner hates her smoking, then I send her away. I ask her to come back when she's ready to give up for her own sake, otherwise I'm wasting my time and her money. Those who sincerely want to quit smoking find that EFT not only gives them a sense of control but a feeling of empowerment.

Dealing with withdrawal symptoms

Withdrawal symptoms is a common excuse to avoid giving up but one that you can deal with by using EFT. With withdrawal symptoms, you don't have to actually experience them; imagining them works just as well.

> 'Even though I have these withdrawal pains, I accept myself and realise they're a small price to pay.'

> 'Even though I feel shaky when I haven't had a cigarette, I feel safe knowing that the feeling won't last and that I'm doing my body good in the long term.'

Feeling the anxiety at giving up

For some people, their cigarettes can be a 'crutch', 'friend', or 'comforter' and the mere thought of not having that support can be too much for them to contemplate and can certainly get their anxiety levels going. If this is the case, you can use EFT first on the fears about losing the 'support' that smoking gives. Assure your client that you'll be showing her how EFT can make her feel good without the need for cigarettes. Explain how she may find it hard at first but not to forget that she doesn't have to believe in EFT for it to work, she just has to tune in to the anxiety.

Clients often say they have no anxieties about giving up. Giving up is why they've come, after all. To test whether this is true, try asking the client to say out loud 'I no longer smoke', 'I don't need cigarettes', or 'I'll never smoke again'. Alternatively, get the client to visualise being in a stressful situation and not having a cigarette. Now, ask the client to notice what comes up and where she feels this sensation. Usually, she can feel anxiety in her stomach and, if this is the case, you can use the Set-up Phrase 'Even though I feel anxious in my stomach about giving up cigarettes, I accept myself'.

Oh, by the way, if the client has a fear of putting on weight after giving up smoking, it's highly unlikely that this will happen. After EFT removes the root cause of the anxiety, the client probably won't look for some other tranquillising substance. For information, though, you may like to know that a person would have to put on an average of 56 pounds before their health was affected to the same degree as it is with smoking.

Recognising the drivers

Having got the initial anxiety about giving up out of the way – and any withdrawal symptoms – proceed to ask when the client first needed this dependency and why. The client's father may have given her that first cigarette, and it made her feel grown up, or she may have reached for a cigarette when faced with bad news, for instance. Dealing with the traumatic memory with EFT should remove the necessity for the comforter. (Chapter 11 deals with trauma.)

If the client needs to smoke on the way to work, for instance, what is it about work that causes the anxiety? Does she smoke because she simply just enjoys it? Ask whether she enjoyed her first cigarette. Probably not, but she carried on regardless because of either the association or the temporary 'fix' it gave. She may have all the excuses as to why she smokes, but that's all they are, excuses – whether it's because she believes it helps her to relax, gives her confidence, or helps with her concentration, they're all a myth. The nicotine leaving the body actually creates the anxiety, as does removing the habit. Ask her whether she can substitute a cigarette for something that doesn't harm her health and she can use at any time, such as EFT – which would she rather choose?

The following sections cover some of the most common reasons why people say they smoke and some suggested EFT phrases to go with them. Use the ones that fit or by all means make up your own. While saying the appropriate phrases, it helps to visualise being in the situation or to bring up the bodily sensations that go with them so that EFT can work more effectively.

Stubbing out your beliefs

Many beliefs surrounding your smoking help you justify carrying on. One is that 'smoking is relaxing'. Did you know the chemicals from nicotine stay in your body for approximately 20 minutes and it's when they leave your body that you start to feel anxious? You can avoid this feeling for so long before you reach for another cigarette. Have a go at:

'Although I've always smoked, it's who I am. I accept myself as a smoker, but I respect myself more by becoming a non-smoker.'

'Even though I smoke like my dad, I forgive myself and choose to copy good things about him instead.'

'Even though I enjoy smoking and inhaling poisonous fumes, I love and accept myself anyway.'

'Although smoking relaxes me, my logical brain tells me this isn't true, but I accept myself anyway.'

'Even though I get tense when I'm pressured, I accept myself and choose to relax instead.'

Watching your emotions go up in smoke

Some people feel the need to smoke to deal with their feelings of anger, sadness, loneliness, and so on. Here are the often-used reasons included in these Set-up Phrases:

'Even though I feel deprived when I see someone else smoking, I deeply and completely respect myself.'

'Even though I need a cigarette when I'm stressed, I completely accept myself and choose to remain calm.'

'Even though I need a cigarette to give me confidence, I choose instead to feel in control.'

'Even though I smoke to numb my feelings of loneliness, I accept and forgive myself.'

Burying your bad behaviour

So, smoking is a habit therefore you can't stop? Well, so was sucking your thumb, but you gave that up, didn't you? The behaviour is the habit, so why not try:

'Even though I like to smoke when in company, I accept myself and I accept that I don't have to damage others' health.'

'Although I smoke when I'm on the phone, I deeply accept myself.'

'Even though I smoke in the car, I accept that there are healthier alternatives.'

'Although I feel guilty about smoking, I deeply and completely accept myself.'

You can tackle any habits or associations with EFT, and help yourself by adopting different behaviours. For instance:

- ✔ **Smoking while drinking coffee:** Try switching to tea or a soft drink instead.

- ✔ **Smoking in the car:** Try chewing gum or holding a pencil instead. Also clean your car, empty ashtrays, and remove cigarettes and any lighters.

- ✔ **Smoking with friends:** Practise at home holding something else in your hand such as a pen. If you hold a glass in your right hand, try switching your glass to your left hand instead.

Hearing voices in your head

Smokers often tell me that a voice in their head tells them to smoke. Here's what you can use:

> *'Even though I have this voice in my head telling me I need to smoke, I decide not to damage my body and respect it instead.'*

> *'Although part of me wants to give up and the voice in my head tells me I don't, I choose to go with the part that wants to give up.'*

Explain to clients and remind yourself, if you're a smoker, that there may be moments of weakness and that giving in isn't a sign of failure. Don't throw your hands up and say 'Well, that's it, I've failed again'. Look at your failure as an opportunity to try again. You just need to do some more tapping, that's all, on 'Even though I have this guilt about having that cigarette, I forgive myself' or 'Even though I feel bad about myself for having that cigarette, I completely accept that I was weak but I choose to be stronger next time'.

Accepting Your Size and Shape

If you're not happy with what you've got then the message out there is to have your teeth whitened, have the fat sucked out of your body, and remove those lines with surgery. Of course, after paying out all that money and undergoing some pain, you're still not guaranteed that you'll feel good about yourself.

Many factors contribute towards how good or bad you feel about yourself and weight is just one of them. Don't believe you have to be the size and shape of a model in order to be loved. Be happy in your own skin and others will see you as the person inside, which is far more attractive. If you're within the recommended levels of weight for your height and your weight isn't affecting your health, yet you still can't accept yourself as you are, then read Chapter 7.

Identifying eating disorders

Toxic thoughts can, but don't necessarily, lead to eating disorders such as anorexia or bulimia. If you suspect you have an eating disorder, you can either deal with your emotional problems yourself through EFT or, if they are severe, seek medical help before consulting an EFT practitioner. Find out more about low self-esteem in Chapter 7.

Some or all these symptoms may be present with bulimia:

✔ Persistent preoccupation with eating and an irresistible craving for food.

✔ Episodes of overeating in which you consume large amounts of food in short periods of time.

✔ Excessive exercise, induced vomiting after eating, starving for periods of time, and/or taking medicines such as laxatives or diuretics to counteract the bingeing.

✔ Fear of obesity, which is also seen in people with anorexia.

Some or all these symptoms may be present with anorexia:

✔ Low body weight for height or age.

✔ Restriction of food intake and fear of becoming obese.

✔ Distorted view of own body weight, shape, or size.

✔ Refusal to maintain minimum normal body weight.

✔ Secretive about food intake.

✔ Excessive exercise.

✔ Denial of feelings of hunger.

✔ Fastidious about cutting up food into tiny pieces.

Feelings of self-loathing and low self-esteem go hand-in-hand with being unable to accept yourself.

If, however, you really do need to lose weight and nothing else has worked, then the following sections can certainly help you.

Understanding why diets fail in the long term

People go on diets because they want to lose weight, but many of those diets fail to deliver on their promise in the long term and you're left wondering why, even though you were so determined. Statistics show that an amazing 95 per cent of diets fail in the long term, mainly because they don't address your emotional drivers behind your eating patterns, and nor do they help you recognise your self-sabotaging behaviours. After you address the underlying reasons as to why your diets fail, your eating habits are determined by you wanting to enjoy a healthy eating lifestyle and are not determined by your emotions.

Comfort eating or *emotional eating* is when you use food to make you feel good. Many people have been conditioned to celebrate happy occasions with cake or something sweet. At the same time, those carbohydrates and sugars release that 'feel good' chemical so you have an immediate association. Next time you need consoling and you're on your own, what better place to look than in the fridge or cupboard for your comforter?

If you carry out this behaviour on a regular basis, you can ultimately develop withdrawal symptoms and need the food to cope with them.

Next time you reach out for something sweet, try taking a step back and look at what you're satisfying? Are you really hungry or is this desire for unhealthy food filling an emotional need? True physical hunger gradually comes on over a period of time and starts with feeling a little 'peckish' to 'really could eat' all the way to 'absolutely starving; could eat anything'. The ideal time to eat is at the 'really could eat' stage because you're more likely to eat the right amount and not eat it too fast. Next time you're thinking 'What should I eat?', ask yourself 'What am I feeding?'.

If you recognise yourself in any of these questions, then you're most likely an emotional eater:

- ✔ Have you lost weight only to put it on again?
- ✔ Do you comfort eat when depressed, upset, or angry?
- ✔ Do you ever reward yourself with food?
- ✔ Do you eat 'naughty' food or more food when on your own?
- ✔ Have you ever eaten out of boredom?
- ✔ Have you ever binged on food only to feel guilty afterwards?

Curbing those cravings

It's unfair, I know, but the very foods that are the most unhealthy are the ones that trigger off those 'must have it' and 'feel good' chemicals, which is why people generally crave chocolate, sweets, and so on. The following exercise is one way you can impress your friends and make more at the same time as you show them how EFT removes the craving simply, swiftly, and elegantly. Try it on yourself first to get the hang of it.

If you're applying EFT on someone else's cravings, be aware that if you lead on this exercise, you may be affected at the same time. (See Chapter 15 for more on this topic.) If you don't want to be put off whatever it is you crave completely, just get your rating down to about a 5. When you're serious about giving it up completely, do it for real and get the craving down to a zero.

Try this exercise on something you can get a craving for if you see, smell, or touch it. Be warned that you can eliminate a craving for good after one or more rounds so make sure you really want to remove the desire. When you've finished the exercise, you'll find your desire has changed somewhat and the food may even smell or taste differently; it may even seem repulsive. If you don't want to remove the craving completely, just get your level of desire down to around a 4 or 5 and then stop.

This example uses a chocolate bar but you can substitute this for whatever it is you crave, even if that means going out and buying that bag of chips.

1. **Take hold of your favourite chocolate bar.**

2. **Take off the wrapping and smell the chocolate or even taste a little of it. Make sure it's only a little to make you want more!**

   This helps to increase the desire, which is what you want.

3. **Notice where in your body you feel the craving or desire.**

4. **Rate on a scale from zero to 10 your desire (with 10 being the highest).**

   The higher the craving, the better.

5. **While concentrating on the craving, carry out a full round of EFT as I describe in Chapter 3, including tapping on the back of the hand, and say the following:**

   'Even though I have this craving in my (stomach), I completely accept myself.'

   Repeat twice more. Tap on remaining points with 'this craving in my (stomach)' or 'this (chocolate) craving in my (stomach)'.

6. **When you've completed the full round of EFT, finishing under the arm, concentrate on the craving and rate it again using the Remaining Phrase of 'Even though I *still* have this chocolate craving . . .'.**

   If the rating has gone down, keep tapping until it goes to a zero (if you want to, that is). If the rating has gone up or you need to eat the food, notice what thoughts or feelings are coming up. Do the words 'deprived', 'needy', or 'lonely' trigger any emotion?

7. **If so, do another round of EFT but this time include the words 'deprived' or 'needy'.**

   'Even though I still have this craving and I feel needy, I completely accept myself.'

Ten sensible diet tips

As well as using EFT, these tips won't go amiss either:

✔ Recognise your 'food moods'. Are you experiencing emotional hunger as opposed to real physical hunger?

✔ Rate your hunger on a scale from 1 to 10. Ideally, eat when it's around a 5.

✔ Stop eating when you feel comfortably full and not 'bloated' or 'stuffed'. Even when you feel stuffed I bet you can always manage that extra sweet dessert?

✔ Drink more water. Your brain can trick you into thinking it's hungry when in fact it's dehydrated.

✔ Take your time and enjoy your food. Eating too fast or too much overrides your brain's control centre so you end up not getting that 'I'm full' message. It takes approximately 20 minutes for the stomach to send a message to the brain to say it's full.

✔ Eat a little something approximately every three hours to counteract any drop in blood sugar levels.

✔ Only put on your plate what you can comfortably eat.

✔ If you can't bear the thought of exercising, move about more or take the stairs rather than the lift.

✔ Ensure you have a breakfast.

✔ Don't deprive yourself of what you enjoy. Remember – a little of what you fancy and all that. As long as you know when to stop, of course.

✔ Don't be dragged into other people's 'comfort zone'.

✔ Lastly, reward your efforts with a manicure, a book, a DVD, or CD – anything, in fact, other than food or drink.

Also include any other words or emotions that may come up, such as loneliness, fear, grief, sadness, control, or abandonment. For example 'Even though I have this sadness and need to fill it with (food), I deeply and completely accept myself', 'Although I have this guilt around food, I accept myself', 'Although I'm ashamed of the way I eat, I forgive myself', and 'Even though I feel lonely and I comfort myself with food, I love and accept myself as I am'.

8. **Consider where these emotions may have stemmed from and what they mean.**

   For example, sadness may indicate loss of something or someone. Perhaps your eating patterns changed after a bereavement. If you can't make a connection, allow EFT to do it for you by just tapping around saying 'I accept myself, even though I don't know why I have this sadness'.

9. **Use EFT on any negative feeling or thought associated with your craving.**

10. **Go back and check the craving again.**

11. **If a little craving remains (around a 3 or 4 on the Subjective Units of Distress Scale – refer to Chapter 3) try using alternative phrases.**

    Start with a negative on the eyebrow with 'I still crave this (food)'; then a positive under the eye, such as 'I feel satisfied'; then a negative under the nose like 'I still have this emptiness'; and so on.

12. **Always end on a positive.**

Even if you have no emotion or memory attached to your eating patterns, you can still carry out this exercise on your cravings.

If you're eating when you're not hungry then you're eating for another reason, which is usually an emotional one.

Table 12-1 gives some 'mix and match' phrases for eating problems.

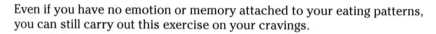

Table 12-1	Phrases to Use with Eating Problems
Even Though . . .	*Positive Follow Up*
'I love eating . . .'	'. . . I respect my body. My body is my temple.'
'I can't leave any food on my plate . . .'	'. . . I choose to be satisfied with less.'
'I eat when I'm bored . . .'	'. . . I choose to occupy myself another way.'
'I'm frightened of failing . . .'	'. . . I have weight to lose and confidence to gain.'
'I have to eat food when I smell it . . .'	'. . . I love and accept myself as I am.'
'I eat when I'm upset/annoyed/ disappointed . . .'	'. . . I accept my feelings and I accept myself.'
'I can't help eating sweet things . . .'	'. . . Giving up puts me in control.'
'I eat all the wrong foods . . .'	'. . . I choose to reject food that's bad for me.'
'I love the taste of ice cream . . .'	'. . . I scream for a healthier body instead.'
'I feel guilty at eating too much . . .'	'. . . I accept myself as I am.'
'I eat to cheer myself up . . .'	'. . . I accept that there are better ways to feel good about myself.'

Always use the exact words that come to mind or that your client comes up with.

Hidden memories and emotions can come up with the craving exercise. Use EFT on any unpleasant or upsetting memories or emotions, even if you can't see the connection at the time. EFT more often than not brings up the connection as you tap along. Don't forget, the answers are within you; the practitioner doesn't have to do any of the work here. If you need help with this, please consult an EFT practitioner.

Battling the bulge and the brain

You may be curious to know why you're regularly successful at losing weight but also regularly successful at putting the weight back on again. ('Understanding why diets fail in the long term', earlier in this chapter, explores the psychology behind this phenomenon.) If this happens to you, then some sabotaging behaviour may be going on either from others or from yourself. Before you shout 'How very dare you!', I have to add that you may not always be consciously aware that you're self-sabotaging; otherwise, why else would you keep going on diets?

So what are these sabotaging behaviours and how do you recognise them? Take a look at these questions and the answers for an insight as to whether or not any sabotaging is going on, and then allow EFT to release the association between the two:

- ✔ **Did something happen in your life the last time you achieved your goal weight?** (You unexpectedly fell pregnant, there was a death in the family, your girlfriend or boyfriend dumped you, or your business went bankrupt.) This question usually brings up the emotional link between a past event and the state you were in at the time, and how it relates to the current state. You may associate an unpleasant experience with your successful weight loss.

- ✔ **Would losing weight mean you could find yourself attracting attention from the opposite sex and you don't like that?** If you're bothered about the opposite sex looking at you, why do you think that is? Could it be because of an unpleasant incident in the past?

- ✔ **Are you the only one within your group of friends or family who has managed to lose weight?** If so, you may have hidden concerns about others being jealous of your success. Do you feel comfortable being the only one who's slim?

- ✔ **Do you believe that if you lose too much weight you'll look unhealthy or haggard and old?** If you lost weight in the past were you bothered about the saggy skin or your face looking drawn? What can you do this time that you didn't do before?

- ✔ **Does talking about your latest diet attract the attention you crave?** Be honest and admit it if you actually like the attention you get by talking about your different diets. It does happen.

- ✔ **When you reach your goal weight, are your negative thoughts getting in the way and telling you it's only a matter of time before you put the weight on again?** These negative voices about yourself are a bit like those limiting beliefs in Chapter 15 and your core beliefs in Chapter 7. They keep you stuck and prevent you from either succeeding or maintaining your weight loss.

Your subconscious carries out your beliefs, whether positive or negative.

Other times you may have heard yourself using these lame (sorry I meant same) excuses: 'This diet is no good', 'I have the fat gene', 'We're an overweight family', 'My metabolism is slow', 'I've got middle-age spread', and 'It's the menopause'.

Well, what a load of rubbish, if you pardon me saying! What you're saying here is 'It's okay to be overweight; it's not my fault; I can take a pill; it's not my responsibility'. If science has proven that a fat gene exists, then it means you just have to try a bit harder, that's all. The more overweight you are, the more metabolism you have, so you actually burn off more calories than thin people. If you firmly believe these excuses, then do some tapping to remove them straight away.

Feeling out of control

Eating disorders are a complex condition that can come from a variety of causes, which makes it difficult to understand. (For more information on eating disorders, see the sidebar 'Identifying eating disorders', earlier in this chapter.) Causes may include feelings of low self-esteem, perceived pressure to be thin, a way of handling stress, suppressing bad memories, or a way of controlling an unsafe environment. Whether it's bingeing, starving, or compulsive eating, for some people, controlling their food is a way of coping with their emotional distress, a way of somehow being in control. Perversely, the food begins to control them.

When using EFT on eating disorders, you can use it to treat the anxiety around eating food, but ultimately you need to dig around and find out when the symptoms first began and what life events may have contributed to the client's eating habits. Was she they teased at school? Did someone once make comment about her weight? Teenagers with anorexic symptoms often come from families who are over-critical, controlling, or overprotective, and someone who's bulimic has a compulsion to eat and then tends to feel guilty afterwards. Some sexual abuse sufferers are determined to remain thin and child-like because this avoids developing womanly curves. Low self-esteem is generally a symptom too, so there may be resistance to saying the Acceptance Phrase (refer to Chapter 3.) Experience has also taught me that clients with eating disorders tend to come to me with other problems and only mention their eating disorder during consultation.

As a therapist, don't try to convince anyone who has a body image problem, or anyone with an eating disorder, that they're not overweight or ugly.

People who suffer from anorexia can also develop bulimia, and vice versa, causing an overlap of the symptoms.

Enough is never enough

Here's an example of an unconscious belief associated with overeating.

Lauren came to see me because she wanted to lose weight. Her weight seemed to have crept up over recent years, mainly because she was now eating out more with her husband. Regardless of the size of the portions of food served to her when she ate out, Lauren not only had to eat everything on her plate, but would often finish off her husband's food too! When she arrived home she'd be consumed with guilt and shame, promising herself she wouldn't repeat this behaviour, but she couldn't help it. Lauren told me she could hear a voice telling her to eat it all up.

I asked Lauren where this voice came from and she told me it was from her mother. Lauren's mother always told her never to leave food and that she must think of all the starving children in other countries. Lauren's belief, of course, was 'I mustn't waste food'.

I asked Lauren to tap using phrases such as 'Even though my mother's voice tells me I have to finish everything on my plate, I forgive myself and I forgive my mother', 'Even though I have to eat the leftovers because enough is never enough, I forgive and accept myself anyway', and 'Even though I have to eat everything on my plate because of those starving children, I accept myself and accept I couldn't feed those starving children with my leftovers'.

After working on her beliefs, I then worked on her guilt: 'Even though I feel guilty at leaving food on my plate, I accept and forgive myself anyway'. When she began to feel more positive, I then asked Lauren to tap and say 'Although I was told not to waste food, I accept myself and prefer to have a tiny waist instead'.

Lauren's attitude to eating changed considerably and she was able to enjoy her food without any of the guilt.

The EFT phrases for an eating disorder may go something like this:

'Even though I eat to numb my feelings . . .'

'Even though I stuff myself with food to avoid the emotional/physical pain . . .'

'Even though I use food to comfort myself . . .'

'Even though I binge because I hate the way I look . . .'

'Even though I deprive myself of food to hide myself . . .'

'Even though I have to control my food because I don't feel safe . . .'

'Even though I hate the way I look . . .'

'Even though I use food to control my anger/fear/hate . . .'

Depending on Alcohol

Just because you depend on having a drink to help you socialise or to cope with a stressful situation doesn't necessarily make you an alcoholic. I suggest, however, that you use EFT for your confidence or stress, because what starts off as an innocent dependency can lead to an addiction.

Apart from the calorie content in alcohol it's a sobering thought that alcohol-related conditions range from liver disease, high blood pressure, and heart disease to osteoporosis and loss of fertility.

Many people know that trying to kick an addiction like alcohol is one of the most difficult, painful, and time-consuming assignments you can undertake. With EFT, however, this isn't necessary. In most cases, as long as you work first on the physical feelings and then on the underlying emotional reasons behind the drinking, you can tackle alcohol addiction. Other support won't go amiss though.

Knowing when one is too many and a thousand isn't enough

Alcoholism implies that you need an alcoholic drink to get you through the day or that when you start drinking you can't stop or find it very difficult to do so. Take a look at the section 'Applying EFT to Addictions', earlier in this chapter, on how to address an addiction to alcohol.

If you have any of the following symptoms after going without a drink for less than a day, you possibly already have a physical addiction to alcohol:

✔ You feel shaky.

✔ You feel or want to be sick.

✔ You feel really anxious or panicky.

Sudden withdrawal effects from drugs are unpleasant. If you have a physical addiction, especially to alcohol, never stop suddenly without consulting your medical practitioner first.

Physical addiction is harder and takes longer to treat with EFT. However, if you use EFT in conjunction with treatment that addresses the psychological or emotional causes of the behaviour, it can produce quick results.

Living with an elephant in the room

Could you ignore an elephant in your living room? How could you carry out your everyday chores with an elephant in the room? Watching TV or having a phone conversation would be impossible. Surely, everyone else must know, so how can it be a secret?

Then why tell a child it's a secret that her parent's an alcoholic?

Children of alcoholics often suffer from tremendous guilt or feelings of low self-esteem. They often feel they're to blame for their parent's/carer's behaviour and display some of the following behaviours:

✔ People pleasing.

✔ Constantly wanting approval.

✔ Able to care for others but uneasy about caring for themselves.

✔ Even when life is going well, anticipating problems.

✔ Feeling more alive when surrounded by chaos or drama.

During your history taking with your client, if she shows any of these behavioural traits, check whether she came from a home where someone abused alcohol.

Suffering from Obsessive Behaviour

Carrying out certain rituals, such as checking over and over again whether you've switched off electrical items or making sure items are in perfect alignment, is a sign of someone who suffers from an *obsessive-compulsive disorder* (OCD). If they don't carry out these rituals and in a certain order then the person with OCD feels an overwhelming anxiety.

Constant nagging doubts, hand-washing, checking that you've switched off electrical items, and checking that everything is in the right place or right order are just a few signs of OCD. Even when you've completed the rituals, the feel-good factor lasts for only a short time before the anxiety starts to build up again.

Although OCD sufferers know that their behaviour is irrational, they're powerless to do anything about it. Although everyone has some form of obsession, you need to recognise when it's getting out of hand and causing you anxiety.

The World Health Organization (WHO) ranks OCD as the tenth most disabling illness of any kind, in terms of lost earnings and diminished quality of life. The medical profession are now more aware of the symptoms so that doctors can make an early diagnosis and start treatment.

The disorder is very distressing for both the sufferer and anyone who lives with someone with the problem. The following symptoms are similar to OCD:

- ✔ Body dysmorphic disorder (extreme anxiety about body image).

- ✔ Trichotillomania (compulsive hair-pulling).

- ✔ Compulsive skin picking.

- ✔ Eating disorders.

- ✔ Hypochondriasis (irrational ideas or fears of having a serious illness).

Like all other anxiety-based behaviour, you can use EFT on the anxiety itself and then on the underlying emotions of guilt, anger, sadness, and so on. Usually, a traumatic experience triggers the disorder, and if this is the case the EFT techniques that I describe in Chapter 5 are an excellent way to deal with this.

A woman developed OCD seven years ago after her dog died. For seven years she felt responsible for his death and all her anxiety and guilt turned into OCD. Her obsession was with feeding and caring for her dogs and horses with a strict routine and order. Her OCD had taken over her life and, because she couldn't sleep for too long, she slept in the car outside the house. As the woman described her desperate situation, her husband looked on as a powerless witness. They had exhausted all other help. I just hope she or her medics read this book!

Looking into the Future

With all addictions, when the anxiety and cravings reduce to zero, use EFT while imagining yourself at a future date as a non-smoker, being your ideal weight, or free from obsessions. Omit the Set-Up Phrase of 'Even though' and start tapping from the eyebrow to under the arm using positive phrases such as: 'I see myself saying no to that cigarette', 'I'm at my ideal weight and I feel good', 'I'm walking into a shop and I don't feel the urge to buy ', 'I see my healthy future before me', 'I feel confident without a drink in my hand', 'I feel liberated', and so on.

Keep tapping until eventually you feel positive and confident about your future without your addictive substance.

If you still can't visualise yourself, you can tap for 'Even though I can't visualise myself as being slim, I forgive myself', 'Although, for whatever reason, I'm not blessed with the power of imagination, I accept myself', or 'Although I have a mental block about seeing myself slim, there's obviously a reason for this that I don't know about and I accept myself anyway'.

Chapter 13

Healing the Body

· ·

In This Chapter

▶ Connecting emotions with physical health

▶ Conquering pain

▶ Dealing with irritable bowel syndrome

▶ Alleviating allergies

▶ Finding a solution to fertility

▶ Coping with a major disease

· ·

*1*f you have an ailment such as a headache or back pain, or you can't sleep, you reach for the appropriate medication for that specific ailment. With EFT you use the same technique for every ailment and symptom. The difference, however, is in the approach and the approach depends upon the emotion or experience causing the ailment or symptom.

This chapter concentrates on how you can use EFT on physical problems. Although I mention only a few here, those that I mention demonstrate how the use of language and emotive emphasis can greatly enhance and speed up results. Using EFT can't make your condition worse, so you have nothing to lose but maybe something to gain. As Hippocrates said, 'The natural healing force within each one of us is the greatest force in getting well.' This chapter, and Chapter 5, contains various techniques that I encourage you to use.

It won't do any harm to take a look at your lifestyle either while you're at it, such as your diet and exercise regime. Begin to recognise patterns in your health and your emotions and how your body tells you when it needs a rest, or why you develop colds at weekends.

EFT isn't a replacement for medical treatments. Where appropriate, always seek medical advice before using EFT.

How old are you?

Here's a tricky question and one to think carefully about before you answer: How old are you? The correct answer, according to recent research, is about 15 and a half. That's the average age of your muscles and guts. Depending on what you read, your body has been replacing its tissues and cells every one to seven years since the day you were conceived.

Did you know how often your body replaces its various parts?

✔ Red blood cells every 90–120 days.

✔ Muscles every six months to three years.

✔ The pancreas every 5–12 months.

✔ Our bones every eight months to four years.

✔ The intestinal lining every 5–30 days.

Combining East and West

If someone told you that an energetic response to a negative emotion can travel at the speed of light (approximately 186,000 miles per second), yet chemicals move through the body at a rate of 1 centimetre per second, which would you rather have? Your thoughts are energy so logic has it that the best method to treat your body is an energetic one. If you find this hard to believe make a note next time you have a negative emotion and see how long it takes for the information to travel from the brain to be experienced in your body.

The Western world has taken it for granted that their methods are the best, but the ancient wisdom of the East can make an important contribution to medicine. The good news is that the Western world is catching on to what the Eastern world has known for 5,000 years and has begun to incorporate both Eastern and Western medicine. Even today, in China thousands of people still have heart surgery every year using only acupuncture for anaesthesia.

Managing Pain

Sudden or acute pain is a signal that something's wrong with the body and you really mustn't ignore it – sometimes it's impossible anyway. For instance, the pain of hitting your thumb with a hammer or spraining your ankle gradually goes away. Any pain that continues for more than a few months, though, can be regarded as *chronic pain*.

Medics recognise the treatment of chronic pain in its own right as a primary problem and have set up pain management clinics. These clinics are in great demand as gradually people realise that they no longer have to suffer unnecessarily. As good as these clinics are, any pain medication merely masks the pain symptoms but can't cure them. Nevertheless, for some chronic pain sufferers, such as those with cancer pain, medication can be very beneficial.

Being adventurous with EFT can bring great rewards. Because it does no physical harm, why not try it on everything and anything from ingrown toenails to cancer pain?

Treating pain with EFT

If your doctor tells you that your chronic pain is in your head, don't be offended – he may be right. Everyone knows of someone who cries at a pinprick yet others who can endure severe pain. How you respond to pain depends upon your previous experiences, upbringing, or learned behaviour. Apart from the physical response to pain, you also have the emotional response such as anxiety, anger, fear, or embarrassment. If your anxiety levels are high, you're more likely to respond to pain than when relaxed.

Using EFT doesn't mask the pain, but focusing on the pain while applying EFT eliminates the body's pain response to emotional trauma and energy blocks – otherwise known as the _chi_ or _qui_.

To use EFT on pain, try focusing first on the pain and ask questions about the pain. Ask, 'When did you first notice the pain?' The answer may indicate an association between an emotional upset in the past and the start of the pain. This is the sort of information you need to help EFT deal with the pain.

You can use any answers that crop up to create the Set-Up Phrases (see Chapters 3 and 4). While doing this you must pay attention to any sensations or feelings that you experience and remember to use EFT on them if they bother you.

Here are some examples of questions with answers and what words to use to set you off:

Q. Where specifically in your body do you get the pain?

A. Top of my right arm; Set-Up Phrase can be 'Even though I have pain in the top of my right arm . . .'.

Q. How would you best describe the pain?

A. A dull ache; 'Even though I have this dull ache at the top of my arm . . .'.

Q. What aggravates it?

A. When I'm tired; 'Even though I get this dull ache when I'm tired . . .'.

If you can't think of an emotion, sometimes just guessing can have the desired effect.

Q. What emotions are attached to this pain?

A. Fear; 'Even though I feel fear with this pain, I accept myself and release the fear, along with the pain'.

Q. Where in your body is this emotion? (You can also add what colour is it or what shape, and include these descriptions in the Set-Up Phrase.)

A. In my stomach and it's heavy; 'Even though I have this heavy fear emotion in my stomach, I deeply and completely accept myself'.

When the pain begins to subside, try adding some positive outcomes:

Q. What would you like to happen?

A. I'd like to be useful again; 'Even though I still have this anger pain in my arm, I deeply and completely accept myself and choose to be useful again'.

Q. If you didn't have this pain what could you do?

A. I could play golf again; 'Even though I still have this anger pain in my arm, I deeply and completely accept myself and choose to release this pain so that I can play golf again'.

Adding the words 'and I forgive myself for anything I may have done to con-tribute to this (problem)' or 'I forgive myself and anyone else who may have contributed to this (problem)' after accepting yourself can be very empower-ing. (You can find more on this in Chapter 6.)

Try to introduce some humour if you can, at the appropriate time, of course.

If addressing both the emotional and physical issues doesn't reduce the physical pain, you probably have some underlying reason to consciously or unconsciously hold on to the pain. You can find out more about this in Chapter 6.

Always be specific when describing the pain, and if applying EFT on some-one else, use their exact words. If they say 'burning fire inside', these are the words to use.

When experiencing pain intensely in the present moment you can often leave out the Set-Up Phrase and Reminder Phrase because your attention is already focused on the problem. Using EFT can calm things down so the treatment can begin. If necessary, tap on the Karate Chop (see Chapter 3 for info on this spot).

Chasing the pain

When you're applying EFT on a physical pain or discomfort, the pain or discomfort can often move to other parts of the body or change in nature. A sharp pain in the arm, for instance, can move to the shoulder and then to the chest and may change to a dull ache. This phenomenon is called *chasing the pain*, mainly because, as the pain or discomfort moves around the body, you simply apply EFT on wherever it moves to.

Observe, as you're applying EFT, whether you feel a reduction in the pain or discomfort, which you must always reduce to zero in intensity. The chase can take some time but is necessary to overcome the pain or to allow any hidden emotions to come to the surface.

Easing Irritable Bowel Syndrome

Irritable bowel syndrome (IBS) is a chronic disorder and the symptoms include recurrent abdominal pain and intermittent diarrhoea, often alternating with constipation. Symptoms worsen at times of stress. Normally, no obvious cause exists and many people don't bother to seek treatment.

Because the condition restricts normal activities, up to 60 per cent of people with IBS also suffer from anxiety or depression. There's no doubt that this disease affects emotional. Here's where EFT can assist with the emotional effects and in the process relieve the symptoms.

Identifying the causes of the IBS is the best place to begin, and then you can treat each one with EFT. Some stressors may include:

 ✔ Depression

 ✔ Anxiety or panic attacks

 ✔ Stress

 ✔ An upsetting incident or traumatic event

 ✔ Low self-esteem

Try introducing phrases with EFT that put the emphasis on 'letting go' or 'releasing', because psychologically you may have a history of holding on to emotions or keeping them hidden. Again, detective work here reaps rewards.

Also, try working on the negative feelings associated with the IBS. The aim is to remove any emotional reaction to embarrassing incidents that bring back memories of shame, embarrassment, or fear.

> *'Even though my IBS caused me embarrassment in the shop, I forgive myself and I forgive my IBS.'*
>
> *'Although I can't let go, I accept myself and choose to relax.'*
>
> *'Even though I'm gripped by this pain, I allow myself to be free from pain and any emotion that goes with it.'*

For the bigger picture on IBS, check out *IBS For Dummies*, by Patricia McNair (Wiley).

Improving Your Eyesight

Lots of evidence exists that connects emotions with eyesight: physical tension around the face restricts the blood flow and oxygen to the eye muscles.

To change or improve eyesight by using behavioural means alone seems almost impossible, yet you know that when you get angry or stressed you say that you can't see straight. If you're open to the possibility that using EFT to remove emotional barriers, and letting go of bad feelings, resentment, and intolerant behaviours, may improve your eyesight, why not try it?

May a secondary benefit, belief, or fear of remembering something visual be preventing your eyesight from improving? Chapter 6 explains about secondary benefits and Chapter 15 talks about limiting beliefs.

Optometrists aren't trained in treating emotional issues, but you can help yourself by clearing out any emotional hang-ups. You don't have to use EFT on the clinical diagnosis of your vision like 'Even though I have glaucoma' or 'Even though I need near-sighted glasses' – just concentrate on anything emotional.

Here are some other suggestions: 'Even though all my family wears glasses', 'Even though my eyesight is deteriorating with age', or 'Even though my optometrist told me that my vision will get worse'. Follow these up with 'I deserve to have perfect vision', 'I choose to see more clearly', or 'I forgive anything or anyone that may have contributed to my poor sight'.

Focusing on improvements

Carol Look (EFT Master) conducted an experiment involving the use of EFT to improve eyesight. The experiment produced astounding results with 75 per cent of participants reporting a 15–75 per cent improvement in their vision by releasing their pent-up emotions such as guilt, shame, anger, and fear.

In her experiment, Dr Look directed 120 people to use EFT daily for eight weeks. Each week, participants received an email with an emotional topic for the next seven days of EFT. Participants spent about five minutes per day doing EFT for a specific emotional issue like anger, fear, guilt, and hurt. Anyone can do EFT by simply tapping on a series of acupuncture points while focusing thought on the emotional issue.

Cheri, a 55-year-old woman, addressed the emotional issues outlined in the EFT experiment by neutralising many unresolved feelings regarding her mother. As she did so, her vision improved in several categories defined in the experiment. Her perception of brightness improved, as did her colour perception and contrast. Her farsighted vision also improved considerably. In Cheri's words, 'It has been many years since I've been able to see clearly the trees and their foliage or to determine if the rattle was a squirrel or a bird.'

Prior to the experiment, Cheri wore glasses for reading 95 per cent of the time but now she no longer uses reading glasses at all.

An appointment with her eye doctor verified Cheri's improvements. Compared to her appointment two years previous, she could read two more lines on the eye chart. She'd been diagnosed with 'vertical muscle imbalance' and ' map-dot-fingerprint dystrophy'. Although he couldn't explain it, the doctor's tests showed that neither condition existed any longer.

Cheri's doctor was very interested in and supportive of using EFT to improve her eyesight. He indicated that, 'emotions play a strong part in the flow of blood to the retina, as well as to different parts of the brain, so increased blood flow (as a result of EFT) to both the retina and the brain would be reflected in the sharpened clarity'.

The experiment isn't a scientific study, but what can you lose by trying this for five minutes a day?

Notice when your eyesight started to deteriorate. Was it after the death of a loved one, for instance, or because you were told it was because of your age? Use EFT to remove any bad feelings, resentment, and intolerant behaviours, and any thoughts, beliefs, or emotions that may have contributed to how your sight is now.

Taking Action on Allergies and Rashes

Researchers at Harvard Medical School have scientifically linked allergic reactions with stress and negative emotions, and EFT has shown remarkable results in the treatment of allergies, including multiple chemical sensitivity (MCS).

Reported findings

Andy Mason's wife was diagnosed with multiple chemical sensitivity (MCS) after suffering with migraine headaches, severe balance problems, and joint pains for 15 years. Visits to allergy specialists, neurologists, and ear, nose, and throat specialists brought her no relief. After an environmental specialist established that she was sensitive to 80 different chemical, food, and airborne allergens, her doctor prescribed stabilising drops and injections, but they offered her minimal protection.

Mason was studying EFT but had never used it for allergies. Because it was easy to do, and EFT has no known side effects, he and his wife systematically used it for each of her identified allergies. Some allergies cleared in 30 minutes, but others required persistence and addressing physical symptoms and emotional issues related to the allergies.

One year after her EFT allergy treatment, Mason reported, 'She has not used any allergy treatments for the past year, and has rarely had any allergic responses. When she has, it is because she has been exposed to a substance that we had not addressed with EFT. Her quality of life (and the dent in our finances from the allergy testing and resultant medication) is much improved since we used EFT to resolve these issues.'

It makes sense that the best way to stay allergy-free is to simply avoid the allergens that cause the allergic reaction. So if, for example, you have a peanut allergy, it makes sense to avoid peanuts or foods that contain them. However, this assumes that you can identify the causative allergen(s) and in many cases such avoidance is impractical, as with a pollen allergy.

Your unconscious mind is very powerful and can influence your immune system by reacting to a stressful situation you want to escape from by using its survival instincts. These psychosomatic factors can cause, or at least exacerbate, some allergic conditions.

Please be responsible with EFT when using it on allergies. Also don't use EFT instead of avoiding allergens or seeking medical attention. If you accidentally come into contact with a substance that causes a severe or anaphylactic reaction, by all means use EFT until medical assistance arrives.

Try using EFT on each symptom of your allergy and make a note of any improvements. It may take time but persistence pays.

When re-introducing the substance that causes the allergy, do so very gently, from a distance, and continue tapping on any fear or anxiety associated with coming into contact with the substance.

Suggested phrases:

'Even though I have this throat swelling . . .'

'Even though I can't breathe . . .'

'Even though my eyes are watering . . .'

When using EFT in an emergency situation, while waiting for medical help to arrive, omit rubbing the Sore Spot or tapping on the Karate Chop (see Chapter 3 for info) and move straight to the remaining points, saying words such as 'this throat swelling' and 'this can't breathe feeling', and all the time follow up with words such as 'I am safe', 'I'm okay', and 'I can relax'.

Question whether any emotional upset or traumatic incident happened at the time the allergy first occurred, and then treat each negative emotion with EFT.

Surviving the Reproductive Years

Despite growing up in a household full of women, the words 'period', 'pregnancy', and 'menopause' were rarely, if ever, mentioned in our house. Instead, we referred to them as 'women's problems'. How grateful I am that we've come a long way since then and my daughters can openly discuss these matters with my husband.

Periods full stop

Menstruation, periods, monthlies, or whatever you want to call them can be painful for many women, and premenstrual syndrome is not only real, but it's downright bothersome. You can treat each of the following symptoms easily with EFT by applying the method I refer to in the section 'Managing Pain', earlier in this chapter:

- Headaches
- Cramps
- Dizziness
- Tension
- Breast pain
- Mood swings

'Even though I have these cramp pains in my stomach, I accept myself.'

'Although I've got this same monthly headache over my eyes, I accept myself as a woman with women's problems.'

'Although I'm angry that it's only women and not men who get these cramps, I accept myself and forgive all men. It's not their fault.'

For appetite and sugar cravings take a look at Chapter 12.

Fighting fertility problems

Finding out that you have a fertility problem can be traumatic, and put a lot of strain and stress on a relationship. You usually focus your attention on the physical aspects of improving diet, rest, exercise, and so on, and ignore the emotional aspects. By subconsciously allowing unhelpful, negative habits to infiltrate your thoughts, you're sabotaging any efforts to get pregnant. Couples often feel angry, guilty, anxious, or stressed and at the same time each is experiencing their own different set of emotions. Researchers have discovered that stress affects the release of sex hormones and lowers sperm count, although they don't know why. All these negatives add to the key factors that cause infertility in the first place, and the next thing you know you're on that merry-go-round.

Knowing that the complex interaction between psychological and emotional factors profoundly influences your ability to conceive consciously works to enhance your ability to become pregnant.

By focusing on the emotional aspects of infertility you can use EFT on those feelings that come up during this emotional roller-coaster ride. Using EFT together as a couple (refer to Chapter 8) and individually on each of your own emotions helps to diffuse the stress, leaving you both emotionally and physically relaxed and allowing your bodies' systems to operate naturally.

Below I identify the most common emotions and give some suggested phrases that you can adapt to suit:

> *'Even though I have this mixture of emotions right now . . .'*
>
> *'Even though I can't cope with the pressure . . .'*
>
> ✔ **Anger:**
>
> *'Even though I'm angry at my body . . .'*
>
> *'Even though I'm angry at why me . . .'*
>
> *'Even though this problem is dominating our lives . . .'*
>
> ✔ **Jealousy:**
>
> *'Even though my friends have no problems getting pregnant . . .'*
>
> *'Even though (name) didn't deserve to get pregnant . . .'*
>
> ✔ **Sadness:**
>
> *'Even though I feel sad when I see mothers with their babies . . .'*
>
> *'Even though I have this ache and emptiness inside . . .'*

✔ **Fear:**

'Even though I fear it won't work . . .'

'Even though I fear my partner will leave me . . .'

✔ **Guilt:**

'Even though I have to go back to work . . .'

'Even though I left it too long before trying to get pregnant . . .'

'Even though I feel inadequate . . .'

Here are some suggested positive affirmations that you can add on after acknowledging the problem:

'I love and accept my body and I accept that this isn't my fault.'

'I love and accept myself and I leave behind the past to concentrate on the future.'

'I deeply love and accept my feelings as being natural.'

'I'm ready to release all my negative emotions and allow my body to heal.'

'I have faith in everyone who's trying to help me overcome this.'

Preferably use present tense statements as in 'I am' or 'I have'.

Another useful method is to try visualisation when saying your affirmations:

'I love and accept myself and see myself holding our baby.'

'I accept my body and accept this egg, warm and snug in my womb.'

Also be aware of any core or limiting belief voices in your head (see Chapters 6 and 15).

Giving birth and pregnancy

Emotions don't go away during and after birth. In fact all those hormones are raging around and certainly need some controlling with EFT. Pregnant women who suffer morning sickness or nausea can also benefit from using EFT as often as possible, even before the onset of the feeling. Here are some suggestions to get you started:

'Even though I'm frightened about giving birth . . .'

'Even though I have this pregnancy nausea . . .'

'Even though all my family have had difficult births . . .'

'Even though I fear it will change our relationship . . .'

'Even though it bothers me how we will cope financially . . .'

'Even though I fear I'll lose my independence . . .'

'Even though I don't think I'll make a good mother . . .'

'Even though I have this nausea . . .'

Some possible positive follow-up affirmations are:

'I accept myself and what my body is going through.'

'I love and accept my body and refuse to believe these voices in my head.'

'I choose to believe that I'll be a good mother . . .'

'I choose to remain calm and relaxed, knowing that it's a natural part of life.'

The jury is out on whether using the ankle point in EFT (see Chapter 4) is unwise during pregnancy. To be on the safe side, avoid tapping on this point.

Surviving menopause and middle-age

Whether you experience natural, artificial, or premature menopause, it marks the end of being able to conceive. Some women sail through the menopause with no emotional changes whatsoever, but others may have psychological issues to contend with – on top of all the strange physical effects. The severity of menopause symptoms and how long they last varies from person to person, but with a bit of help from EFT, you can help minimise the symptoms associated with the menopause.

Use EFT on 'hot flushes' and 'night sweats' by saying:

'Even though I'm going through the change, I accept myself deeply and choose not to react.'

'Even though I have this hot flush going on, I accept my bodily changes and choose to remain calm and cool.'

'Even though I feel like I'm on fire, I choose to put the fire out with EFT.'

Middle-age, like the menopause, also defines a change in life. This milestone can cause you to look back on your life and, in turn, brings with it a busload of emotions. Sadness, confusion, guilt – you name it and you probably have it.

While all this negative stuff is going on, remind yourself of your achievements (no matter how small), how life expectancy is extending year-on-year, your wisdom, new-found freedom, and so on. Conquer those limiting beliefs that I refer to in Chapter 15.

Remember to 'chase the pain' with EFT if physical symptoms move around the body.

Dealing with Symptoms Arising from Chronic and Serious Diseases

Using EFT on the symptoms of anyone who has a chronic or serious disease, such as cancer, calls for an experienced practitioner. I've witnessed the many, many occasions where physical symptoms have improved or have gone after EFT released past emotional traumas. Some of these have been instantaneous and others have taken their time. The wait is worth the reward, however.

In this section I give a few examples of how you can use EFT on chronic and serious diseases.

Understanding emotion and illness

Practitioners demonstrated advanced EFT applications on clients with serious diseases at a series of workshops in the US and England. Between 250 and 400 people attended, with a variety of diseases ranging from Parkinson's disease to multiple chemical sensitivity, diabetes, and chronic fatigue syndrome, to name but a few. Many people found that their symptoms relieved during these workshops. Although EFT does work rapidly on most issues, when working on serious diseases you remember that it takes skill, patience, and persistence. It also takes a broader understanding of what the underlying causes are.

You can see the most profound interaction between physical health and emotional health in the way in which your body responds to an illness, and you can find out more on this in Chapter 2. The desire for your body to heal is perfectly natural. EFT rebalances your energy system, thus allowing the free flow of energy – vital to both health and vitality.

Physical ailments often disappear or improve when you treat emotional problems with EFT – and the other way around.

Some questions that may get to the emotional cause of the illness include:

- ✔ What major traumatic events have happened in your life or around the time you developed the disease/illness?
- ✔ Are you holding on to any anger or resentment with this disease/illness or anyone else for that matter?
- ✔ Do you blame anyone or anything for you having this disease/illness?
- ✔ In your own words, what's your worst symptom?
- ✔ What would you like to happen?

The following observations from clients whose symptoms disappeared after using EFT demonstrate the connection between physical symptoms and the mind:

- ✔ A woman has unexplained chronic backache. In her life she has to take on unwanted responsibility and support everyone in her family. The EFT phrase she uses is 'Even though I've had to support everyone in my family and now my back can't support me, I accept myself and forgive anyone who may have contributed to it'.

- ✔ A man's hands are constantly stiff yet investigations into whether he has rheumatoid arthritis come back negative. Further questioning reveals that he's a very inflexible person with rigid views. The EFT phrase is 'Even though I have to be rigid in my views, I accept that others are entitled to their opinions and I ease up on myself and my fingers'.

- ✔ A woman has repeated chronic throat infections. During questioning, she reveals that she was never allowed to speak up when she was a child. Her mother always said that 'little girls should be seen and not heard'. The woman has difficulty asserting herself. First she uses EFT on 'Even though little girls should be seen and not heard, I'm grown up now and I can be heard'. Then she did more work on the childhood problems before getting full relief.

Cancer

Approximately 200 types of cancer exist, along with hundreds of causes and contributors to the disease. Pay close attention to any emotional issues that come up and watch out for any subconscious secondary benefit as I describe in Chapter 6. EFT can help minimise the distress and pain associated with cancer.

Touch and Breathe

Sometimes, when someone is in a great deal of pain or discomfort, tapping physically is impossible because it can cause more pain and discomfort. In these instances, you can get around the problem by using a technique called 'Touch and Breathe'. It works by just holding your fingers on the appropriate points rather than tapping or rubbing. Patients can still enjoy the comforting effects of EFT.

I work voluntarily for a cancer care centre and have trained their volunteers and nurses to use EFT with cancer patients. I find the work to be very rewarding and satisfying as EFT works very effectively not only with cancer pain and associated emotions, but also with the side effects of chemotherapy. Symptoms such as nerve damage, tremors, joint pain, digestive problems, nausea etc have been dramatically reduced or removed with EFT which is why the technique is being used in many hospitals and hospices. You can use the techniques for pain that I describe earlier in this chapter. These are only suggestions and you can create your own as you progress.

Waiting for diagnosis

Use EFT on the anxiety symptoms, both physical and emotional, leading up to the tests, during the waiting period, and even in the waiting room. Some suggestions of what to say may include:

> *'Even though I'm scared of what the result will be, I love and accept who I am and why I feel this way and I choose to remain calm and focused.'*

> *'Even though I have this panic in my chest, I love and accept myself for having this emotion and I choose to feel safe.'*

Undergoing treatment

Again, applying EFT on the effects of the chemotherapy and any emotional symptoms can greatly benefit the sufferer's pain and distress. Remember, the least EFT can do is to instil a feeling of calm, which in itself is beneficial. Here are some EFT phrases to use on the side effects of chemotherapy:

> *'Even though I have this nausea in my stomach, I accept that I need this chemotherapy but I don't accept that I have to have this nausea.'*

> *'Even though I have this sad emotion at losing my hair, I accept my bald self and I accept that my hair will grow back again – it's a small price to pay.'*

> *'Even though my food tastes bland, I deeply love and accept myself.'*

Sometimes using EFT is difficult when parts of the body are sensitive to touch. You can use a simple technique called 'Touch and Breathe' (see the nearby sidebar for more on this technique). This technique entails simply placing fingers on the appropriate EFT points rather than tapping while saying the phrases.

Tapping by proxy, which I mention in Chapter 16, also works very well with patients who you can't tap on or who can't tap for themselves.

Energy

Tiredness, exhaustion, and lethargy are all symptoms of cancer and can have a negative impact on cancer management.

> *'Even though I feel exhausted, I choose to feel energised and strong.'*

> *'Even though I have no motivation, I choose to increase my motivation with tapping.'*

> *'Even though I have no energy because of this cancer, I deeply accept myself and I'm determined to beat it.'*

Visualisation

You can use visualising, such as 'seeing' the cancer cells being destroyed, with the Set-Up Phrase. Some patients give their cancer cells names of people they don't like or descriptions such as 'arrows' or 'black ants'. An example may be:

> *'Even though I have these rogue cancer cells, I now see them being destroyed and replaced with healthy cells.'*

> *'Even though these ants are invading my space, I choose to imagine them leaving and allowing myself to heal.'*

Encourage a safe healing haven in your mind to which you can take yourself when you need, and use it in your Set-Up Phrase. An example may be:

> *'Even though they told me that my treatment isn't working, I choose to retreat to my safe healing haven, where I know that I'll heal.'*

Chapter 14

Secrets of Successful Sleep

. . . .

. . . .

Do you dream of having a good night's sleep? How many times have you lain awake trying to sleep and the harder you try, the more difficult it becomes? Most people have suffered from some type of sleeplessness but when it becomes a long-term problem it can interfere with your health in general, cause you to have an accident, and can even be the cause of some marital breakdowns.

No matter how much sleep you need, if you don't get enough, you suffer the effects of sleep deprivation. A good night's sleep truly makes an enormous difference to your quality of life, and countless clinical cases show that EFT helps people fall asleep and stay asleep, even in times of stress and adversity.

Taking active steps to improve your sleep may be all you need. If you still can't sleep after taking the actions I describe in this chapter, and you have no recognised medical condition, then you need to look at the underlying cause. If you address the underlying cause at the onset of your sleep problems, you have a better chance of preventing your sleeplessness turning into a habit.

If physical pain is keeping you awake refer to Chapter 13 for some help and advice.

Helping Yourself to a Good Night's Rest

Sleep problems can be a consequence of not being able to drift off to sleep for hours or going to sleep immediately but waking up and not being able to go back to sleep. You may feel as if you've had a good night's rest but feel tired the next day as a result of unproductive sleep. Everyone's sleep pattern is different, so six hours' sleep may be okay for one person but not okay for another. Sleep patterns change as you age or when on medication, for instance.

Before you help yourself or someone else to get a good night's sleep with EFT, you need to examine what's causing the sleep problem. Here are some helpful questions you can use to establish the cause. If you can't establish a pattern, try keeping a sleep diary for a week or two.

✔ When did your sleep problem start?

✔ Have there been any recent changes in your life that may coincide with your sleep problem? (New baby, different work pattern, stress, worries, illness, and family problems can all have an effect.)

✔ Does it take you a long time to fall asleep?

✔ Do you fall asleep easily and then wake up in the night?

✔ When you wake up, do you find it difficult to go back to sleep?

After you establish the problem, you need to use EFT on whatever's causing the problem. The sections in this chapter help you find what you're looking for, or you can refer to the index at the back of this book.

More than one cause may exist.

Inducing sleep with EFT

By using EFT daily you notice an improvement in your sleep as a consequence. Using EFT each evening before you go to bed, or when awake at night, at the very least deeply relaxes you. If you use EFT daily on everyday or long-term worries or problems, you should notice an improvement in your sleep as a consequence.

If you don't know the cause of your sleep problem, you can induce sleep by practising the following steps. Keep in mind that the phrases in the steps are only suggestions and you need to use the words that best describe how you feel at that time and follow it up with the outcome that you want. Try these phrases to help you, but familiarise yourself with Chapter 3 before carrying out this exercise because it helps you understand the process.

✔ **Before going to bed:**

 'Even though I won't sleep tonight, I accept myself and decide to relax instead.'

 'Even though I'll wake up during the night because that's what happens, what if I choose to remain relaxed until morning.'

'Although I'll lie awake again tonight, I accept myself, knowing that rest will come soon.'

✔ **While in bed:**

'Even though I can't get to sleep right now, I choose to relax.'

'Although I can't go to sleep, what if I just relaxed.'

'Although I'm still awake and sleep won't come, what if I allow myself to simply drift into a deep, deep rest.'

Although I find it hard to sleep, I accept that my body deserves a rest.'

When you've finished your Set-up Phrase, you can tap on the remaining meridian points using negative words such as 'I won't sleep tonight', 'Sleep eludes me', 'I never sleep right through', 'I'll wake up because that's what I do', 'I'm still awake', 'I'm waiting for the sun to come up', and 'I don't deserve sleep'. Just use whatever negative thoughts come into your head.

If you introduce a positive (as opposed to a negative) 'sleep' statement in your EFT Set-up Phrase, it most likely won't work. The reason for this is if you said, for example, 'Even though I'm wide awake I choose to sleep', this is giving your subconscious a command it doesn't agree with, so it rejects the idea. This is why it's best to use positive phrases such as 'Even though I'm wide awake, I choose to feel pleasantly drowsy', 'My body feels heavy', or 'I feel deeply relaxed' instead.

When you feel relaxed, then you can try introducing positive words as you tap on the remaining meridian points, such as 'I feel gently relaxed', 'I accept I need rest', 'My body feels heavy', or 'I'll operate more efficiently when rested.'

If you're having trouble getting a good night's sleep, start by trying to exclude anything that may interfere with your goal. I offer some suggestions here but you may have your own. Before retiring to your bed:

✔ Remove any distractions (pets, light, TV, and so on) from your bedroom.

✔ Avoid alcohol or caffeine.

✔ Make sure that your mattress and pillow are comfortable and give you enough support.

✔ Ensure that the room temperature is comfortable and that your bedroom is uncluttered.

✔ Keep the room as dark as possible if light tends to wake you up.

✔ Make sure that your feet are warm.

✔ Do whatever it is before bedtime that helps you relax, such as a warm bath, reading, or listening to music.

Calming your mind

Do you have a *monkey mind* in which your thoughts jump from one to another like a monkey jumps from tree to tree? Do you have to pay attention to all the thoughts that pass through your mind?

Set some time aside to identify what anxious thoughts keep you awake at night and try to establish whether a pattern exists. For instance, do you have difficulty in sleeping on a Sunday before your first day back at work on a Monday? Or the night before you're due to visit someone or travel somewhere?

Modern-day concerns awake the primal fear in you so that when you start to think anxious thoughts, your body is in a state of alert. Of course you mustn't go to sleep right now; you have to be vigilant and on guard – it's a primitive response and one that keeps you awake.

Do you know someone who worries when they have nothing to worry about? Most worriers have an imaginary list of worries a mile and a half long. Chronic worriers can develop this pattern of behaviour into a habit, so the sooner they get rid of this type of behaviour, the better.

If anxious thoughts are interfering with your sleep, consider whether worrying benefits you. The idea of a benefit from worrying may seem silly but some people feel that, in order to please others, they have to make sure that everything is perfect – and unless they worry it won't be. Others may feel that they have to work hard in order to prove that they're worthy – and worrying makes them feel that they're working hard. And some people deliberately burden themselves with worry to draw attention to themselves to reinforce the feeling of being needed or wanted. If any of these reasons apply to you, then you need to use EFT on them to ensure a good night's sleep.

To use EFT on your worries, you first need to identify them. This scale measures how much you worry. You score yourself from 1 to 5 on the following statements. A rating of 1 means the statement doesn't describe you at all, and 5 means it describes you perfectly. Higher total scores mean higher worry levels. If you're worried on a constant basis, you may want to take a look at Chapter 9 on fighting fears, phobias, and anxieties.

This is only a guide – don't use it to determine whether you have an anxiety disorder.

- ✔ If I don't have enough time to do everything, I don't worry about it.
- ✔ My worries overwhelm me.
- ✔ I don't tend to worry about things.
- ✔ I know I shouldn't worry about things, but I just can't help it.

✔ When I'm under pressure, I worry a lot.

✔ I'm always worrying about something.

✔ I find it easy to dismiss worrying thoughts.

✔ As soon as I finish one task, I start to worry about everything else I have to do.

✔ I never worry about anything.

✔ When there's nothing more I can do about something, I don't worry about it any more.

✔ I've been a worrier all my life.

✔ I notice that I've been worrying about things.

✔ Once I start worrying I can't stop.

✔ I worry all the time.

✔ I worry about projects until they're finished.

When you've identified your highest scoring statements, try using EFT on each of them. The following steps give you an idea of how to go about it:

1. **Complete the following thoughts:**

   • 'Even though I'm worried about . . .'

   For example, say you're worrying about work. Then you may use a Set-up Phrase in the following way: 'Even though I'm worried about a project at work, I accept myself and choose to rest, knowing that rest will help me concentrate . . .'.

   • 'Even though I can't stop my mind worrying . . .'

   The Set-up Phrase may be 'Even though I can't stop my mind worrying, what would happen if I allowed my mind to relax for once'.

   • 'Even though I've been a worrier all my life . . .'

   The Set-up Phrase may be 'Even though I've always been a worrier, I no longer want this job because I have better things to do with my time'.

2. **The section on 'Inducing Sleep with EFT', earlier in this chapter, section has some EFT ideas you can use.**

3. **You can also ask yourself who else could do the job of worrying better? Apart from losing sleep, what do you achieve by worrying in the middle of the night?**

The key is to name the problem and focus on the positive outcome that you want.

Dealing with restless leg syndrome

Restless leg syndrome (RLS) is a debilitating condition suffered by many millions of people. If you or someone you know suffers from RLS, you no doubt understand how it interferes with your sleep, causing daytime fatigue. Typical symptoms are an involuntary urge to move your leg accompanied by tingly prickling sensations that can become worse during periods of inactivity. This restless feeling can also affect arms and the torso. Many people also experience RLS while flying, which can be quite uncomfortable. If you're in a deep sleep you may not be fully aware of your jerking limbs, but they can wake you up or disturb your sleep as you move to a more comfortable position.

The cause of RLS and how to treat it is a matter of much controversy among physicians. Medication is usually temporary and can even aggravate the condition. Research is continuing but no known cure exist – yet this doesn't seem to stop many advertisers who offer a cure within days.

You can use EFT on RLS and you may want to know the best way to tackle it.

Symptoms can be difficult for the sufferer to describe, which makes it important to use your words, whether it's 'itchy legs', 'creepy crawly legs', or even 'this feeling in my legs I can't describe'.

First, at the onset of RLS, try carrying out the full EFT routine (see Chapter 3), including finger points, Nine Gamut Procedure, inside wrist, and top of head while fully concentrating on what's happening and where. Your Set-Up Phrase may be something like:

> *'Even though I have this uncomfortable feeling in my (state specific part of leg), I deeply and completely love and accept my body and my leg.'*

> *'Even though this twitching is driving me mad, I accept myself and my leg, knowing that it will soon be rested.'*

You may need to do about three or four rounds of EFT using the negative phrases until you find some relief. When you do start to feel some relief, try introducing some positive phrases as you tap on the remaining meridian points, using words such as 'My leg feels rested' or 'My legs feel calm'.

Handling Dreaming and Nightmares

Dreams can be wonderful, frightening, disturbing, and powerful. In your dreams you can be anyone you like, do what you like. Nightmares are vivid dreams that can cause feelings of fear and anxiety, although not all nightmares are disturbing. Did you know that the most common emotion experienced in dreams is anxiety? Probably because you have no control during your dreamlike state!

Famous dreamers

On the morning of 22 November 1963 I was only 9 years old. I came downstairs and told my mother about a disturbing dream I'd had about President John F Kennedy. (In case you're wondering how I knew about him at 9 years of age, my family were Irish Catholics and they put photos of John F Kennedy alongside those of the Pope in our house.) I told my mother that I saw the president in a car, waving, and crowds were shouting and waving back. The next thing I heard a bang and the picture in my dream went blurry. I then saw Jackie Kennedy bending over the president, and she was crying. Then I woke up. I thought no more of this dream until early in the evening when a news bulletin appeared on TV showing 'my dream'. I had other 'premonition type' dreams before and after that but none were as memorable as the death of President Kennedy.

I'm not famous because of my dreams but some people are:

- **Paul McCartney:** Woke up with the song 'Yesterday' in his head as a result of a dream. The song went on to become the most covered version of any song ever written.

- **Abraham Lincoln:** Dreamed about his own death.

- **Elias Howe:** Had a dream about a bunch of natives with holes in the tips of their spears. This solved his problem of where to put the hole in the needle and led to the invention of the sewing machine in 1845.

- **Jack Nicklaus:** Improved his golf handicap after trying out a new golf swing that he visualised in a dream.

- **Stephen King:** Gets many of the ideas for his horror books from dreams – or should that be nightmares!

- **Robert Louis Stevenson:** Conceived the classic novel *Dr Jekyll and Mr Hyde* from a dream.

- **Morgan Robertson:** Wrote a novel in 1898, which he called *Futility*. The novel was based on a dream he had. In his dream there was large cruise liner that carried many people. It was sailing across the Atlantic at a speed of 23 knots on a foggy night. He observed with nervousness that there were only 24 lifeboats for the 2,000 passengers and crew. He heard the words 'unsinkable', and then saw an iceberg. Just before he woke up he saw the name on the ship – *The Titan*. Notice the similarities with the sinking of the *Titanic*?

Considered the father of psychoanalysis, Sigmund Freud believed that dreams are an outlet for the subconscious, and the repressed emotions that lie there. For example, you can repress a bad relationship or loss of a close one, and redirect the anger for the loss towards the 'inner self', so that it only emerges during dreams or through regression. Freud's theories are difficult to prove, but while no one can disprove them, they're very popular among many psychologists, and the relevance of some dreams to people's lives indicates that they're of some significance. So the next time you're battling it out with a big monster in your dreams, it may be because you're fighting for a pay rise with your boss.

You can use EFT on your dreams and nightmares in many ways. Before you go to sleep, tap on the anticipation of having the dream or nightmare. When you wake up, tap on the emotion you feel then or felt during that dream. Even tap on the part of the dream or nightmare that causes you distress. (For more on the EFT approach, see Chapter 3.)

If you're still feeling disturbed the next day by a dream or nightmare, use EFT on the negative feelings.

If recalling the dream or memory is causing some distress, try using one of the gentle approaches of EFT that I give in Chapter 5.

Part V
Exploring Other Avenues

The 5th Wave   By Rich Tennant

"I'm almost certain you're not supposed to perform EFT while eating 'Cheese Puffs,' unless there's some therapeutic value to having yellow spots all over your face."

In this part . . .

Ever felt you could make more of yourself? This part walks you through using EFT to break down barriers to personal success, whatever you might want to do with your life.

Read on to get a handle on how to empower others too, whether by using EFT with your kids, or sizing up the possibilities of EFT as a career or business.

Chapter 15

Empowering Yourself and Others

. . . .

. . . .

*F*eelings of not going anywhere in life or a belief that something's holding you back are quite common complaints from most people and yet EFT can remove them. If the words 'I feel empowered' or 'I'm motivated' get stuck in your throat, this chapter helps you recognise how you can free yourself from your own and others' beliefs that are restraining you. This chapter also introduces language techniques that you can use to great effect with EFT. At the end of the day, empowerment comes from within – you just have to know how to access it, that's all.

The Law of Attraction

The Law of Attraction works on the basis that your conscious or unconscious thoughts, actions, or beliefs attract corresponding negative or positive experiences. A major film called *The Secret* is based on this concept and tells us that sending out positive messages to the universe brings back positive rewards.

Well, I can tell you that the real secret is knowing that no one thinks positively all the time. With the majority of people an inner dialogue is going on, sabotaging every attempt to succeed. You can wish for success but if you're scared of what you'll do with it when you get it or you've been ' programmed' into believing that you're not good enough, you're wasting your time and efforts.

I expect you can remember the times you've talked yourself out of doing what you wanted to do and done something else instead – and then wondered why you never achieved your goal. You've nothing to worry about if this happens very infrequently, but when it happens more often than not, you won't move forward. Do you think people are driven and motivated because they don't like themselves, their shortcomings, or inadequacies? No, people become driven after they change their negative thinking about themselves.

What you need to do is remove all self-doubts with EFT beforehand and the following sections help you with this. Helping your client discover how to apply EFT on himself is about as empowering as you can make him feel.

Putting a Lid on Limiting Beliefs

A *belief* is a thought you hang on to that you trust deeply. Believing in Father Christmas is harmless; believing that when dark clouds loom overhead it's likely to rain is sensible. You seldom question your beliefs because you hold them to be truths, right? What about the other beliefs you have in general that may be 'All girls who wear low-cut tops and lots of make-up are easy', 'Anyone over 40 is old', or 'Young boys who drive flash cars must be drug dealers'. These generalised beliefs aren't only unfounded, they can be dangerous.

Much like negative core beliefs (see Chapter 7), negative limiting beliefs are what you hold buried deep within your subconscious, and they're often tied in with self-image or perceptions about the world. As a result, they trigger automatic reactions and behaviours.

You can see limiting beliefs both in animals and people. For example, Washington DC zoo kept a magnificent white tiger named Mohini, the first to be kept in the US, in a 12 foot by 12 foot cage. Eventually, the zoo built a new habitat for her with several acres of hills, trees, a pond, and vegetation. The zookeeper released Mohini from her cage into her new environment, but to everyone's dismay Mohini continued to pace back and forth within her 12 by 12 area.

Here's a sample of limiting beliefs you may have:

✔ You hold stubborn and often unreasonable opinions: 'All rich people are dishonest.'

✔ You have specific capabilities, traits, or behaviours that you believe you can't change: 'I'm hopeless at driving.'

✔ You believe a particular action or result is the only way to resolve a problem: 'Spare the rod and you spoil the child.'

✔ You'll never succeed so why bother: 'I'm not going for that new job because they'll only want someone with better qualifications than mine, so what's the point.'

Breaking the barrier

In the year I was born, 1954, the sporting world still didn't believe that a human being could run a mile in under four minutes. They said it wasn't possible, it couldn't be done, and that it was beyond human endurance. On 6 May 1954 the English athlete Roger Bannister became the first person to break the four-minute mile barrier. Within 56 days, John Landy broke Bannister's record in 3 minutes and 57.9 seconds in Finland. By 1957, 16 other runners had also broken the four-minute mile. These results show that, after you remove your mental barriers or limiting beliefs, anything is possible.

An interesting connection exists between your conscious mind and your subconscious. Your subconscious is tasked with the responsibility of making what you consciously believe is true, actually come true – well, at least to the best of your subconscious mind's ability to make it true. In other words, if you think you can do something, you can, and, if you think you can't, you can't, or as Henry Ford said, 'Whether you can or you can't – you're right.'

Look out for clients who cling on to limiting beliefs for safety reasons. Hidden behind these beliefs may be fear of death, loneliness, low self-esteem, poor self-image, ignorance, guilt, childhood trauma, or bad childhood memories. You need to use EFT on these.

You may not always be aware of your limiting beliefs so you can tap and ask yourself 'Even though I don't know what's stopping me from (action), I accept myself'. If you can remember, why not try this:

1. **Write down the limiting belief you have.**

   For example 'Rich people are dishonest'.

2. **Listen to your inner dialogue that goes with that phrase.**

   It may be telling you 'In order for me to be rich, I need to be dishonest'.

3. **Ask yourself what past experiences reinforce that belief?**

   Examples may be 'My landlord made lots of money by being dishonest' or 'My boss who owned the company used to fiddle his accounts'.

4. **Consider whether any of these experiences have lead you to your belief.**

   If yes, use EFT as follows: 'Even though I believe all rich people are dishonest, I accept that I'm basing my opinion on my landlord and my boss and not all people who are rich.'

   If any 'ifs' and 'buts' remain, refer to the later section 'Hearing the "Ifs" and "Buts"'. If you think you may be scared of failing or succeeding, you can find information and advice on this further into the chapter also.

Acting like you own the place

Possessing a thick accent, a surname like Schwarzenegger, and coming from a childhood that was anything but privileged hasn't interfered with Arnold becoming a successful body-builder, Hollywood actor, and governor of California. As he says, 'The mind is really so incredible. Before I won my first Mr Universe title I walked around the tournament like I owned it. I had won it so many times in my mind, the title was already mine. Then when I moved on to the movies I used the same technique. I visualised daily being a successful actor and earning big money.'

Tuning into Your RAS

Have you heard of your *reticular activating system* (RAS)? It's in the oldest part of your brain and is responsible for your sleeping, eating, arousal, and motivation. It also acts as your inbuilt radar system. Have you ever been in a crowded room with people talking and laughing, music going, and other distracting noises, yet don't take much notice of any of it until you hear your name being mentioned? Suddenly, your ears prick up. This sudden alertness is because you've subconsciously instructed your RAS to listen out for your name. A similar thing happens after you buy a new car. Before you bought this particular make and model you probably didn't notice many on the road, but now they're everywhere – or so it seems.

What's interesting about your RAS is that you can programme it to achieve your goals. More interestingly, because your RAS can't distinguish between what's real and what isn't, it basically believes anything you tell it, whether this is true or not. If you don't believe me, try telling a child not to spill their drink whatever happens, or telling yourself you mustn't mention so and so's name in conversation. How often does the opposite happen?

If you want something in life, try focusing your attention in the future on what you want as opposed to what you don't want.

If you think it's that simple then why doesn't this concept work for everyone? Read the later section in this chapter 'Putting a Lid on Limiting Beliefs' to understand why.

Developing Your Ultimate Truth Statement

Sometimes intangible issues exist, generally around your beliefs, that are difficult to measure. If you have a problem with your own confidence, for example, and you want to use EFT to improve this, how do you apply EFT for it and how can you measure whether it's effective or not?

The Ultimate Truth Statement is a statement of your belief in the outcome. So, if you lack confidence, you start off by making a statement about where you want to be, such as 'I'm 100 per cent confident'. Now, do you really believe that statement? Probably not, so you measure your belief in the statement. This time, rather than measuring improvements by how the numbers go down, you're aiming to go from a zero to 10.

This is mostly for intangible issues and not efficient to use for trauma, depression, or other complex problems.

The following steps walk you through the exercise. (I suggest studying the tapping routine in Chapter 4 before embarking on this exercise.)

1. **State the phrase where you want to be.**

   For example 'I will sleep well tonight' or 'I'm 100 per cent confident I'll achieve my goal weight'. Don't measure on what you feel at this very moment, but measure on where you want to be.

2. **Rate the belief of your statement, with 10 being 100 per cent belief and zero no belief at all.**

   Your rating will probably be around 5 or 6 and your ultimate aim is to get to 10 and not the usual zero.

3. **Tap for 'Even though I'm not 100 per cent confident, I'll achieve my goal weight. I love and accept myself.'**

4. **After two or three rounds using the Reminder Phrase start introducing positive phrases such as 'I'd really like to be confident' and 'I'm gradually moving towards where I want to be'.**

5. **As you complete these steps, check your rating.**

   Your rating should be moving up. If it's not moving up, check whether any hidden issues (refer to Chapter 6) are in the way and use EFT on each to eliminate them.

6. **When your rating is 7 or higher, start with the Set-Up Phrase from Step 1 and switch to a Choice Phrase (see 'Choosing for yourself', later in this chapter).**

   For example 'Even though part of me is still not 100 per cent confident, I choose to find it within me to eliminate this lack of confidence', 'I choose to let the bigger part of me win', or 'Even though part of me is still resistant . . .'.

7. **Check the rating again and if it is at 8 do more choices.**

   For example, tap on the eyebrow and say 'remaining resistance . . .'; side of eye: 'I choose to believe . . .'; under eye: 'remaining resistance . . .'; under nose: I choose to believe . . .'; and so on. Then rate the belief again.

8. **If you're up to 9, tap on any remaining lack of confidence or whatever is in the way with the Nine Gamut Procedure (the back of hand and eye roll; see Chapter 3).**

9. **Finish with one round of all positive phrases.**

You know if it's worked when you can say the statement out loud and mean it.

If you see little or no movement, check whether fear of success or failure may be getting in the way.

You can use this technique for times when you can't progress, lack confidence or motivation, procrastinate, and – one that was familiar to me – have writer's block!

Hearing the 'Ifs' and 'Buts'

If you're not getting anywhere with EFT on your goals or aspirations, maybe your subconscious is setting up an objection. Although on a conscious level you have a desire to change, your subconscious voice is coming up with objections in the form of 'ifs' and 'buts' for a variety of reasons. These objections may sound like excuses and they're in a way, but they have underlying reasons that you must address in order for EFT to work.

The annoying thing is that you or your client may not realise that these 'ifs' and 'buts' are there, but when EFT doesn't work they may well be the reason for your lack of success. Removing the objections with EFT clears the way to work on the positive outcome.

Table 15-1 shows some examples:

Table 15-1	Using EFT to Remove 'Ifs' and 'Buts'
Positive Outcome with Added 'Ifs' and 'Buts'	*EFT Set-up Phrase to Remove 'Ifs' and 'Buts'*
'I want to be promoted but if I'm promoted I'll lose my friends.'	'Even though I may lose my friends if I'm promoted, I completely accept myself.'
'I want this backache to go away but if it does I'll be expected to help around the house.'	'Even though I'll be expected to do my share of the work when this backache goes, I still accept myself.'
'I want to be happy but when I'm happy bad things usually happen.'	'Even though I want to be happy but when I am bad things happen, I accept that these are my beliefs based on past experiences and I choose to change my beliefs.'

Fearing Success

For a moment, imagine achieving a long-awaited goal or desire and being in the state of feeling, hearing, and seeing that achievement. How does it honestly make you feel? Does it make you feel motivated or slightly uncomfortable? If you feel uncomfortable then you most likely have a fear of success.

Just like the psychological reversal that I describe in Chapter 6, fear of success, or failure for that matter, can hinder progress with EFT. You may not even recognise that you have a fear of success until you start using avoidance behaviours and expressions such as:

- ✔ If I make a lot of money, my friends won't want to know me any more.
- ✔ If I'm promoted, there'll be a lot of jealousy. They'll say I've got above my station.
- ✔ If I end this relationship and meet someone else, I may be going out of the frying pan into the fire. I'm best staying with who I know.

Perhaps you prefer to avoid responsibility or believe that achieving your goal in life means change. Many people find change difficult to handle and it can bring on all sorts of fears. Being in your 'comfort zone' is far safer.

You can find out if you have a fear of success if you agree with any of these statements:

- ✔ You have no faith in your own ability to maintain your progress and the accomplishments you've achieved in your life.
- ✔ Even if you accomplish all that you set out to, you still won't be happy, content, or satisfied.
- ✔ You don't deserve all the good things and recognitions that come your way, even though they're a result of your accomplishments and successes.
- ✔ You fear that what you've achieved so far can self-destruct at any time.
- ✔ No matter how much you're able to achieve or accomplish, it's never enough to sustain success or happiness.
- ✔ Obviously, there are others out there who are better than you, who'll replace you if you don't maintain your success.
- ✔ Success is an end in itself; yet that end is not enough to sustain your interest and/or commitment.
- ✔ After you achieve the goals you've worked diligently for, you fear the motivation to continue will fade.

Your emotions are the language of your subconscious mind and they function in every cell of your body, giving you continual feedback about your non-conscious or hidden self. You need to apply EFT to each and every fear that's stopping you reaching your goal. If necessary, seek the help of an EFT practitioner.

An EFT phrase for a person who fears success is 'Even though I fear my achievements (be as specific here as you can) will self-destruct at any time, I deeply and completely accept myself.'

Use EFT on all the experiences that have attributed to these fears.

Being Scared of Failure

Adults become preoccupied with the opinions of others because of society's difficulty in accepting failure. People believe that they have to work harder, and accomplish more, in order to please the boss. The boss replaces the parent, and people see their boss as the approval giver.

Fear of failure often comes with low self-esteem and with it comes rejection, perfection, shame, not being good enough, and guilt issues. It can even come in the guise of arrogance. EFT takes care of these easily, but you need to be thorough. For others, a fear of failure can be equally de-motivating and can prohibit them seeking challenges or opportunities.

If you have doubts about your worthiness then check out Chapter 7, which deals with low self-esteem. If you have feelings of being stuck in life, you may find Chapter 6 helpful.

When you take on a challenge begin by writing down all the positives and negatives. Starting up in business was daunting for me, which brought up a whole host of questions in my mind and most of them, I admit, were negative. To put them into perspective, I sat down with a piece of paper and wrote down all the negative thoughts I could think of. I then used EFT on each and every one until I realised my real fear was what other people would think if I failed. After I got those worries out of the way I could hear a different voice saying, 'How do you know the answer to these questions unless you try?' That reminded me of Michael Jordan saying, 'I can accept failure but I can't accept not trying.'

Recognising that you have a fear of success or failure is a big step in the right direction. Using EFT on the fear itself enables you to remove any sabotaging thoughts or actions. You can then use some positive phrases to feel better about yourself.

You need to use EFT daily for both fear of success and fear of failure because of the many hidden issues surrounding them.

Driving ambition

As a boy Gordon was physically beaten and verbally abused by his father, who was always telling Gordon he was no good. Gordon grew up determined to make his father proud of him and gain his approval. This boy became Gordon Ramsay, the famous chef, who openly attributes his relentless drive and ambition to his fear of rejection by his father. Although Gordon's father died in 1999, he still relentlessly keeps striving for perfection.

Running with EFT

Depending on your issue, you may be using EFT up to 15 or 20 times a day but find that you can't set this time aside easily. You don't always need to set time aside; in fact, you can use EFT during the course of your everyday activities. If you can use 'your point' (refer to Chapter 4) this is quicker, but if not, even tapping on some of your meridians will hardly raise eyebrows. I've often performed EFT on myself and others in a variety of places including a crowded hospital waiting room.

Here are some of my suggestions on where you can use EFT:

- During a walk, especially if you're clearing the air after a disagreement.
- In the lift.
- While waiting for a bus, train, or tram or as a passenger.
- In the sauna or steam room. (You can also concentrate on your health issues.)
- While sitting in the cinema or theatre. (You can also use EFT for any emotion that comes up from what you're watching!)
- In the shower (also, to get you motivated in the morning).

If you're too busy to use EFT on a regular basis, check out whether or not you're using the avoidance tactics I mention in the next section. Busy people don't have the chance to look at their underlying problems, so people with self-esteem issues often hide their true feelings of inadequacy by staying busy, busy, busy. Try using EFT to give yourself permission (refer to Chapter 6) to stop or slow down. Your body will thank you for it.

Dragging Your Feet

Procrastinating, hesitating, and deliberating all mean the same thing – you're putting off until tomorrow what you can do today. I admit, I too can easily be distracted by what, to my mind, are more interesting things.

Of all the reasons that exist as to why you put things off, the one thing they all have in common is that they're all emotional. When you use avoidance behaviour you're probably feeling anxious, but other emotions may be attached as well. You need to ask what or who is causing the procrastination. If you have feelings of inadequacy, for instance, find out where these feelings originated, if you can, and use EFT on each one. Here are some emotions that may be lurking behind the procrastination:

✔ Anger at being criticised or at yourself.

✔ Guilt at not being motivated.

✔ Anxiety about making a wrong decision.

✔ Shame at not achieving your goal.

✔ Feelings of inadequacy – not being good enough.

✔ Resentment at always being responsible.

Take a look at the other headings within this chapter to see what else may also contribute to procrastination. Above all else, remember to accept yourself for who you are.

De-cluttering Your Life

Feeling 'stuck' in life, having a tendency to procrastinate, or feeling that you're unable to move forward is an indication that you need to de-clutter your life. Putting things off to another day only drains you of your energy, and when you're able to let go, you'll notice a huge emotional lift.

When we, as a family of four, sold our family home after 25 years, we were able to remain emotionally detached because I explained to the family that objects and bricks and mortar didn't mean anything. It was us staying together as a family that was important.

If you have difficulty letting go, whether it's clutter in your house or heart, EFT can be of enormous benefit.

Whether it's tidying your house or organising your wardrobe, your finances, or your relationship, could some underlying emotion be preventing you from sorting it out? Could your procrastination stem from not wanting to confront unpleasant memories? Here are some EFT phrases:

'Even though I have this sad feeling at throwing these memories out, I can still have my memories without these objects.'

'Even though I have this anxiety just thinking of throwing (object) out, I completely accept myself.'

'Even though I have this fear of letting go of, I deeply and completely accept myself.'

Consider recycling items or giving them to charity.

Objects only have the meanings that you give or attach to them.

Improving Your Game

Regardless of whether you play golf, cricket, football, rugby, hockey, tennis, or any other sport, the difference between an average performance and an outstanding performance lies within your head. You can avoid your emotions interfering with your skills and talents.

Many golf players, for instance, sit within their *comfort zone* – the place they regard as being within their level of ability. This comfort zone can apply to a scoring range or a handicap. Whether these players have the ability to improve on that perfect pitching shot or not doesn't matter, because it's much safer to keep within their comfort zone. By doing so, they avoid anxiety and tension creeping in. When they try to improve on their performance, they end up making a lousy job of it. Is it any wonder, when self-doubt sabotages all efforts?

No matter what your doubts or negative beliefs are, EFT can eliminate them. Here are some phrases that you can use for many sporting emotions:

'Even though I'm holding my anger in my stiff back, I deeply accept myself and choose to release this anger.'

'Even though my golf swing is useless, I recognise that I'm working within my comfort zone and I choose to break free.'

'Even though I have a weak backhander, I accept myself and I'm willing to be strong.'

'Even though my emotions get in the way of my performance, I forgive myself and anyone else who may contribute to this.'

But why stop there? Don't forget to tap on any physical symptoms, like a stiff back, as well as the emotional blockages.

Borrowing Benefits from Someone Else's Session

While working on a volunteer in an open session, Gary Craig, the founder of EFT, discovered by accident that, when the audience tapped along at the same time, the audience's issues reduced or cleared, even though their issues were different to the volunteer's. The term became known as *borrowing benefits* simply because you benefit from someone else's EFT session.

If you're conversant with and have sufficient knowledge of EFT to conduct a borrowing benefits session, here's a suggested format:

1. **Explain to the participants what's going to happen.**

   The session should last approximately 2½ hours, which gives time to introduce EFT and demonstrate on a few people from the audience, plus have a debriefing session at the end.

2. **Ask the participants to bring along a list of approximately four or five issues that they'd like to work on.**

   See Chapter 6 on clearing your own issues.

3. **As the EFT practitioner, act as the group leader and invite a volunteer out front to demonstrate EFT on his problem.**

4. **Ask the audience to focus on their problems and rate them.**

5. **Use the shortcut technique (refer to Chapter 4) on the volunteer.**

6. **As you do Step 5, have the audience tap along using the words you and the volunteer use.**

   In effect, they're tapping along with the volunteer while keeping their own problems running in the background.

7. **Tell the audience to rate their problems again, and where they see no change, to use the remaining phrase.**

Although very rare, using this technique may bring up some other hidden issues with a member of the audience. If this happens to you, stop immediately and either take the opportunity to dig deeper into this issue or, alternatively, seek the help of an EFT practitioner as soon as you can. If you can't identify the problem, try tapping for 'Even though something else bothers me about this and I don't know what it is, I completely accept myself'.

Cleaning Up Your Words

Words can be very empowering and no more so than in a therapeutic situation. When you use constant emotional words you cause experiences within you that take you in the direction of those words. Clients use metaphors to describe how they feel because it's easier, so you need to be on the look out for them.

A *metaphor* is is a figure of speech in which the expression used refers to something it only resembles. An example is 'Life is just a bowl of cherries.' Remember, though, not to confuse a metaphor with a simile. Although they're quite alike, a *simile* is a comparison to something else, such as 'That building is as tall as the Eiffel Tower'.

I scatter metaphors liberally throughout this book. Think about the words you use to describe your energy levels, for instance. They often make comparisons to a battery: 'feeling *flat*', 'need to *recharge*', or even 'I feel *powered up*'. For centuries people have used metaphors as a natural way of describing health – With descriptions such as 'this *knot* in my stomach' or 'this *stabbing* pain', for example. Metaphors not only provide the therapist with an accurate description of the client's symptoms, but you can also use them with imagery techniques to promote self-healing.

Imagine that a client tells you he has a feeling of 'being stuck' – where do you go from there? For a start, the words 'being stuck' have different meanings to different people, depending on their experiences in life. To you they may mean 'standing still', to another they may mean 'facing a brick wall', and to your client they may mean 'unable to find my way out'.

The late psychotherapist David Grove developed a style of questioning called *clean language*, aimed at eliciting answers from the client without the therapist 'contaminating' the meaning. Using questioning techniques is a great way of gaining an understanding into what your client actually means and where the meaning has come from.

Here are some basic language question from David Grove's method that I've adapted to fit in with EFT. (You can bring in any questions of your own as long as you remember to use the client's own words.)

✔ And (client's words) is like what?

✔ And what does (client's words) remind you of?

✔ And when you hear (client's words) where do you feel (client's words) that in your body?

✔ And is there a relationship between (client's words) and (client's words)?

✔ And what happens just before (client's words)?

✔ And where does this (client's words) come from?

✔ And what would you like to have happen?

✔ And what needs to happen for (client's words) to happen?

Going back to the client 'feeling stuck', here's an example of questions that you can use and an illustration of using EFT at the same time. While asking the questions and listening to the answers, the therapist taps on the client's meridians from eyebrow to under the arm:

Therapist: And feeling stuck is like what?

Client: It's like I can't find a way out.

Therapist: And what does not finding your way out remind you of?

Client: The time I failed my exams.

Therapist: And where did that 'failed your exams' come from?

Client: It came from my dad who said I'd never find my way in the world.

Therapist: And do you feel your dad's words 'never find your way in the world' anywhere in your body?

Client: Yes, they're in my head. Him saying that makes me angry.

Therapist: And what would you like to happen?

Client: I'd like these words out of my head so I can be free.

Therapist: And what number from zero to 10 would you give these words in your head, with 10 being the highest?

Client: They're an 8.

The therapist then uses the Set-Up Phrase 'Even though I'm angry because my dad said I'll never find my way in the world, I've decided to let go of these words in my head so I can be free', or 'I let go of these words and any anger; I forgive my dad'. Then carry out a Reminder Phrase of 'never find my way in the world', 'It's in my head', 'I can't find a way out', 'It's stuck in my head', 'this anger', 'my dad's words', and so on until the client can recall the same words without any emotion. Then do a round of alternate positive and negative phrases (see the later section 'Combining the negative with the positive'), always ending on a positive, followed by a full round of positive phrases.

ANECDOTE

Maybe it's a good thing – or maybe not

A very old Chinese Taoist story describes a farmer in a poor country village. He was considered very well-to-do because he owned a horse, which he used for ploughing and for transportation. One day his horse ran away. All his neighbours exclaimed how terrible this was, but the farmer simply said, 'Maybe.'

A few days later the horse returned and brought two wild horses with it. The neighbours all rejoiced at his good fortune, but the farmer just said, 'Maybe.'

The next day the farmer's son tried to ride one of the wild horses; the horse threw him and broke his leg. The neighbours all offered their sympathy for his misfortune, but the farmer again said, 'Maybe.'

The next week conscription officers came to the village to take young men for the army. They rejected the farmer's son because of his broken leg. When the neighbours told him how lucky he was, the farmer replied, 'Maybe.'

The meaning that any event has depends upon the 'frame' in which you perceive it. When you change the frame, you change the meaning. Having two wild horses is a good thing until you see it in the context of the son's broken leg. The broken leg seems to be bad in the context of peaceful village life, but in the context of conscription and war, it suddenly becomes good. This is called reframing: changing the frame in which a person perceives events in order to change the meaning. When the meaning changes, the person's responses and behaviours also change.

Taking a tip from Tom Sawyer

In *The Adventures of Tom Sawyer*, Tom had to whitewash a fence while his friends went to play. Tom's friend Ben laughed at Tom for having to work.

Tom: 'Well, what do you call work?'

Ben: 'Why, ain't that work?'

Tom continued to whitewash and said in a casual manner, 'Well, maybe it is and maybe it ain't – all I know is it suits Tom Sawyer.'

Ben: 'Oh come on now, you don't mean to let on that you like it?'

Tom: 'Like it? Well I don't see why I oughtn't to like it. Does a boy get the chance to whitewash a fence every day?'

That put things in a new light for Ben and soon Ben and the rest of Tom's friends were even paying to whitewash the fence.

Your subconscious mind has to have a reason or validate meanings. Whether true or untrue, conscious or unconscious, your conscious has to validate and give a reason for your actions so it validates the meaning to make it fit. You need to use EFT on each of the beliefs to bring about a change.

Another creative way of using words is to incorporate those that are personal to the client. Take a look at this scenario: An army officer came to see me because he had a fear of heights. The therapy session revealed that his fear began when he nearly fell out of a window when he was 5 years old. To begin with I worked on the memory of his fear as a 5-year-old with 'Even though I have this fear in my stomach of falling out of a window when I was 5, I accept that 5-year-old fear and I accept myself'. The words I incorporated during his EFT session were 'marching', 'ordering', 'lining up', and so on.

Reframing to See Things Differently

Reframing isn't about making everything wonderful and rosy; it's about viewing behaviours or situations from a different perspective to the one you're used to. For example, say that you have an old painting lying unnoticed in the attic and one day you decide to put it into an expensive frame and suddenly it's become a work of art. By reframing that painting you've changed its meaning. Most people learned the meaning of words and how to reframe them from an early age, and you'll find some examples in this section. Milton Erickson, the famous hypnotherapist, often used reframing in his work with clients to bring about a subconscious change.

Reframing isn't new. Many fables and fairytales include behaviours or events that change their meaning when the frames around them change. The different-looking chick seems to be an ugly duckling, but he turns out to be a swan – more beautiful than the ducks he's been comparing himself to. Reindeer Rudolph's funny-looking red nose becomes useful for guiding Santa's sleigh on a foggy night.

With EFT you can use reframing during the Set-Up Phrase to help shift a perspective from negative to positive. Table 15-2 lists some examples.

Table 15-2	Real-Life Reframing Examples
Scenario	*Possible Reframe*
'Even though my wife is too willing to help others . . .'	'I may need that sort of help one day.'
'Even though my son always has an opinion . . .'	'At least he'll be able to stand up for himself when he leaves home.'
Even though my boyfriend is mean with money . . .'	'I feel safe knowing that he'll never give it all away.'
'Even though after several attempts I still fail . . .'	'At least I'm tenacious and determined.'

Try writing down some phrases and possible reframes to give you some practice.

'What If' Statements

Using 'What If' Statements during EFT is a great way of opening up the possibility of achieving a goal. Introduce them when any 'limiting beliefs' exist. Similar to other techniques that I describe within this chapter, 'What If' Statements bypass any inner conflict and you can use them for physical and emotional issues. Here's an example for someone who's been told that they'll have pain for the rest of their life:

> *'Even though I've been told this pain is with me for life, I love my body as it is.'*
>
> *'Even though the pain will never go away, I deeply accept myself anyway.'*
>
> *'Even though I believe this pain is there for a reason, I absolutely and completely accept myself with this belief.'*

> Eyebrow: *'What if I have held on to this pain because of my belief?'*
>
> Side of eye: *'What if I can heal my body with EFT?'*
>
> Under eye: *'What if I choose to be free?'*
>
> Under nose: *'What if I let go of this pain?'*
>
> Chin: *'What if this pain just goes?'*
>
> Collarbone: *'What can I do when I'm free of this pain?'*
>
> Under arm: *'I can choose to be pain free.'*
>
> Crown of head: *'What if I can release this pain right now?'*

If, after saying the last statement, you believe this to be true, then you can finish. If some doubt or some 'yeah buts' as described in the earlier sections remain, then do some more EFT.

Choosing for yourself

What does the word 'choice' mean to you? For me, it describes freedom, empowerment and right. For others, it can also mean release or grown-up independence. I've heard people use the word 'alternative', but to me that implies that only two choices exist. An alternative is what Elizabeth is given in Jane Austen's novel *Pride and Prejudice* when she's told 'An unhappy alternative is before you, Elizabeth. . . . Your mother will never see you again if you do not marry Mr Collins and I will never see you again if you do'.

In today's society of 'do as I say', it's not often you have a choice in matters, which is why this word can be so empowering when used with EFT. Dr Patricia Carrington recently introduced this into her work on EFT and it has been extremely useful ever since. Using the word 'choose' somehow allows you to accept the phrase you use more readily.

The traditional way of saying the Set-up Phrase, as I describe in Chapters 3 and 4, is to use the negative words such as:

> *'Even though I'm deeply ashamed . . .'*
>
> *'Even though I'm angry . . .'*
>
> *'Even though I have this pain . . .'*

You usually follow the first part up by saying an affirmation such as 'I deeply love and accept myself', or similar words of acceptance that you feel comfortable with.

The Choice Phrase combines the negative with the positive, and you can add it at the end of a phrase, for the whole round, or simply on its own as an affirmation as follows:

> *'Even though I'm deeply ashamed, I choose to release this emotion.'*
>
> *'Even though I'm angry, I choose to feel at peace with myself.'*
>
> *'Even though I have this pain, I choose to accept that it's my body's way of healing itself.'*

I generally introduce the Choice Phrase when the intensity on the Subjective Units of Distress Scale (refer to Chapter 3) is around a 3.

You can also introduce the combination of positive and negative phrases here, as I explain in the next section.

Combining the negative with the positive

If you're arguing with yourself or refusing to change, give this technique a try – it can be fun. If you want to know more about conflict, refer to Chapter 6.

Where your client refuses to do something, first do one full round of EFT starting with the Sore Spot or Karate Chop (refer to Chapters 3 or 4), saying 'Even though I refuse to (whatever the issue is), I love and accept myself anyway'. After you've followed this through for a few rounds with EFT, you see a shift in the subconscious towards a positive choice of wanting to change. When you can't see a noticeable change towards the positive (usually, this is when you're more inclined to want to change) try introducing the Choice Phrase that I referred to the previous section. These phrases are merely suggestions – use words that make sense to you.

To help you understand the process more clearly, the following describes a conflict situation with a smoker who's undecided whether to give up or not.

1. **Using Sore Spot or Karate Chop, begin by saying 'Even though I refuse to give up smoking, I love and accept myself anyway' three times.**

2. **Now move on to the first round (all negative):**

> Eyebrow: 'I refuse to give up smoking.'
>
> Side of eye: 'I'm not even interested in giving up.'
>
> Under eye: 'No one can make me.'
>
> Under nose: 'If I don't want to, I don't have to give up smoking.'
>
> Chin: 'I won't change.'
>
> Under arm: 'I'm fed up with everyone having a go at me.'
>
> Top of head: 'I absolutely refuse to give up smoking.'

3. **Second round (combination of negative and positive).** On the second round of tapping, try introducing some choices:

> Eyebrow: 'I refuse to give up smoking.' (negative)
>
> Side of eye: '*I* choose to give up, not anyone else.' (positive)
>
> Under eye: 'No one can make me.' (negative)
>
> Under nose: 'As I can choose, I choose to believe that I can give up smoking.' (positive)
>
> Chin: 'I won't change.' (negative)
>
> Collarbone: 'I choose to accept that I can change if I want to.' (positive)
>
> Under arm: 'I absolutely refuse to change.' (negative)
>
> Top of head: 'What can be so bad about wanting to change?' (positive)

Keep repeating the alternative pattern until you notice a move towards a positive change, and then introduce a third round as follows.

4. Third round (all positive)

> Eyebrow: 'I choose to give up smoking.'
>
> Side of eye: 'Choice is very empowering.'
>
> Under eye: 'Choices are good.'
>
> Under nose: 'Positive choices are even better.'
>
> Chin: 'Choosing to be a non-smoker is my choice.'
>
> Collarbone: 'I accept change.'
>
> Under arm: 'Change is good.'
>
> Top of head: 'I want to change to be healthy.'

These phrases bring up a lot of 'tail enders'. These 'ifs' and 'buts' that come up prevent healing. After you identify the 'ifs' and 'buts', you can then use EFT on each of them.

When using the combination of negative and positive phrases, always end on a positive statement.

I explain the 'Touch and Breath' technique technique in Chapter.

Getting what you want

When formulating your Acceptance Phrase, do get into the habit of using empowering words. (The first half of your Set-up Phrase is acknowledging the problem with 'Even though . . .' and the second half is 'I accept myself . . .'; you can find more on this in Chapters 3 and 4.) Using positive words such as 'choose', 'desire', 'want', 'intend', 'deserve', 'challenge', 'committed', 'can', 'will', and so on, rather than weak words such as 'will try', 'should' 'maybe' 'attempt', or 'must', is more likely to achieve your objective.

Chapter 16

Treating Children with EFT

. . . .

In This Chapter

▶ Discovering that ignoring emotions in children doesn't pay

▶ Showing your child how to use EFT

▶ Doing your own homework

. . . .

*W*hether you're 2 or 102, you can still benefit from using EFT. Children are wonderful students of EFT and don't have the same inhibitions with discovery and understanding as adults. In today's society children aren't only growing up faster but they're witnessing an ever-changing world. They have their growing pains and emotional turbulence to deal with as well. Adults have a certain amount of freedom and choice when dealing with their emotions but children are restricted by rules, embarrassment, and shame. If you ignore their feelings, their frustrations can lead to serious emotional problems and ultimately displays of anger, defiance, and destruction can manifest. The experts now say that, by the age of 3, all the early implantation of ideas, beliefs, prejudices, emotional responses, and behaviour is complete. Pretty scary when you think about it.

If you're pregnant, you can refer to Chapter 13 for helpful EFT advice.

Where I refer to 'children' I mean anyone aged 16 years or under.

Becoming a Better Parent

Every parent knows that parenting is no 'walk in the park' and that nothing quite prepares you for the role of parenthood and the responsibility of raising a child. As you constantly battle with your own emotions, you never know whether you're doing the right thing or making the right decision, but in the end you go with what you know best, usually guided by your own upbringing.

Parenting can also awaken many of your own unresolved issues from childhood. When you don't explore and deal with these issues, you can act them out towards your children, sometimes in painful ways. Being over-protective, competitive, strict, or judgemental are just a few of the results of those unresolved issues in you. All the emotions you experienced as a child can sometimes come back to haunt you. But remember, you're not powerless and you can change with the help of EFT.

Consider the answers you give to these questions and whether they influence your relationship with your child:

- Was your childhood a happy one?

- Were your parents emotionally demonstrative?

- Do you follow rules or find yourself saying things your parents did, even though you don't agree with them? 'Do as I say and not as I do', for instance?

- Are there rules you'd rather change?

- Are you ever upset by your behaviour towards your child?

If problems exist in this area you can use EFT on any that you want to change. Don't see this as a sign of failure – see it as an opportunity to put wrong things right and to make a fresh start. If you'd like some help with starting again, refer to Chapters 7 and 10.

No one believes that a perfect parent exists – or they shouldn't! Everyone makes mistakes, which is why you can also use EFT for those times when you don't get it quite right. Using the following Set-up Phrases and the basic EFT tapping technique (see Chapter 3 for details), you can release yourself from the guilt of getting things wrong:

> *'Even though I was wrong to be so strict with Johnny, I completely accept what I did and forgive myself.'*

> *'Even though I pushed Leanne too much so she'd do well in her exams, I accept myself as a parent who was trying their best.'*

> *'Even though I shouldn't have grounded Kate when I did, I have to accept that the decision I made seemed the right one at the time and I forgive myself.'*

> *'Although I should have talked to Mary more often, I accept myself; I was doing the best I could with the resources I had.'*

Here are some ideas on raising emotionally healthy kids:

- Show interest in your children and what they have to say.

- When appropriate, apologise to your children and admit you make mistakes sometimes.

✔ Comfort and protect them to make them feel safe and secure.

✔ Acknowledge their achievements.

✔ Punish or criticise the behaviour and not the child. 'I don't like you *shouting* (behaviour)' is preferable to saying 'I don't like *you* (as a person) because you shout'.

✔ Remain consistent and in partnership. Your partner and family members should follow your family rules where possible.

✔ Show your love every day with hugs, kisses, and saying 'I love you'.

✔ Provide regular routines with mealtimes and bedtimes. Children can't thrive without routine.

✔ Spend quality time with your children. Activities don't have to cost anything – walking, reading, or playing board games are all free and help you engage with your children. If children know they can have your attention some of the time, they won't always seek it through bad behaviour.

✔ Discuss boundaries with your child and explain that they're put there for a reason, which is to keep them safe and because you care for and love them. Keep boundaries age appropriate, reasonable, and always consistent.

Introducing EFT to Children

How do you introduce your child to achieving emotional health by using EFT? The best way to introduce EFT is for your child to see you, as a parent, doing it for yourself. If the child asks what you're doing, you tell her that you know a simple technique that can make you feel better.

Here are a few additional ideas:

✔ Mention that you're sure the child's favourite hero uses EFT.

✔ Depending on the age of the child, try introducing EFT like a game, saying 'I've heard that tapping on certain parts of your body can help make you feel better when someone upsets or annoys you' (or can improve your test results, or increase your game, or whatever gets the child's interest) or 'If you want to follow me in a "monkey see, monkey do" fashion you can even amaze your friends with this'. When I've shown children what to do, I then say something like 'Now you have a go on something like your fear of spiders or the horrible feeling you get when you have to read in class and let's see if it works for you'.

EFT teaches children to be responsible for their own feelings about what happens to them. Teaching children to acknowledge their feelings and how to deal with them lessens the chances of them reaching for other self-soothing habits such as smoking, drinking, and worse when they get older.

Of course, before you work with children, you need to follow a few guidelines. Paying attention to these guidelines now pays rewards and saves headaches later.

- ✔ If you're a therapist, depending on which country you work in, check what the law and licensing regulations are in relation to working with children. The rules may be complex and time-consuming but you need to follow them to stay within the law.

- ✔ Whether you're a parent or a therapist you must clear your own emotional issues first, because doing this makes all the difference. (Chapter 6 has more on clearing issues.) Remember, babies and children have an inbuilt radar tuned in to your negative emotions.

- ✔ Generally, most children are already tuned into their problem, so the Set-Up Phrase isn't always necessary, especially for babies. (See Chapter 3 for more on the Set-Up Phrase.)

- ✔ Make the child comfortable and respect her opinions, feelings, and wants.

- ✔ Keep the session relatively short because most children have a short attention span.

- ✔ Ask the child to tell you where she feels the sadness, hurt, anger, and so on in her body. Then ask her to measure it. But if you say 'Rate the intensity of your emotion on a scale from zero to 10 . . .', she's not likely to understand. Instead, children find it much easier to measure how they feel by spreading their arms apart to say how big their problem is or how they feel. If they choose, they can give their feelings a shape or colour. Use these measurements before then after using EFT.

- ✔ Ask if the child's ever had this same feeling before and what it reminds her of.

- ✔ In terms of who does the tapping, ask the child – let her decide what's best for her. If you're not permitted to touch the child, she can copy you. You can tap on yourself as she taps on herself, or you can tap on her. Use any variation that the child is comfortable with. You can also gently rub the EFT points instead of tapping on them. If the child doesn't want to tap, you can tap on her as she tells you what's bothering her, asking along the way 'Where do you feel that right now?' or 'How does it feel now?', and then use EFT.

- ✔ Get into a routine using EFT with children and they'll soon become familiar with it. If you're working on your own child, this routine builds up a special bond and promotes greater communication between you both.

Young Children: Tapping at Bedtime

The best opportunity you're going to have in using EFT with young children is when you're putting them to bed. As you tuck the child in, and before you read a bedtime story, ask her what sort of day she's had. If she comes up with something like 'Jimmy kicked my lunchbox around the playground', you can ask her what feelings she has as she's saying that. She may come up with 'It hurts in my stomach', and then you can tap on 'I have this Johnny feeling in my stomach, but I'm still a good kid'. Tap on whatever has made her feel sad, upset, or in pain. Sometimes, the story you're reading may bring up some emotions and this again is an ideal time to use EFT.

Children under 7 years and especially between the ages of 2 to 4 years take what you tell them literally and can't put things into context.

Explain to your child that problems are like pieces of a jigsaw and that you need to treat each piece with EFT. However, you don't have to complete all the jigsaw to see the picture.

The Tween Years: Caught in the Middle

Between the ages of 8 and 12 you find you're either too young or too old to do certain things. You want to be grown up yet you like the security of being a child. You like new clothes but you're not old enough to earn money to pay for them. You may act grown up but you don't like the responsibility that goes with it. In essence, you're caught between leaving your childhood behind and entering your teen years. What a conflicting and confusing time! It's not all bad news, however, because this section helps you recognise the signs so that you can prepare for what lies ahead, and it also shows you how you can deal with emotional problems with EFT. I outline a few problems that tweens may encounter with a selection of EFT phrases that may go with them. You can find ones that I've left out in the 'Helping Your Teen' section, later in this chapter.

Fears

Fears abound at this age – fear of growing up, violence, uncertainty, war, and sex, to name a few. Here's an example of EFT phrases to use with a fear of growing up:

> *'Even though I'm frightened of growing up, I accept that I don't want to remain a child forever either.'*

> *'Although I'm frightened of all the violence in the world, I choose to feel safe.'*

Objections and wants

'Want' and 'don't want' are frequently used words in a tween's vocabulary.

> *'Although I don't like Aunty calling me 'cute' because I'm not a child, I accept and forgive her.'*

> *'Even though I want designer clothes to be like my friends, I accept that no amount of designer clothes makes me a better person. It's who I am that matters.'*

Awareness

Suddenly, it dawns upon tweens that the world and the people in it aren't quite as they thought they were. Here are some phrases to try:

> *'Even though I've discovered that people don't always tell the truth, I choose not to be like them, and understand that they must have their reasons.'*

> *'Even though I've realised that my parents aren't perfect, whose are?'*

Helping Your Teen

The period between the ages of 13 and 16 is when children are influenced not only by their peers, but also by their elders. In other words, they copy and model themselves not only on their friends or heroes, but also their parents. No, I'm not talking about your clothes or taste in music, but how you behave. Your children subconsciously take in your values and morals.

This age is the crucial time to engage and support your child because this period shapes her future.

As difficult as this may be, communicating your love for your teen is the single most important thing that you can do. At this age teens decide how they feel about themselves largely by how you react to them. Which is why it's also important to communicate your values and to set expectations and limits, such as insisting on honesty, self-control, and respect for others, while still allowing teenagers to have their own space.

When my two daughters decide to kick against the rules, I know that getting the right balance to deal with the situation is difficult. However, they both appreciate that I set out the rules for their own good. Parents of teens often find themselves noticing only the problems, and they may get into the habit of giving mostly negative feedback and criticism. Although teens need feedback, they respond better when you give it positively and speak with love instead of 'You'll do as I say, or else'.

When teens have low self-esteem or family problems, they're at risk of developing self-destructive behaviours such as using drugs or alcohol or having unprotected sex. Depression and eating disorders are also important issues for teens. (See Chapter 7 on tips relating to low self-esteem.)

Plenty of books out there discuss parenting skills, which is great for the parents, but the one thing EFT does is give children control and choice, and they don't often get a lot of that. They get to do EFT when and if they want, which I'd say is another good selling point. Having persuaded my two teenage daughters to use EFT, then I believe anything is possible.

Here are some of my favourite phrases that you can adapt to suit. You can leave out the 'Even though' and 'Although' words to make them more acceptable if you like.

> *'I can't see the point of doing this stupid tapping, but I'm cool.'*

> *'I get scared sometimes about growing up, but I'm still worthy of my parents' love.'*

> *'I want to do things my way and it causes arguments. I accept myself and I accept that I'm loved in spite of this.'*

> *'I want freedom to do what I want sometimes – even if I don't know what to do with it when I've got it. I just want to rebel.'*

> *'My job is hating my parents' rules, and their job is to keep me safe, so it looks like we're both doing a good job.'*

> *'Although I get anxious when friends ask me to do things I don't like, I accept myself as a unique individual who's not afraid to say no.'*

At one time, not many teens would like to admit to using EFT, but that's slowly changing, thank goodness, as the technique grows in popularity. Learning EFT from an early age means children grow up with it. If they're still a little reticent, show them how to use EFT when they're in a receptive mood and get them to try it out in the privacy of their own room. Do emphasise that they still need to talk about some problems with you as parents/adults.

Introducing EFT into Schools

If I could, I'd put EFT on every school curriculum – not only for the pupils but for the teachers as well. Imagine if every teacher used EFT to calm her emotions before entering the classroom. Even better if the teachers taught the pupils and let the pupils use it on themselves. School teachers have come on my training courses and some schools are now incorporating EFT into their school programme, and I'm sure others will follow suit.

You don't need to touch a child when showing her how to use EFT on herself.

Because EFT has no research base to confirm its efficacy, it can be difficult to get through the educational door. The American Red Cross took 12 years to acknowledge and include the Heimlich manoeuvre (which has saved thousands of lives), so never admit defeat!

If you're in a position of authority and want to know more, you can discuss how you can introduce EFT with a qualified EFT therapist or trainer.

Here are some ideas on how you can introduce EFT into schools:

- ✔ Spread the word at every opportunity, whether at the school gates, PTA meeting, or school fete.

- ✔ If you're trained in EFT, offer an introductory workshop to parents and invite children as well.

- ✔ Write articles for the school magazine on the benefits of using EFT on children.

- ✔ If you're a teacher, speak with your head of school about using EFT as a study project to measure performance. Have some evidence or case studies handy from other schools that have used it.

Handling Specific Situations

When you're familiar with the EFT routine that I describe in Chapters 3 and 4, and have used it on your own issues, you can then show your own or other children how and when they can use EFT to control their own emotions. This gives them a wonderful sense of confidence and empowerment, as well as peace.

You can use the shortened tapping routine that I describe in Chapter 4 in any situation, but you need to simplify the phrasing for the Set-Up Phrase and change the affirmation (or self-acceptance). Don't be too strict about the order of tapping either, because at this stage you just want the children to take part and not to feel conspicuous or fear they'll get it wrong. Anyway, the order isn't that important – it's the results that count. (You can find more on the tapping order in Chapter 4.)

When I work with young children I often ask them to bring along their favourite teddy bear or doll. Doing this not only puts them at ease and acts as a comforter but also acts as a surrogate toy for EFT. With their permission, I put sticky pads on the bear or doll where the meridian points would be and show the child where to tap. If they don't bring their own, I have a teddy bear that I use with markers on its meridian points. Children find this quite funny and cute.

A child may find it difficult to identify with or say 'I deeply and completely accept myself', and if you ask her to say these words, she'll probably refuse. If she's too young she may not understand either. If she refuses, it doesn't necessarily mean she has low self-esteem issues; it's more than likely out of embarrassment. Use other affirmations that fit in with their language style, such as 'I'm an okay kid', 'I'm cool', 'I'm a cool dude', 'I'm wicked', or whatever is in fashion at the time.

The child doesn't always have to tell you what the problem is and Chapter 5 has some clever techniques to use in these circumstances.

I've covered only a few issues in this chapter but EFT can help children with many more issues. The following are some examples where you can use EFT; you just have to adjust the Set-up Phrases to fit:

- ✔ Returning to school
- ✔ Test or performance anxiety
- ✔ Separation issues
- ✔ Pain
- ✔ Frustrations
- ✔ Thumb-sucking
- ✔ Nail-biting
- ✔ Toilet-training/bedwetting
- ✔ Eating problems
- ✔ Teen love
- ✔ Teacher problems
- ✔ Fear of the dark or ghosts
- ✔ Stammering or stuttering
- ✔ Stage fright

Nightmares and night terrors

Nightmares and night terrors are quite different. Nightmares tend to occur after several hours of sleep; screaming or moving about is very uncommon; the dream is usually elaborate and intense; and the dreamer realises soon after wakening that she's had a dream. Night terrors, on the other hand, occur during the first hour or two of sleep; loud screaming and thrashing about are common; and the sleeper is hard to awaken and usually remembers no more than an overwhelming feeling or a single scene, if anything.

Nightmares and night terrors arise from different physiological stages of sleep. Children who have night terrors may also have a tendency to sleep-walk and/or urinate in bed. Psychologists don't fully understand the causes of night terrors, though children usually stop having them by puberty.

You can treat nightmares and night terrors in much the same way as I describe in Chapter 14. If you're concerned about these night terrors, please consult your doctor.

Calming babies with EFT

When babies cry, you don't always know what's wrong with them because they can't communicate any other way. This can cause distress in you and your baby. Whether it's to calm your baby from a traumatic birth, relieve her teething or colicky pains, or ease her sleepless nights, you'll be relieved to know that you can use EFT on them all. If you practise tapping on yourself and massaging your baby every day, you'll both notice a profound difference.

Calm yourself first with EFT before treating your baby.

Don't use the additional tapping point on the crown of the head (the fontanelle) with babies.

Because babies don't usually like you to tap on them, especially around the face area, you can either use the tip of your ring finger (less pressure); massage the points; use tapping by proxy (see the section 'Tapping by Proxy', later in this chapter), or the 'Touch and Breathe' technique (see Chapter 13) while using soothing words such as:

> *'Even though I'm hungry/tired/scared/wanting attention, I'm still a loved baby and choose to feel calm and relaxed.'*

> *'Even though I have these wind pains, I'm still a good baby and my mummy loves me.'*

> *'Even though my birth was difficult, I'm here now and I'm safe.'*

You can also use EFT on yourself as a parent:

> *'Even though (name of baby) is crying and I don't know why, I accept myself as a good mother and choose to remain calm while sending (name of baby) my love.'*

> *'Even though (name of baby) is having trouble sleeping I choose to send him/her peace and contentment.'*

> *'Even though (name of baby) is tetchy and restless, right now mummy loves you very much.'*

After a few rounds of tapping on the remaining meridian points with EFT using negative phrases, you can change the words to all positive. For example, words for the baby as you tap on yourself or on the baby may be 'I'm a good baby', 'I'm loved', 'I communicate the only way I know how', or 'I'm new to the world and all its rules'.

School phobia

Children who don't like school often feign an illness to get out of going. As a working mother I had little choice but to send them off, saying, 'You'll be okay when you're there and if you still don't feel well ask the school to call me.' However, that tummy ache may be real and can actually be caused by an emotional reaction, especially if your child is suffering from a recognised disorder known as *school phobia*. School phobia is such a concern among some educational authorities that they've set up special units to deal with a problem that was once almost unheard of.

At the root of any phobia is an anxiety, so the first thing to do is to find out what or who your child is anxious about. Most children don't want to upset their parents and may be resistant to talking about the intensity of their feelings, so choosing the right moment is the key. If this doesn't work, try talking with their friends or the headteacher.

Rewarding your children when they're sick, or buying them gifts, only internalises the idea that illness equates with love and attention, which teaches your children to use being unwell as a manipulative tactic.

Beating the bully

Bullies can be teachers, fellow pupils, club or gang members, family members – in fact, anyone, and that includes you. How do you recognise a bully? A bully does any number of things to make another person feel sad, depressed, or lonely, such as calling names, spreading false rumours, and making threats or belittling comments. Bullies often come from families who are emotionally crippled and whose parents, or even themselves, may be sufferers of abuse. In order to vent their anger, bullies prey on individuals they perceive to be weak.

If your child complains of being bullied, take the problem seriously so that you can deal with it in the appropriate way. A bully can only survive on the existence of a victim.

Laws are in place to protect children and adults from bullying, but if you need some emotional support this is where EFT can come in. EFT can't solve the problem but it can help your child to cope.

Either ask the child to tap on herself or you can tap for her as she tells you her concerns.

If your child allows you to, try tapping on her as she tells you her concerns. (Chapter 5 has details of how to carry out the 'Tell the Story' technique.)

> *'Even though Henry calls me names, I'm a good kid and I choose to put up a brick wall so he can't hurt me.'*
>
> *'Even though I'm angry at my teacher, I'm the one in charge with this tapping and I can be cool.'*
>
> *'Even though Molly's bullying me and she leaves me out of everything, I can forgive her because she needs help.'*

A little bit of a bully lives in everyone, so don't forget to tap for:

> *'Even though what I did to Massoud was wrong, I forgive myself and I choose to change my behaviour.'*
>
> *'Although I got Samira into trouble, I can forgive myself because I won't do it again, knowing it was wrong.'*

Learning and behavioural difficulties

In this section I outline the most common learning and behaviour problems that can occur in childhood and that you can carry through to adulthood.

If you want to use EFT on any of these conditions, please don't change or stop any medication without the doctor's consent. Again, I have to stress that there's no harm in trying to alleviate emotional issues with EFT, but if you don't feel qualified or capable of dealing with these issues, please consult a qualified EFT practitioner or professional therapist.

Attention disorders

Most children with attention deficit and hyperactivity disorder (ADHD) and attention deficit disorder (ADD) have great difficulty remaining still, taking turns, and keeping quiet. They may also demonstrate aggressive and defiant behaviour as well as having sleep problems. Symptoms must be evident in at least two settings, such as home and school, in order for a doctor to diagnose either disorder.

After the diagnosis, what help is there for parents and teachers? Parents learn management techniques and receive advice on medication or psychological treatment. The teachers receive educational management. At this stage EFT gets interesting.

Don A. Blackerby has been working on students with ADHD and ADD for around ten years with a 90 to 95 per cent success rate using EFT. He reckons that if the symptoms persist over time, then you need to look at the deeper issues such as current traumas in school. If none exist, then you need to investigate past unresolved traumas. Anger, anxiety, rage, fears, and guilt all come from some unresolved and unconscious trauma. He also believes that the symptoms of ADD/ADHD are simply ways of acting out the unconscious and unresolved trauma. You can effectively treat these unresolved traumas with EFT.

If you can't find a trauma, then some of the causes may be allergies, toxins in the body, high stress and anxiety, lots of sugar or junk food in the diet, or just the stress of not being able to cope with life. As well as changing the diet, you can use EFT on the stresses.

Dyslexia

Dyslexia is based on language difficulty, which makes it hard for those affected to understand written words. A person with dyslexia may read a 'b' as a 'd', or write the number '21' as a '12', or they may have difficulty distinguishing right from left. Hundreds of celebrities suffered from dyslexia at school, including Sir Richard Branson, who focused on his talents to become one of the world's richest men. Here are some others:

- Anthony Hopkins
- John Lennon
- Susan Hampshire
- Hans Christian Andersen
- Agatha Christie

Sophisticated approaches with EFT are usually necessary in complex cases like these. However, you have nothing to lose by trying with the skills you have and using some of the techniques that I refer to in the nearby sidebar 'Unscrambling words with EFT', to see how you get on. If instant results don't come with EFT, you're likely to see some improvement.

Unscrambling words with EFT

A 12-year-old boy who'd been diagnosed with both dyslexia and ADHD had never learned to read words comprising more than two or three letters, and even these were a struggle. He had issues with teachers and became easily angered and frustrated in class.

He explained that the words were moving up and down about 3–4 centimetres on the page, and each of the letters had an outline around it. If that weren't bad enough, there were also letters within the letters that were moving around. When asked what his emotional response was looking at the page, he replied that he was scared. He also became noticeably agitated.

Using EFT turned into a game where he had to follow the tapping of different points. He used either hand on either side on any of the points in any order. The only rule was that he had to mirror the practitioner exactly, using these words:

'Even though the words move up and down, I'm still a good kid.'

'Even though I can see outlines around the letters, I've done nothing wrong.'

'Even though I can see letters within the letters, I can still have fun.'

'Even though the words scare me, I can be brave.'

After five to ten minutes of work, the boy said that most of the words were much clearer now. He did some more work on the remaining outlines and movement. The page came into focus clearly for him for the first time in his life. Some fear remained, which apparently came from a particularly strict teacher before his dyslexia diagnosis. After he dealt with that fear using EFT, he no longer had any emotional reaction from trying to read.

Although he still couldn't read, because he'd never really learned how, he felt much more confident that he'd be able to.

A week later only a small amount of movement and faint outline had returned. After spending 15 minutes on this, it disappeared and the boy has had no problem since. He was no longer in as much trouble at school and came top of his science exam.

This case study is provided courtesy of Leon Jay.

Attachment disorders

John Bowlby, a British psychoanalyst, theorised that attachment disorder (AD) and later a more severe form diagnosed as reactive attachment disorder (RAD), was the result of a breakdown in the affectionate tie of bonding between mother and child. In other words, if you don't meet a child's basic needs of love, food, and security in the first few months of life (for whatever reason) or the child suffers neglect or abuse, the child shuts off her emotions and takes control of her life in order to feel safe. This need to control is what causes significant problems with parents or new caregivers.

Children with AD or RAD show most of the following symptoms:

- Don't respond to reason or logic.
- Crazy lying.

✔ Superficial charm.

✔ Food hoarding.

✔ Defiant behaviour.

✔ Unable to recognise right and wrong.

✔ False allegations of abuse.

✔ Indiscriminate affection towards strangers.

✔ Lack of affection towards new parents/caregivers.

✔ Learning difficulties.

✔ Inability to secure friendships.

✔ Avoiding eye contact.

The two most common feelings triggered in adults with AD or RAD tend to be fear and sadness. After something triggers these feelings, defences go into action to protect the sufferers from those feelings. Adults with attachment difficulties want to be loved and accepted but don't have the tools to achieve that goal. They sabotage what they want and need, which is why traditional therapy doesn't usually work.

EFT can work, however, on changing the maladaptive thought processes that result in negative behaviour. You need to:

✔ Identify feelings (sadness, anger, fear, and so on) and find out where they've come from.

✔ Acknowledge those feelings with EFT: 'Even though I have this sadness because . . .'.

✔ Include the reframing techniques that I refer to in Chapter 6 to switch the cognitive thoughts.

✔ Use EFT on any grief and loss issues.

✔ Use EFT for feelings of abandonment (see Chapter 8) if the child is adopted or orphaned.

✔ Enhance self-esteem (Chapter 7 can help you here).

Parents or caregivers also need emotional support and can use EFT on their feelings of frustration. Due to the attachment issues, they too can feel rejected or manipulated by the child.

Children with AD or RAD are very manipulative and can lie very convincingly. They can behave as though they've been starved of affection and display overtly charming behaviour. That is until they realise that they can't manipulate you.

Tapping by Proxy

Tapping by proxy was discovered by a mother who was sitting by the incubator of her tiny premature baby, who doctors said wouldn't survive the night. The mother was an EFT therapist and she began to tap on herself while concentrating on the baby. As she continued to tap, the baby began to change colour and move a little. The baby didn't die and continued to thrive. The mother was convinced that somehow she'd created the change in her baby by *tapping by proxy*. Since then, tens of thousands of others have used the technique.

If you don't believe it, why not try it on that annoying barking dog that keeps you awake at night? You can tap by proxy on babies, animals, someone who's too ill to tap on themselves, those you come into conflict with, or anyone who needs help. Here are the instructions on how to tap by proxy:

Before you begin you'll be interested to know that you don't have to be in the same room, but you do need to concentrate and focus your attention on the child's problem.

1. **Establish the Set-Up Phrase that best describes the problem, such as 'Peter is very nervous'.**

2. **Use the Set-Up Phrase three times – as an example 'Even though Peter is very nervous, I love and accept Peter as he is'.**

3. **Tap on the remaining points with 'nervous Peter'.**

4. **When you've finished, reassess.**

5. **If necessary carry out a remainder round ('Even though Peter still feels nervous') and change the words to suit (check out Chapter 3 for more on the Remaining Phrase).**

Chapter 17

Doing Business with EFT

. . . .

. . . .

*H*ow many therapists does it take to change a light bulb? Only one, but it must want to change!

I know it's an old joke, but although therapy work has its lighter moments (no pun intended) and can be very rewarding, it isn't all a barrel load of laughs either. Whether you're contemplating training as an EFT practitioner or you want to incorporate EFT into your existing therapy practice, this chapter gives you practical advice and support. You'll also find this chapter helpful if, having used this book on your own emotional problems, you've come to the decision that you need the help of a professional. Whatever your reason, this chapter explains most of what you need to know about seeking EFT therapy or practising EFT professionally – and if I haven't covered something here, I give you directions on where to find the information.

Seeking Help for Yourself

You may have decided, for whatever reason, that you need the help of a professional and are wondering where to start.

Too many people blindly pick a therapist out of a telephone directory and plunge right in without any hesitation. I know that it's a minefield out there but you're not having your drains unblocked – you're putting your health in someone else's hands, so a little time invested now reaps rewards later.

Seeking a professional

Due to the growing awareness of EFT, you'll find a wealth of information on the Internet about the subject and websites where you can seek help from a professional.

When looking for EFT practitioners on a website you may find them listed as 'EFT therapist', 'psychotherapist' or 'energy psychologist', and you'll notice I've used both 'practitioner' and 'therapist' in this book. At a basic level no differences exist between descriptions because all are licensed professionals trained to help clients to solve their problems. At a higher level, significant differences can exist in terms of education and training, which I talk about later in this chapter. I haven't addressed legal issues here because they differ from country to country.

If friends or relatives recommend a therapist, make sure you come to your own decision as to the therapist's suitability. Asking questions is perfectly acceptable and indeed any reputable therapist encourages this. If you haven't been to see a therapist before and are unsure what questions to ask, the next section can assist you.

Ultimately, what determines the effectiveness of EFT treatment lies as much with the client's determination to overcome his problems as it does with a therapist's qualifications.

Making contact

Your first contact with your practitioner/therapist will probably be over the phone. If the therapist can't answer the phone, you should be able to leave your name, telephone number, and the best time to return the call either on the answering machine or with a receptionist. You don't need to leave any other details at this stage and you'll ideally receive a call back the same day or first thing the next day. During that call the therapist may ask for a brief outline of your problem (stop smoking, confidence, and so on) and make an appointment for a free consultation.

Your first meeting should be a free consultation with an opportunity to get to know one another, giving you an opportunity to describe your problem and the sort of outcome you'd like. You also want to know:

- ✔ **Is the therapist able to resolve your problem?** A good EFT therapist will refer you on to an EFT therapist who specialises in certain problems if he's not fully confident that he can help you.

- ✔ **What's the cost and length per session?** Cost depends upon the therapist's experience and location. An average session lasts approximately one hour and most therapists end the session at a natural break and not abruptly on the hour.

Legal regulations or requirements may exist in your state or country with regard to what you charge for EFT sessions, and you may want to educate yourself about any such requirements before proceeding with a professional career as an EFT practitioner.

✔ **Are there any sliding scale charges?** You may be a pensioner or senior, you may be a child, or alternatively you may not be working. Some therapists gladly reduce their fees in some or all these circumstances. There's no charge for asking.

✔ **Are the therapist's qualifications or insurance certificates on display?** Any reputable therapist displays his credentials for you to see. I've never been asked yet but I do put them on the wall and point them out to assure them I'm qualified and insured. Qualifications vary, depending in what part of the world you live. The Association for the Advancement of Meridian Energy Techniques and the Association for Meridian Energy Therapies have a list of therapists who've trained with them. You are, of course, free to approach anyone who has sufficient experience in EFT; that's entirely your decision.

✔ **Do you feel comfortable with your therapist and feel you can be open and honest with him?** It's very important you have a rapport and level of trust with your therapist. Do tell your therapist if at any time you feel uncomfortable. If you feel that he's gone beyond the ethical boundaries, report him to his associating body, if he's a member of one.

Run a mile if any therapist suggests 'memory recovery techniques' based on the expectation of past sexual abuse of which you have no memory, or if he says any of the following:

✔ You have the symptoms of someone who was abused.

✔ Studies show that most people with your symptoms were sexually abused.

✔ If you think you were abused, then you probably were.

✔ Remembering is essential if you want to be healed.

Meeting your therapist for the first time

If you have a free consultation, use this time as an opportunity to ask any questions of your own or any that I give in this chapter. Don't feel obliged to proceed with any pre-arranged appointment following this consultation if you feel you need more time, or you're not comfortable with the therapist or the environment.

Typically, your first paid-for EFT session involves the practitioner asking what your symptoms are, what your desired outcome is, and taking a note of your general history. The practitioner gives a brief explanation of EFT and a demonstration of the technique, which, in some cases, can be in a 'monkey see, monkey do' fashion. If the practitioner is conducting the technique on you as opposed to you doing it yourself – or even a combination of both – he'll ask for your permission first.

EFT works whether you do the tapping or the practitioner does it for you. Some practitioners tap on the client (with his permission) so the client can concentrate on his issues.

Before the end of the session the practitioner shows you how to carry out the tapping routine (see Chapter 3) and he may ask you to practise this at home. Being shown how to use the technique makes it much easier to use when having a go yourself. The therapist may give you a set number of times to practise, or not, depending upon your therapist. He may give you suggested phrases on a sheet of paper or he may give you a recording of the session.

After the session, you may make another appointment and these are generally about a week apart because this gives time for you to practise EFT and report back on any noticeable changes.

Joining the Professionals

If you're not seeking help for yourself but are interested in becoming an EFT practitioner or therapist, where do you start?

Many people can attest to the effectiveness of EFT as a self-help therapy, and people are using it widely within specialist areas of the medical profession, with drug counsellors, prison wardens, therapists, and psychologists, to name but a few. Despite these endorsements, you obviously want to know whether you can make a living from EFT, whether you possess the necessary qualities to train as an EFT practitioner, and what's involved to become one. First, you don't need any other qualifications before training to become an EFT practitioner.

Qualifications

Alarming as it may seem, practically anyone can call themselves a therapist, because in many countries no regulations or licensing laws are in place. For this reason, the Association for the Advancement of Meridian Energy Techniques (AAMET) and the Association for Meridian Energy Therapies (AMT) set themselves up to regulate standards of training and certification. If a practitioner is a member of either of these associations, you can report them if you feel they've breached the association's strict codes of conduct, which you can find on their respective websites (www.aamet.org and www. theamt.com).

In some countries, such as the US and Canada, attending training sessions can be difficult because of travelling distances. For this reason, both organisations allow you to obtain a qualification by correspondence courses.

For your clients' benefit, display all certificates and insurance details for your clients' inspection.

Location, location

Whether you hire a room, have your own clinic, or work from home, it needs to be clean, comfortable, and free from too much noise or disturbance. Neutral colours and a few artificial plants (remember allergy sufferers) and paintings can all add to looking professional and helping the client feel comfortable. Make a clean washroom available and a plentiful supply of fresh water is essential for both you and your client. Boxes of tissues are always necessary to have close by for those emotional moments.

Great expectations

For many people, going to see a practitioner or therapist is usually the last resort after they've explored all other avenues and they've either failed or not come up to their expectations. The client will generally be feeling at an all-time low, but as a practitioner, in addition to being qualified, trained, and insured, your client expects you to:

- ✔ Take an interest and understand their problem.
- ✔ Ensure that he feels comfortable and at ease with you.
- ✔ Be emotionally healthy.

Getting the session started

It's very important to know as much as possible about the client's life psychologically, even if he's come to see you urgently. You may also want to know whether the client has support from family or friends, and whether he has any pre-existing conditions likely to affect recovery. A consultation form prepared beforehand with tick boxes against a variety of symptoms acts as a guide to other problems that may be going on in your client's life. You'd be surprised at how many clients are totally oblivious of how many problems they really do have.

One of the best ways to describe EFT to clients who are new to EFT is to compare it to acupuncture but without the needles. I find the best way to introduce EFT is to just show the client how it works on a simple issue to begin with, such as constricted breathing (refer to Chapter 6).

Conveying a sense of caring

Keep these points in mind as you work with your client, both privately and publicly:

- ✔ If you meet a client outside a therapy session, walk past or avoid him. If he wants to acknowledge you, respond briefly and walk on. Doing this is a mark of respect for your client.

- ✔ Always ask your client if he's sought medical help for his condition prior to seeing you, and advise him not to stop taking any medication.

- ✔ Remember that you've never finished learning! Ensure that you practise continuous personal development.

- ✔ Seek the help and support of a supervisor or mentor if you've recently qualified.

The following behaviours are unhelpful to your client and don't encourage him to open up to you, nor do they enhance your success with EFT:

- ✔ Putting your own slant on his problem from your own experiences ('Oh, I know what you mean, when I had that problem . . .').

- ✔ Adding your own words or definitions. For instance, if a client describes his problem as a 'dicky' shoulder, then use his words and not your own interpretation.

- ✔ Reacting with horror or disbelief when your client reveals something shocking or revolting.

Closing the session

Summarising the session after each one and discussing with your client what worked and what didn't is an excellent way of getting feedback. All feedback is constructive and you can use it to improve on what you already know. I'm not egotistical enough to think that I know it all and my mantra is that there's always room to learn and make improvements.

Some practitioners give their clients a recording of the session, brief notes, or homework for them to work on between sessions.

At the end of therapy, follow up your sessions with your client. Generally, I find that my clients are very grateful when I contact them several weeks after the therapy ends. This contact makes the client feel valued and offers the opportunity for added feedback. It's also a good opportunity to ask the client, now that he's seen that EFT works, to pass on your details to others!

Payment, please

Because EFT works so quickly and doesn't involve months of therapy, fees work out favourably compared to many other therapies. Base how much you charge on your own experience, level of training, location, and overheads.

Most EFT therapists charge by the hour and I know of some therapists who use such a tight schedule that they have clients queuing up. There are obvious risks here, not only with timing if a client turns up late, but a session should end at a natural break, within reason, of course. I mean, it wouldn't do for me to be looking at my watch just as my client was about to reveal something important. So my suggestion would be to charge for a 'session' and explain how long a session generally lasts. You'll be surprised what you can treat in a one-hour session.

Friends or family may ask how much you charge and whether you're going to offer a discount. Just tell them that you're running a business and need the money to get started – or you can give them 'EFT vouchers' as presents. By all means consider a discount if they've introduced a client to you. As for how much to charge, do some research as to what other EFT therapists in your area are charging first. As a beginner, you may want to charge less but increase your fees as you become more experienced.

Keep in mind that you've invested a lot of time and money on your way to becoming a practitioner and may also have trained in other therapies or specialist areas of EFT to augment your skills. If you still feel uncomfortable about charging a reasonable fee, see Chapter 15 on how to overcome fear of success.

Knowing me, knowing you

After you've trained and qualified as an EFT practitioner or trainer, in all probability you'll want to start earning some money. Advertising can be costly but you can use other ways to get your name and practice known. Here are some suggestions:

- ✔ Build or get someone else to build your own website.
- ✔ Register with the therapy-related websites that are free to join. Some are free if you agree to advertise their website on yours.
- ✔ Join your EFT associated body website.
- ✔ Give free talks to local clubs and organisations.

✔ Run introductory workshops that give an overview of EFT and a chance to see it in action.

✔ Hire a stall at a therapy trade fair.

✔ Approach your local radio station and offer to talk for free on EFT.

✔ Offer your services for free to hospices, addiction groups, and other charitable groups.

✔ Submit an article to your local (or national) newspaper.

✔ If you're a trainer consider:

- Sending newsletters to trainees or other interested therapists.

- Offering free places to members of a charitable organisation.

- Reducing your fees for those on a low income.

Taking Care of Yourself as a Practitioner

Ideally, looking after yourself is at the top of your list. Listening to people's emotional problems day after day can have an impact on your own emotional and physical health and, accordingly, you need to be on your guard for any danger signals.

Any significant changes in your behaviour or thinking patterns may indicate that you're running the risk of endangering your own health and your clients' treatment.

A friend of mine was putting lots of energy into her research work and with her clients. She began to feel constantly tired and exhausted and wasn't focusing clearly. Admirable as her intentions were, I reminded her of the need to help herself before being able to help others.

Spotting the signs of problems

Do yourself and your clients a favour by checking out your own emotional health on a regular basis and addressing any problems before they get worse. Remember, coming back from gaining a poor reputation as a therapist can be very difficult, or sometimes impossible.

In particular, watch out for the following:

✔ *Burn out* or *emotional fatigue/overload* can happen when a therapist is emotionally drained or saturated. Putting too many demands on yourself can make you feel as if your emotional resources are depleted and you can feel overwhelmed by clients' expectations. Ultimately, feelings of failure set in and can cause depression.

✔ *Counter-transference* happens as a consequence of the therapist transferring his own unconscious feelings onto the client. A therapist whose own father was an abuser, for instance, may transfer his own feelings or anxieties onto a client who has a similar problem with his father.

✔ *Compassion fatigue*, otherwise known as *vicarious trauma* or *secondary trauma*, was first recognised during the 1950s when a nursing magazine used the term to describe nurses who were worn down by everyday medical emergencies. As a consequence of being exposed to their clients' description of traumatic events and their post-traumatic stress symptoms, the therapist can suffer secondary traumatic stress symptoms similar to their clients'.

Research has shown that rabbis and other members of the clergy who spend more time with people exposed to extreme stressors such as rape, robbery, and abuse are more likely to suffer from secondary traumatic stress.

Be assured that these conditions aren't a sign of weakness, but show your compassion and empathy. Nevertheless, please seek help if you're showing any signs of damaging behavioural or mental changes. They're treatable.

Chapter 6's section 'Clearing your own Issues' shows you how applying EFT on yourself on a regular basis can alleviate the stress associated with therapy work. Also watch out for some other signs:

✔ **Inability to shut off:** When you find yourself speaking to your friends or family in 'therapy speak', it's time to realise that you're bringing your work home. My family don't want me to speak to them like they're my clients and neither will yours.

✔ **Isolation:** If you're working on your own, especially from home, get out more or even talk on the phone to someone.

✔ **Not attending own needs:** You're dealing with everyone else's needs and don't leave enough time to tend to your own or your family's. It's not necessarily a conscious decision; there can be times when, in your desire to help other's needs, you may forget your own.

Treating yourself

In treating yourself, imagine what you'd be telling your best friend if they were doing your job:

✔ Be aware of changes in your behaviour or thinking patterns.

✔ Take 'time out' and change scenery.

- Become a member of an EFT group.
- Discuss the problem with your family or friends.
- Create for yourself a work–life balance.
- Get to know your neighbours and local community.
- Eat and drink healthily.
- Enrol on a course to advance your skills.
- Practise what you preach!

Conducting EFT over the Phone

After you've mastered EFT, there's no reason why you can't use this technique over the phone. You don't need to go out and buy expensive equipment like webcams, computer software, or a video phone unless you want to and you feel them to be necessary or to add professionalism. You and the person at the other end of the phone can manage just as well with a normal hand-held phone.

A very high percentage of EFT therapists are prepared to work over the telephone because phone sessions are as effective as face-to-face sessions.

Personally, I find telephone work more effective and advantageous than face-to-face sessions. I somehow feel more 'connected' with the client and that may be because there are fewer distractions. There can be difficulties with body language working over the phone, but quite honestly I do get indications from a client's breathing, pace, volume, and tone of voice. I also ask continually how the client is feeling.

A selection of pros and cons, to help you decide, may include:

Pros of working over the phone:

- It increases the number of people you can treat.
- It allows you to operate wherever you are in the world.
- You can do it in a lunch hour.
- There's greater anonymity.
- You can treat the person there and then with their problem. This can be especially effective for phobias, fears, or distressing circumstances (mobile phones can be a great asset here).

> ✔ It reduces travelling time and costs.
>
> ✔ It takes care of childcare problems.
>
> ✔ You're generally more focused on the problem in a home environment.

Cons of working over the phone:

> ✔ The other person may not like, or be able, to speak over the phone (infirmity, hearing or speech problems, for instance).
>
> ✔ It can be difficult to build rapport, especially with children.
>
> ✔ Certain physical problems aren't suitable for telephone work – where a client is prone to seizures, for example.
>
> ✔ In certain parts of the world, insurance companies won't cover therapy work conducted over the phone if outside the country.
>
> ✔ Unless you put rules in place, you may get calls at unexpected times.
>
> ✔ The person at other end can forget to call you.
>
> ✔ Installing computer-based phone applications, speakers, or similar, can be expensive if you don't check out the free offers.
>
> ✔ You may have difficulty assessing body language.

Usually, the practitioner/therapist makes initial contact over the phone and then conducts the first session face-to-face, as I describe earlier in this chapter.

The client needs to have to hand a diagram of the tapping points and the instructions on how to apply EFT. You can email this information to the client or the client can download the instructions off your website well before the first session, so the client is acquainted with the technique.

Clients usually pay for telephone sessions either by credit card at the time of the appointment or directly following it, by a cheque sent to the practitioner before the appointment, or through PayPal. Telephone sessions cost exactly the same as office visits because they require the same investment of time and the same degree of expertise on the part of the practitioner.

If you're unsure about whether telephone sessions will work with you, try one first on a friend as a trial run.

Part VI
The Part of Tens

The 5th Wave   By Rich Tennant

"I learned my EFT tapping technique from my neighbor's uncle, and he should know. He was a Morse code operator during World War II."

In this part . . .

This Part of Tens is a source of useful EFT info. Check out the other therapies which work well with EFT, the questions everyone asks about EFT, and the ways in which EFT can improve your life.

Chapter 18

Ten (or so) Other Therapies That Harmonise with EFT

In This Chapter

▶ A quick reference to other therapies

▶ Becoming aware of how other therapies blend with EFT

Many EFT practitioners use other healing techniques during a session. Don't be surprised if your EFT therapist is skilled in other therapies and combines these with EFT during your sessions.

Practising only one therapy doesn't mean that the therapist isn't competent – she's invested a lot of time, money, and effort into perfecting the therapy she's chosen to specialise in. However, EFT is very flexible and you can combine it with many other healing techniques.

In this chapter I outline a number of therapies that I feel harmonise with EFT. They're not part of the original teachings of EFT but some EFT practitioners introduce them to enhance their skills. EFT comes under the umbrella of 'meridian and energy therapies' and some of the therapies that I include here also come under that name.

This chapter is like trying to fit an elephant into a matchbox so I can give only a brief synopsis of each therapy. However, a quick search on the Internet gives you more information on those therapies that you're interested in.

Healing with Theta

In 1995, Vianna Stibal discovered a way to heal her body from a serious disease and then pioneered and refined a method of healing called Theta healing.

Theta healing acknowledges that your magnetic forces attract what your subconscious mind believes. For instance, when someone tells you 'You're beautiful', how do you react? Are you energised and strengthened by it, or do you feel pain in the chest or throat? Or do you reply with, 'No I'm not; you're just saying that,' and reject the energy sent to you?

When hearing the news 'You're redundant from your job', do you feel hurt and angry, like you've been kicked in the stomach? Or do you handle it gracefully, let it go, move on with wisdom and insight about what that particular life experience was all about?

Known as the 'no-nonsense, pragmatic approach to healing', Theta healing works on these four levels:

- **Core beliefs:** Beliefs in the subconscious mind from conception to the present.

- **Genetic:** Everything that your ancestors handed down to you.

- **History:** Including promises, vows, and memories from your present or past life.

- **Soul:** The real you, the one that continues after you die.

Your brain produces electrical frequencies (measured by units of hertz – the number of cycles per second), which change according to the state you're in. By entering the theta brainwaves, theta healing can take place. It claims to transform emotional blocks, clear limiting genetic and family patterns of beliefs, and heal physical ailments. You may have experienced a theta state when feeling that sense of oneness when surrounded by natural beauty.

- **Beta waves (14–20 hertz):** This is the state you're in when you're going about your normal day-to-day activities – recognised as normal waking consciousness.

- **Alpha waves (8–13 hertz):** If you're experiencing this level of activity then your mind is in a state of light meditation, similar to daydreaming.

- **Theta waves (4–7 hertz):** At this level your brainwaves are in a heightened state of creativity, similar to being in a deep meditative state.

- **Delta waves (1.5–3 hertz):** If your brainwaves are at this level you're in a deep sleep, unconscious, or in a deep state of meditation.

Eyeing Up Eye Movement De-sensitisation and Reprocessing

American psychologist Dr Helen Shapiro developed Eye Movement De-sensitisation and Reprocessing (EMDR). She noticed that using certain eye movements was an effective treatment for trauma and post-traumatic stress disorder. It's one of the most significant and exciting developments in the treatment of psychological trauma and is supported by extensive research.

There's more to EMDR than meets the eye (pardon the pun). The goal of this therapy is to leave you with the emotions, understanding, and perspectives that lead to healthy and useful behaviours and interactions. Some practitioners of EMDR use the technique to bring traumas to the surface, and then use EFT to remove the emotional response.

Communicating with Be Set Free Fast

The acronym for Behavioural and Emotional Symptom Elimination Training for Resolving Excess Emotion Fear, Anger, Sadness, and Trauma is *Be Set Free Fast*. It's a highly focused energy therapy developed and refined by psychologist Larry Phillip Nims.

Be Set Free Fast effectively treats every psychological, physical, and spiritual problem that has emotional roots. Treatment involves communicating with the subconscious mind using thought energy. In case you're wondering what *thought energy* is, it's the energy you create with your own emotions, ideas, and beliefs. Thought energy even has a positive and negative charge, just like physical energy. People sometimes describe this process as the *Law of Attraction* – see Chapter 15 for more on this.

Flowing with Emotrance

Developed by Sylvia Hartman, *Emotrance* is more of a meditative approach to healing than EFT and works on the basis that energy flows into, through, and out of your body. The principle is that you're only aware of your strong emotions when they turn into physiological sensations. When you're on the receiving end of a distressing comment or upsetting message, the body's energy is disturbed, you feel a sensation, and you react accordingly.

Imagine someone telling you 'Your house has been burned to the ground'. This 'shock' is kept in your energy system. In Emotrance, the practitioner asks you to show with your hands where the problem (anger, grief, pain, and so on) is. The technique works by focusing your thoughts on parts of your body and guiding the energy towards an even flow of movement.

Looking into Tapas Acupressure Technique

Tapas Acupressure Technique, or TAT, is an elegant energy psychology treatment that's simple to use. Based on Taoist principles of balance and wholeness, TAT is said to bring a sense of integration, connectedness, and oneness. TAT links meridians with the vision centres to change your perception about problems in your life.

Tapas Fleming created the therapy in 1994 as a result of her own major life crises. The aim of TAT is to resolve inner conflict, unblock areas where you feel stuck, heal trauma, and treat allergies.

Influencing with Neurolinguistic Programming

Richard Bandler and Dr John Grinder developed neurolinguistic programming (NLP) in the 1970s, and people still use it today for personal and business issues.

No single definition of NLP exists – NLP contains an array of different techniques but in a nutshell NLP explores the way you communicate with yourself and how you can influence communication in others. It examines how you create negative thoughts and shows you how to turn them into more useful positive ones. There's a lot more to NLP than I can cover here. You can check out *Neuro-linguistic Programming For Dummies* by Romilla Ready and Kate Burton (Wiley) if you want to find out more.

Because NLP looks at how external experiences affect your internal state, you can use it to good effect with EFT. I include some NLP techniques throughout this book and the 'Dissociated Technique' in Chapter 5 is just one.

Switching On to Cognitive Behavioural Therapy

Cognitive Behavioural Therapy (CBT) uses a structured approach to help you identify negative thoughts and feelings and their connection with your negative behaviour. You can use the principles effectively in EFT therapy sessions. CBT is a combination of behavioural and cognitive therapy, which put simply means that by challenging negative thoughts and replacing them with more positive you can change your negative behaviour. CBT is a gradual process where you are given home assignments to help you overcome your problems. For the bigger picture on CBT, check out *Cognitive Behavioural Therapy For Dummies* by Rob Willson and Rhena Branch (Wiley).

Waking Up to Hypnotherapy

This is a highly respected therapy that heals during a trance-like state. Basically, *hypnotherapy* is hypnosis but with therapy. Hypnotherapy can help with problems such as anxiety and Irritable Bowel Syndrome (IBS), and provide pain control without drugs.

Despite what you may have heard, during hypnosis you're aware and in control at every moment and can terminate the session at any time. You can't get 'stuck' in a state of hypnosis, and the therapist can't make you do something that's against your will, so forget all that stuff about 'I had to take my clothes off – I was hypnotised'.

Hypnotherapy accesses a person's subconscious much the same way that EFT does. You can use EFT appropriately before and during a hypnotherapy session. Before the session, you can calm and relax your client with EFT. During hypnosis the client may become distressed and this is the perfect opportunity to use EFT on the issue and collapse any excessive distress in the process. Chapter 5 describes techniques that you can use. For more on Hypnotherapy, take a look at *Hypnotherapy For Dummies*, by Mike Bryant and Peter Mabbutt (Wiley).

Get your client's permission to tap on her beforehand and explain how EFT works.

Meeting Your Inner Child

Practitioners often perform inner child work during a hypnotic trance and they use it with EFT or as a stand-alone therapy. During this therapy your therapist safely guides you towards meeting with your own inner child and you have the opportunity to comfort and support him or her. The therapy is very cathartic and rewarding because it allows healing to take place in a gentle, almost dissociated way. This therapy is not new and the concept of the inner child was first mentioned in ancient mythology. Some psychotherapists refer to it as the 'True Self' and psychologist Carl Jung called it the 'Divine Child'.

Sometimes being abandoned, neglected, traumatised, or unloved as a child stays with you as you grow up, developing into feelings of inner sadness, loneliness, anger, or fear. Many adult problems stem from an event that occurred in childhood. You can use EFT to connect with the inner child as you gently tap.

Here's how it works:

1. **Visualise yourself as that lonely, fearful child.**

2. **Allow yourself to be comforted by hugging a pillow, cushion, or teddy bear while releasing all the pent-up emotions with EFT.**

3. **During the EFT session, you can insert words into your EFT phrases to remind you that your only responsibility as a child was to be carefree, enjoy yourself, and leave the responsibility and the proper upbringing methods to your parents.**

   You need to recognise that you're in no way at fault for what happened to you as a child, especially if it involves your parents.

4. **Use whatever experience it was as a way to improve the adult life you're living now.**

5. **Remind yourself on a regular basis of how no one on this earth is perfect, that everyone makes mistakes, and life can throw experiences at you that make you feel helpless, but this doesn't make you any less of a good person.**

Handing It to Reiki

The Japanese word *reiki* is universal terminology used in Japan to refer to the many types of healing and energy work. Anyone can easily learn reiki, and it involves the therapist placing the hands in various positions over the fully clothed client, who's either lying or sitting down. Reiki is a gentle energy that you can safely use on most people regardless of their state of health.

People disagree over where reiki originated from and who introduced it to the Western world, but one name that crops up often is that of Dr Mikao Usui, who developed the technique in the early 20th century.

During a reiki session you may feel a flow of energy, but even if you don't, you feel deeply relaxed. Have a course of treatments over a specified period, depending on your needs.

EFT can bring resolution to any unresolved emotional issues that surface from reiki therapy. For more on Reiki, check out *Reiki For Dummies* by Nina L. Paul.

Sole-searching with Reflexology

Reflexology is an ancient healing technique, based on the same principles as acupuncture. You practise it as a pressure-point massage of the feet or hands.

Dr William Fitzgerald introduced this therapy to the Western world in 1913 and the American physiotherapist Eunice Ingham took the idea further in the 1930s, maintaining that you can treat all parts of the body by pressing certain areas of the foot.

Reflexology has grown in popularity ever since because people receive relief from stress, anxiety and stress-related conditions like insomnia and migraine, asthma, sinusitis, eczema, wound healing, back pain and general pain relief, PMS and other menstrual problems, infertility and constipation.

You may need a number of weekly treatments because occasionally symptoms may worsen before improving. This is a sign that the body's natural healing processes are removing unwanted toxins.

Chapter 19

Ten Frequently Asked Questions about EFT

● ●

In This Chapter

▶ Finding out what EFT can do for you

▶ Carrying out EFT on yourself

▶ Feeling the after-effects of EFT

● ●

*I*n this chapter I've put together ten questions that I'm frequently asked that you may not find the answers to in this book or, if they're there you'll have to thumb through to find. My aim is to make sure you're informed and enlightened about EFT as much as possible without any nagging questions.

As I've Only Used My Imagination to Relieve My Problem, How Do I Know EFT Works in a Real Situation?

Your subconscious is very literal and doesn't recognise the difference between what's real and what's imagined. After the EFT technique works on the imaginary situation, it will work in a real life one too. If you don't want to take my word for it, why not test it out for yourself?

Will EFT Work For Me and How Many Sessions Do I Need to Clear My Problem?

Nothing works for absolutely everyone and that includes EFT. A micro percentage of the population don't respond to EFT, but many reasons may exist for this, and you can find some of the most common reasons in Chapter 6. Saying that, compared to most therapies, the results from EFT are often much faster and, in most instances, you can see them immediately. This has caused a widespread rumour that you can treat all problems in the same way, which is, of course, not the case. You need to have a realistic expectation that some problems take longer than others to deal with, and the number of sessions also depends upon your own expectations as well as the experience of the practitioner. As a guide, though, in the high majority of cases you definitely see some improvement in your first session.

Acknowledge any small or insignificant positive changes before deciding that EFT isn't working. Also ask friends and family whether they've noticed any changes in you. Occasionally, it may take a couple of days to notice any changes due to the use of EFT.

Can I Use EFT That My Second-Cousin's Father-In-Law's Best Friend Showed Me?

You make the choice, but don't be surprised if you don't get the results you'd expect. If you're offered 'hand me down' EFT, at least use it alongside this book. It's frustrating to hear people say that EFT didn't work for them and dismiss EFT because they learned from someone who used their own interpretation of the technique.

Will EFT Still Work if I Miss Out a Point or Get It Wrong?

Chapter 3 describes the tapping points involved when using EFT and, although the EFT routine is very simple in its basic form, until you get used to it you may tap in the wrong order. You'll be relieved to know that you can switch from left to right, you can jump about from the top of your head to your collarbone to under your eye, and still find that EFT works. The words don't matter either, as long as they're your own words about how you feel. After you're familiar with the routine in Chapters 3 and 4 and are getting results, by all means experiment at your own pace and see what you come up with. Maybe you'll find one point that does it for you.

What If I Suddenly Get an Unexpected Emotional Surge in the Middle of a Meeting?

First of all, thank your body for releasing this. Secondly, try to treat it with EFT, even if it means excusing yourself to go to the bathroom. If you can't excuse yourself, try tapping your Karate Chop (side of hand) under the table while saying to yourself 'I am calm; I can deal with this later', to bring the emotion down.

Remember to make a note afterwards of what came up and what intensity rating you gave it. Whatever happens, don't ignore it and push it to one side. Treat it like a wound that needs healing, because as sure as eggs is eggs, it will come up again and maybe at another inappropriate time.

I'm Not Comfortable with Tapping for Negative Affirmations; Can I Use Positive Ones Instead?

EFT works best when you focus on the negative as you tap on the meridian points that I describe in Chapters 3 and 4. Of course, you can tap for 'I'm happy', but if your subconscious says otherwise it will start to put up objections and stop EFT working, as I describe in Chapter 6. There's no point in introducing positives until your subconscious is ready to change. Chapter 15 can help you here. Listen to those objection, however, and tap for them by all means.

Why Do I Feel So Tired After Using EFT?

You've experienced the equivalent to a good workout, that's why. Through releasing energy blocks with EFT, your energy can now flow freely, leaving you feeling very relaxed. Some people feel more relaxed than others. Drinking water and going with what your body is telling you helps you feel more energised.

Does Any Scientific Research Validate EFT?

If you need science to prove that EFT works, why search around for this when you can get the answer by trying EFT out for yourself? You don't even need to believe in it either for it to work. If you still have a compulsion to read the science stuff, then visit the Association for the Advancement of Energy Therapies website at www.aamet.org, where they have a synopsis of energy therapy research.

Does It Matter Whether I Tap on Myself or Someone Else Taps on Me?

I always teach clients how to use EFT on themselves, but sometimes even when they're doing it in front of me they just don't get any movement in their emotional intensity. As soon as I tap on them they feel the emotional blockage move almost immediately. I don't put that down to me being any better at using EFT than they are; I feel it must be something to do with the body's energy, plus confidence in using the technique. Practise, practise, practise is the best advice I can give.

Do Any Limitations Exist on Using EFT and What If I'm on Medication?

Despite the amazing results you can achieve through EFT for a wide variety of psychological and physiological problems, EFT is a complementary therapy. Don't view it as a remedy or a substitute for medical treatment in the case of acute problems.

As long as your medication allows you to understand and comprehend what's going on, then there's no reason why you can't use EFT or benefit from someone using it on you. Many people are on anti-depressants while using EFT and continue to use EFT to gradually wean themselves off them – always with a medical practitioner's advice, of course.

The mantra is 'try it on everything', but unless qualified avoid treating anyone with a history of epilepsy, schizophrenia, or other severe mental health problems. EFT can't cure cancer or any chronic illness. However, it can reduce, or even eliminate, the stress and fears surrounding the illness and in the process it can ease symptoms.

Chapter 20

Ten Ways EFT Can Improve Your Life

. . . .

In This Chapter

▶ Using EFT to your advantage

▶ Improving your health and changing your life

. . . .

*T*here are times when EFT has such a profound affect on your life it can literally take your breath away, but sometimes changes are going on that aren't always so obvious and can be so subtle that you barely notice them. This chapter outlines just ten ways in which using EFT on a regular daily basis can improve your life.

Achieving Success

You can use EFT to achieve success in many ways, whether it's to boost your business or to improve your golf score. After you know how to use EFT on your limiting beliefs (as I explain in Chapter 15), you have no qualms about stepping outside your comfort zone. In addition, you can set yourself specific and achievable goals with conviction and belief. There's a saying that money attracts money, but after you remove any limiting beliefs around your guilt, fear of being noticed, or even that you don't deserve success, you understand what was really in your way.

As an employee, no longer do you have to be scared of cold calling clients, speaking up in the boardroom, or meeting sales targets. When you're called to play golf at your corporate event day, you can apply EFT to your nerves about the game and use it on any areas of your game that need improving. As a confident communicator, you can voice your opinions, offer guidance and support to others, and not take criticism personally.

Gaining Self-confidence

One thing everyone wishes they had more of is confidence, yet here you can have it, literally, at your fingertips. Can you recall the last time you sat an exam, went for an interview, went on your first date, or maybe took part in an audition? Can you remember how you felt beforehand? Now imagine all those horrible feelings just melt away and are a thing of the past. Imagine that this time you don't want to be sick, you're not sweating buckets, and you can actually remember what you have to say because your head hasn't become a mangled mess or your tongue hasn't stuck to the roof of your mouth. You go from being a 'yes person' to someone who asserts themselves with authority and receives respect from colleagues.

Developing a Positive Outlook

Everyone prefers to see someone who's happy rather than grumpy. Seeing someone else smile cheers you up in the process and it's not difficult to do. This doesn't mean you have to pretend to be happy; it means focusing on what you do have in life rather than what you don't have. Ridding yourself of those negative feelings with EFT puts a positive, peaceful outlook on your life. You discover how to accept letting go of those things in life that are holding you back.

Clinging on to fears and phobias is bound to have a detrimental affect on your outlook on life and can prevent you living life to the full. You appreciate how wonderful life can be after you have release from your fears and phobias.

Improving Your Relationships

Use EFT for all your relationship problems, whether it's with your partner, child, mother, or great aunt. Discover the joy of teaching your child how to use EFT to cope with anxieties, uncertainties, and fears. EFT also helps you recognise what drives your emotions, and this in turn increases your understanding of your own and others' emotions. You see situations from the perspective of other people, including the people you live with. This non-verbal type of communication plays an important part in developing good relationships. As you remove your own emotional barriers you understand how to express yourself without fear of judgement or criticism.

During times of loss or heartbreak you also have the therapeutic tool of EFT to help you through the bad times by removing the excess negative emotions but leaving you with the fond memories.

Living a Healthier Life

EFT can help you to stop smoking and lose weight. By using EFT to improve your own emotional health, you can make an impact on your physical health as well. EFT can help decrease blood pressure, stress, and other contributors that lead to serious diseases. That in itself is something worth taking seriously. You can also build up your immune system, resulting in fewer days off work due to sickness, colds, and flu. Generally, people who feel good about themselves make healthier lifestyle and dietary choices, so one good thing actually leads to another.

Because EFT taps into your brain, it can hinder the message from the brain to the body telling you that you're in pain. The benefit of this is that you can use EFT on any physical pain from headaches to childbirth.

Getting Motivated

You know when you don't want to do something because you make all the excuses under the sun not to do it. EFT can take away this feeling of being stuck in life and give you the motivation you need to take the first step. It doesn't matter whether you want to give up smoking, move house, or join the gym, EFT can help you overcome any procrastinations you have. As a consequence you widen your horizons in life.

Losing Weight

EFT not only takes away the cravings associated with food but it also unearths the true reasons causing the emotional eating patterns. Understanding what emotions drive you to eat takes you one step closer to achieving and maintaining your weight loss.

Finding Happiness

Using EFT to get rid of those negative thoughts about yourself and others, and learning the true meaning of loving yourself and being able to accept yourself, is the only real way to find happiness. You recognise that no amount of money in the world can make you happy – it's what's inside that counts. EFT helps you change your underlying negative behaviour and, in the process, discover your true self.

Relaxing More

Certainly one of the easiest and most noticeable benefits of using EFT is that you immediately feel more relaxed. Simply by removing those energy blocks, you increase the positive flow of energy. You can also feel relaxed and uplifted knowing that your problems are no longer causing you anxiety, and that in itself feels like a great relief. By using EFT on a regular basis in your daily life you can become more balanced and able to confront unpleasant events and situations in a logical and composed manner.

Appendix

Resources

● ●

*I*n this Appendix I've included a selection of material to help you get the most from this book. Kicking off with a guide to monitoring stress levels, I also include a glossary of terms and a handy list of addresses and websites to help you to enhance your developing EFT skills.

If you want to get in touch about anything in this book, you can contact me at therapy4me@hotmail.co.uk, or by telephone (0845 838 1399 or 07934 593 389). You could also look up my website, www.therapy4me.co.uk).

Monitoring Stress Levels

The scale in Table A-1 was drawn up in 1967 by Doctors Holmes and Rahe as a way of predicting whether certain life events cause more stress than others. Their findings were converted into a scale and scores were given against each stressful event experienced over the past 12 months.

This scale cannot be totally relied upon, as our lives have changed considerably since 1967. For instance, holidays are given a score of 13 but I bet you could double that after you've spent days trawling through and booking your holiday online, struggling with parking at the airport and then waiting hours in the airport lounge as your flight is delayed, and the kids scream – need I go on?

However, the list and scores give you some insight into the stressors that you barely notice as changes at all. But when accumulated, theses stressors can have a profound effect on your health and well-being. The scale can be used in conjunction with Chapter 11.

Table A-1	The Holmes and Rahe Scale
Events that have happened during the past 12 months	*Stressor rating*
Death of a spouse	100
Divorce	73
Marital separation	65
Death of a close family member	63
Major personal injury or illness	53
Marriage	50
Marital reconciliation	45
Retirement	45
Major change in health or behaviour of a family member	44
Pregnancy	40
Sexual difficulties	39
Gaining a new family member (birth, adoption, relative moving in)	39
Major change in financial status (lot better, or worse, off)	38
Death of a close friend	37
Changing to different kind of work	36
Changes in number of arguments with spouse	35
Taking out a significant mortgage or loan	31
Major changes in work responsibilities	29
Son or daughter leaving home	29
Trouble with in-laws	29
Outstanding personal achievement	28
Trouble with boss	23
Change in working hours	20
Change in residence	20
Change in schools	20
Change in recreation	19
Change in church activities	19
Change in social activities	18
Small mortgage or loan	17
Major change in sleeping habits	16
Major change in number of family get-togethers	15

Events that have happened during the past 12 months	Stressor rating
Change in eating habits	15
Holiday	13
Christmas	12
Minor violations of law	11
Total:	

Results:

- **0 –149:** No significant change in health likely;

- **150 –199:** Mild stress and a 35 per cent chance of illness;

- **200 –299:** Moderate stress and a 50 per cent chance of illness;

- **300 +:** Major stress and an 80 per cent chance of illness.

Experts estimate that it takes a year to replenish the energy expended in adjusting to any of the changes described in the list.

Glossary of Terms

A handy, quick reference guide to the list of the most commonly referred to terms throughout the book.

Abreaction: A negative response to a memory which can range from as becoming emotionally upset to a severe reaction similar to a full blown panic attack.

Anchoring: Connecting a stimulus with a positive state, for example rubbing forefinger and thumb together whilst thinking of the happiest memory you've had. The association of the action will eventually automatically connect to the feeling.

Apex: Refers to the situation when a client's problem is cleared up so quickly that they claim they either didn't have the problem in the first place, or if they did, they don't remember having any emotional intensity associated with it. The situation is extremely frustrating for practitioners and I would suggest you write down the problem and intensity number to show them afterwards.

Aspects: A problem has more than one part, a bit like a jigsaw puzzle. These parts are known as *aspects*. Although each 'aspect' needs to be neutralised with EFT, more often than not it's only necessary to reduce a few before the rest collapse on their own.

Calibration: Measuring changes in a person's facial expression or body language during therapy.

Chasing the pain: A phenomenon during EFT when energy shifts around the body and is felt physically. A person who feels fear in their stomach at the beginning of a session may notice it shifting to their chest then their throat before disappearing altogether, for example. Pain also travels in much the same way.

Cognitive shift: When there has been a logical acceptance of the problem.

Core issues: Every problem presents itself as a symptom. Getting to the core issue is like peeling the layers off an onion to get to the root of the problem. A skilful Practitioner has the ability and experience to get to the core issue quickly. Asking questions and practicing EFT will greatly improve your technique.

Full routine: Tapping on all the meridian points and sometimes including the crown of the head, inner wrist, chest, and inside ankle points.

Generalisation effect: An effect experienced when one problem has been cleared with EFT yet the effects are felt in other areas. For example, if you had a fear of failing and this was removed with EFT then any other common theme around fear of failing will also be removed.

Karate chop: The fleshy part at the side of the hand which is tapped on during an EFT routine.

Meridians: Channels of energy that circulate around your body which are invisible to the naked eye.

9 Gamut: Point located in the 'valley' on the back of the hand between the little finger and the ring finger. Not always used by practitioners but re-introduced when dealing with more complex cases or when intensity levels are not moving.

Polarity reversal: When energy in your body is reversed or is flowing the wrong way. This can create chronic negative thinking and can interfere with EFT working.

Psychological reversal: Effect experienced when the subconscious mind interferes with the conscious mind to sabotage any efforts to overcome the problem.

Reminder phrase: Words that are used as you tap on the meridian points after you've used your Set-up phrase. The reminder is a way of keeping you focused on your problem as you tap around the body.

Remainder Phrase: Phrase used when you've completed a round of EFT and there's still some of the problem left, after measuring on the SUDs scale. Usually contains words such as 'still' or 'remaining'.

Secondary Benefit Syndrome: A subconscious belief that there's more to gain by having the problem than not having it.

Set-Up Phrase: An acknowledgement of the problem followed by an acceptance phrase performed whilst rubbing the Sore Spot or the Karate Chop. Using a Set up phrase can also help with any psychological reversals.

Sequence: Order in which meridian points are tapped. After carrying out the Set up phrase, the sequence consists of tapping on the remaining meridian points: eyebrow, side of eye, under eye, under nose, chin, collar bone and under arm. Additional points can be tapped on such as the crown of the head, the wrist, liver and ankle points.

Shortcut: Performing the EFT routine but leaving out the finger points, 9 Gamut and eyes rolling method.

Sore Spot: The place between the nipple and the shoulder, where you'd probably wear a badge or place your hand when giving a pledge.

SUDS (Subjective Units of Distress Scale): Scale used as a guide in measuring emotional or physical intensity. The person with the problem would rate their feelings ranging from 0–10. Zero would indicate being calm and having no distress, 5 would probably be moderately uncomfortable and 10 would be finding it difficult to talk about the problem or feeling highly anxious.

Validity of Cognition: Scale measuring intangible issues such as belief, procrastination, motivation, and so on.

Training Centres and Organisations Worldwide

This section introduces the main sources of training and research information exist for those with a keen interest in EFT.

The Association for the Advancement of Meridian Energy Therapies: www. AAMET.com. This website provides information for both lay persons and practitioners to find out more about energy therapies. Book reviews and research articles are provided covering all aspects of Meridian and Energy Therapy. Access is made available to various Practitioner and Trainee lists plus you can find details of EFT Training workshops around the world.

The Association of Meridian Energy Therapies (AMT): www.AMT.com; Tel: (+44|0)1323 729 666; 18 Marlow Avenue, Eastbourne, East Sussex, BN22 8SJ, United Kingdom;

The Association for Comprehensive Energy Psychology (ACEP): www. ACEP.com; E-mail: acep@energypsych.org; 303 Park Avenue South, Box 1051, New York, NY 10010-3657 USA;

AMT and ACEP are both professional bodies who organise training to aid further interaction and research in the field of meridian energy therapies. ACEP is an international non-profit organisation of licensed mental health professionals and allied energy health practitioners who are dedicated to developing and applying energy psychology.

Other Useful Websites

Gary Craig is the founder of the Emotional Freedom Technique and his website, www.emofree.com contains case studies, listings and much more. A treasure trove of information on EFT.

Dr David Lake and Steve Wells are internationally recognised as innovative leaders and skilled practitioners in the new field of Energy Psychology. David and Steve have been using Energy Psychology techniques for the past nine years and have developed their own unique integrative energy approach, Provocative Energy Techniques (PET). You can find their website at www. eftdownunder.com.

The EFT Register website at www.EFTRegister.com (Tel: 0845 838 1399) lists details of all energ therapists in the uk and will eventually include the rest worldwide. Within this Register, you can locate an EFT Practitioner or Trainer near to where you live, regardless of which association they belong to.

Books

In terms of self help and further understanding emotions, these books will be valuable additions to your library. There are many books written on emotions, and energy therapies but these are the ones I believe you'll find most helpful:

You Can Heal Your Life by Louise L Hay (Hay House Inc): Louise Hay was diagnosed with cancer more than 20 years ago and believes it's our thoughts that create our illnesses. You can use this book to look up your own illness and find the positive affirmation to use with EFT.

Molecules of Emotion by Candace B Pert (Simon & Schuster): A book that looks at how the brain, immune system, and endocrine system link and communicate with each other. Candace discusses how body chemicals form an information network that links how emotions affect the mind and how the mind affects emotions. Interesting stuff.

Trusting Ourselves: The Complete Guide to Emotional Well-Being for Women by Karen Johnson (Atlantic Monthly Press): Written by a woman, a book aimed at women who know why they've got their emotional problems. This book cuts out the medical jargon and tells you as it is and how you can facilitate change. Although a little dated now, there's still some inspiring information.

Feelings Buried Alive Never Die by Karol K Truman (Brigham Distributing): A practical book on the connection between emotions and physical diseases. Contains useful tools you can incorporate with EFT for turning negative emotions into positive ones.

Index

• *D* •

FOR DUMMIES®

Do Anything. Just Add Dummies

UK editions

BUSINESS

Starting a Business For Dummies, 2nd Edition
978-0-470-51806-9

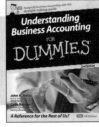

Understanding Business Accounting For Dummies, 2nd Edition
978-0-470-99245-6

Business Plans For Dummies
978-0-7645-7026-1

FINANCE

Investing For Dummies, 2nd Edition
978-0-470-99280-7

Tax For Dummies
978-0-470-99811-3

Bookkeeping For Dummies
978-0-470-05815-2

PROPERTY

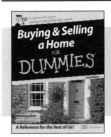

Buying & Selling a Home For Dummies
978-0-470-99448-1

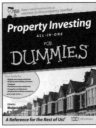

Property Investing For Dummies
978-0-470-51502-0

DIY & Home Maintenance For Dummies
978-0-7645-7054-4

Body Language For Dummies
978-0-470-51291-3

Building Self-Confidence For Dummies
978-0-470-01669-5

Children's Health For Dummies
978-0-470-02735-6

Cognitive Behavioural Coaching For Dummies
978-0-470-71379-2

Counselling Skills For Dummies
978-0-470-51190-9

Digital Marketing For Dummies
978-0-470-05793-3

Divorce For Dummies
978-0-7645-7030-8

eBay.co.uk For Dummies, 2nd Edition
978-0-470-51807-6

Emotional Freedom Technique For Dummies
978-0-470-75876-2

English Grammar For Dummies
978-0-470-05752-0

Fertility & Infertility For Dummies
978-0-470-05750-6

Genealogy Online For Dummies
978-0-7645-7061-2

Golf For Dummies
978-0-470-01811-8

Green Living For Dummies
978-0-470-06038-4

FOR DUMMIES®

A world of resources to help you grow

UK editions

SELF-HELP

Cognitive Behavioural Therapy For Dummies

978-0-470-01838-5

Neuro-linguistic Programming For Dummies

978-0-7645-7028-5

Personal Development All-in-One For Dummies

978-0-470-51501-3

HEALTH

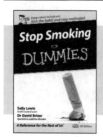

Stop Smoking For Dummies

978-0-470-99456-6

IBS For Dummies

978-0-470-51737-6

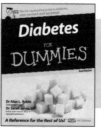

Diabetes For Dummies

978-0-470-05810-7

HISTORY

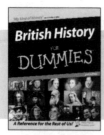

British History For Dummies

978-0-470-03536-8

Twentieth Century History For Dummies

978-0-470-51015-5

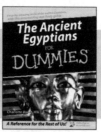

The Ancient Egyptians For Dummies

978-0-470-06544-0

Hypnotherapy For Dummies
978-0-470-01930-6

Inventing For Dummies
978-0-470-51996-7

Job Hunting and Career Change All-in-One For Dummies
978-0-470-51611-9

Motivation For Dummies
978-0-470-76035-2

Origami Kit For Dummies
978-0-470-75857-1

Patents, Registered Designs, Trade Marks and Copyright For Dummies
978-0-470-51997-4

Psychometric Tests For Dummies
978-0-470-75366-8

Raising Happy Children For Dummies
978-0-470-05978-4

Starting and Running a Business All-in-One For Dummies
978-0-470-51648-5

Sudoku For Dummies
978-0-470-01892-7

The British Citizenship Test For Dummies, 2nd Edition
978-0-470-72339-5

Time Management For Dummies
978-0-470-77765-7

Wills, Probate, & Inheritance Tax For Dummies, 2nd Edition
978-0-470-75629-4

Winning on Betfair For Dummies, 2nd Edition
978-0-470-72336-4

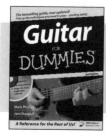

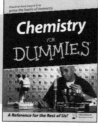

FOR DUMMIES®

Helping you expand your horizons and achieve your potential

COMPUTER BASICS

978-0-470-24055-7

978-0-470-13728-4

978-0-471-75421-3

DIGITAL LIFESTYLE

978-0-7645-9802-9

978-0-470-17474-6

978-0-470-17469-2

WEB & DESIGN

978-0-470-08030-6

978-0-470-11193-2

978-0-470-11490-2

Access 2007 For Dummies
978-0-470-04612-8

Adobe Creative Suite 3 Design Premium
All-in-One Desk Reference For Dummies
978-0-470-11724-8

AutoCAD 2008 For Dummies
978-0-470-11650-0

C++ For Dummies, 5th Edition
978-0-7645-6852-7

Excel 2007 All-in-One Desk Reference For
Dummies
978-0-470-03738-6

Flash CS3 For Dummies
978-0-470-12100-9

Laptops For Dummies, 2nd Edition
978-0-470-05432-1

Mac OS X Leopard For Dummies
978-0-470-05433-8

Macs For Dummies, 9th Edition
978-0-470-04849-8

Networking All-in-One Desk Reference For
Dummies, 3rd Edition
978-0-470-17915-4

Office 2007 All-in-One Desk Reference For
Dummies
978-0-471-78279-7

Search Engine Optimization For Dummies,
2nd Edition
978-0-471-97998-2

Second Life For Dummies
978-0-470-18025-9

The Internet For Dummies, 11th Edition
978-0-470-12174-0

Visual Studio 2008 All-in-One Desk
Reference For Dummies
978-0-470-19108-8

Web Analytics For Dummies
978-0-470-09824-0

Windows XP For Dummies, 2nd Edition
978-0-7645-7326-2

Available wherever books are sold. For more information or to order direct go to
www.wiley.com or call +44 (0) 1243 843291